check w/ veg

Spinach

cream.

COOKING
FOR TWO

COOKING
FOR TWO
WHEN MINUTES MATTER

❈ LUCY COLE ❈

WINGS BOOKS
New York • Avenel, New Jersey

This 1994 edition is published by Wings Books,
distributed by Random House Value Publishing, Inc.,
40 Engelhard Avenue, Avenel, New Jersey 07001,
by arrangement with Frederick Fell Publishers, Inc.,
a division of Lifetime Books, Inc.

Random House
New York • Toronto • London • Sydney • Auckland

Printed and bound in the United States of America

Library of Congress Cataloging-in-Publication Data
Cole, Lucy.
    Cooking for two : when minutes matter / Lucy Cole.
           p. cm.
    Originally published: Hollywood, Fla. : F. Fell, c1986.
    Includes index.
    ISBN 0-517-11879-3
    1. Cookery for two. 2. Cookery, International. 3. Menus.
I. Title. II. Title: Cooking for 2.
TX652.C7126 1994
641.5'61—dc20
                                       94-10844
                                          CIP

8 7 6 5 4 3 2

For my daughter,
   Julie

CONTENTS

Layered Spinach, Onions, Tomatoes, and Mushrooms
Green Hungarian Wine
Brandied Cherry Sherbet Sundaes

MEDITERRANEAN MENU
Smoked-Oyster Appetizer Salad
Swordfish Kebabs
Green Rice
Roasted Red Peppers with Pine Nuts
Sauvignon Blanc
Melon and Peaches Anisette

INDIAN MENU
Chick Pea and Rice Soup
Spicy Sole Fillets
Sherried Tomatoes
Broccoli with Cashews and Sesame Seeds
Pineapple Yogurt Drink
Bananas in Cardamom Orange Sauce

ORIENTAL AMERICAN MENU
Spinach, Mushroom, and Bean Sprout Salad
Stir-Fried Scallops and Vegetables
Rice
Sake
Almond Ice Cream with Lychee Sauce

CHICKEN MENUS

WINTER MENU
Grapefruit and Artichoke Green Salad
Herb-Roasted Chicken and Potatoes
Broccoli and Cherry Tomato Sauté
Gamay Beaujolais
Winter Fruit and Cheese Dessert

GREEK MENU
Spinach, Tomato, and Feta Salad
Lemon Broiled Chicken with Walnut Honey Glaze
Vegetable Pilaf
White Demestica
Brandied Apricot Sundaes

PORK MENUS

SAUSAGE AND CURED-MEAT MENUS

Beaujolais
Lemon Puddings
Irish Coffee

COOKING
FOR TWO

INTRODUCTION

Gourmet Cooking When Minutes Matter is a book for today's active men and women, married or single, working in or out of the home or both, who appreciate good food but have limited time for cooking it. A splendid variety of exciting and creative menus is included, as a quick glance through the pages will show you. You'll find easy, step-by-step instructions for such enticing dishes as veal chops with currants and pine nuts; stir-fried pork, lychees, snow peas, and tomatoes; rack of lamb with sherried mushroom sauce; herbed salmon and vegetable sauté; grapefruit and artichoke green salad; Valencia consommé; layered spinach, onions, tomatoes, and mushrooms; melon and peaches anisette; chocolate rum custard; and more.

What is it that lifts meals out of the ordinary? One of the most effective ways of creating imaginative dishes in a minimum of time is through the skillful use of herbs and spices. Thoughtfully selected seasonings can lend distinction to simple foods: tarragon, thyme, and parsley turn roast chicken and potatoes into a festive dish; cinnamon and cloves spark an entrée of pork chops with peaches and sour cream; cumin butter adds a new fillip to a sauté of corn, zucchini, and tomatoes.

Another way of breaking the monotony of quick dinners is to garner ideas from the world's great cuisines. You'll find this book liberally sprinkled with international themes, from an exotic Tunisian lamb-chop couscous dinner to a Greek lemon-broiled chicken glazed with honey and walnuts.

An important aspect of producing good meals quickly is time management.

1

And that's just what this book helps you to do—get the most out of the time you spend. You can prepare each menu suggested in this book, from appetizer to dessert, in about an hour. Here are the timesavers provided:

Menus. When time is short, every minute you spend thumbing through recipes and trying to decide on an appropriate menu shortens the time you have left to cook. You're one step ahead when recipes are already packaged into harmonious combinations, as they are in this book. You can easily use the recipes independently, if you like, or refer to the section on Menu Planning for more ideas.

Shopping Lists. While this book can't do the grocery shopping for you, it does provide an accurate, categorized shopping list (with a checklist of staples) for each menu. The list saves you time and helps prevent your overlooking a needed staple, such as coffee or plastic wrap.

Preparation Sequences. A choice of preparation schedules is given so you can begin preparation an hour before dinner or the day before, as you choose. The best sequences have been worked out to assure a smooth pace of work with everything coming out at the right time.

Efficient Recipes. The recipes have been selected for ease of preparation and carefully formulated to avoid unnecessary ingredients and steps. Tedious or messy procedures, such as sifting, sieving, and deep-fat frying, have been eliminated.

Practicality. You don't need to have on hand a supply of homemade stock, crêpes, pie crusts, cooked rice, or other prepared items—the raw materials that you'll need can be readily purchased.

Timesaving Tips. Some specific timesaving ideas are listed in the next section.

Thus, through the expert use of herbs and spices, an infusion of international culinary ideas, and good time management, you can produce memorable meals for two in a minimum of time. When you're in the mood for good food, but feel you haven't the leisure to prepare it, try the menus in this book. A whole new world of elegant and easy dining awaits you.

TIMESAVING TIPS

GETTING ORGANIZED
USING THIS BOOK
HANDLING INGREDIENTS

The three sections that follow offer suggestions for managing your time effectively.

Getting Organized deals with actions you can take now that will pay dividends later.

Using this Book lists three important guidelines for using this book to best advantage.

Handling Ingredients describes fast ways of accomplishing six routine cooking tasks.

GETTING ORGANIZED

• Have good knives, appropriate to the tasks required, and keep them sharp. Razor-sharp edges make peeling, chopping, slicing, and boning quick and satisfying tasks.

• Have at least one kitchen timer that you can set to remind you when a particular cooking step is expected to be completed. You can concentrate better on what you're doing at the moment if you don't have to keep reminding yourself that the almonds are almost brown and the vegetables are almost done.

• It's trite but true that "a place for everything and everything in its place" is a great timesaver. This applies to the refrigerator and freezer too. Designate certain areas for certain foods and keep them there.

• Keep herbs, spices, and flavorings on a convenient rack in alphabetical order. You can save five minutes by not having to dig out a spice jar from the back of a cabinet or drawer that's full of other things.

• Keep the most often used basics, such as flour, sugar, salt, cornstarch, and white rice, in canisters with lift-off tops. Use the top to level ingredients in measuring cups or spoons. (If weevils are a problem in canisters with loose-fitting tops, a fresh bay leaf, placed on top of the contents, will keep them away.)

• There are a few ingredients called for in this book that might not be available at your local grocery store. They can all be purchased well in advance, however, so if you'd like to be aware of them for your next visit to a gourmet shop or Oriental market, here they are (see Index for recipes using these ingredients):

* powdered saffron (expensive; you can substitute turmeric)
* Swedish preserved lingonberries (expensive; you can substitute wholeberry cranberry sauce)
* shelled pine nuts (expensive; you can substitute slivered almonds)
* couscous (a semolina of wheat; you can substitute rice or cracked wheat)
* Italian Arborio rice (expensive for rice; you can substitute long-grain white rice or converted rice)
* wild rice (expensive)
* cracked wheat (Ala)
* mango chutney (Major Grey's)
* ground cardamom
* ground turmeric
* ground coriander
* ground white pepper
* Oriental sesame oil
* oyster sauce
* hoisin sauce
* Japanese rice vinegar
* canned lychees (11 oz. size)
* preserved kumquats

USING THIS BOOK

• Use the shopping list that's given with each menu to assemble necessary ingredients before starting food preparations for the meal.

• The recipes are designed for you to prepare as you go. Do *not* do the basic preparations ahead of time, unless specifically stated in the recipe or unless you have extra time. For example, the first instruction in a recipe might be to brown a piece of meat. While this is taking place you will have plenty of time to chop an onion or slice the mushrooms that are called for in a later step.

• Relax when following the countdowns. It's not intended that you be in a race against time. Times shown are merely averages, rounded to the nearest five minutes. If you fall behind schedule, nothing dreadful will happen; just continue at a comfortable pace. You may also notice that the total working times in a given menu may be greater than the suggested starting time to do the menu at the last minute. This is because some preparation takes place after the start of a meal, as for example, five minutes spent after dinner to assemble an ice cream sundae.

HANDLING INGREDIENTS

• Once you are proficient at boning chicken breasts, many quick dishes are possible, as the boned breasts cook in about 4 minutes, or 2 minutes if cut for stir-frying. Here's how to bone them quickly and easily:

  A. Grasp the chicken skin with your hand and pull it off. Cut away any patches of fat from the chicken flesh.

  B. Place the breast, bone side down, on a flat surface. Make a small cut at the top end of the breast (where the wing was attached) to separate the flesh from the bone.

  C. If the breast has part of the wishbone or breastbone attached, cut the membrane down the length of the bones at the outside edge. With your thumb, loosen the flesh from the wishbone or breastbone.

  D. Using a knife when needed, loosen the flesh from the ribs starting from the top end of the breast and continuing down about 3 inches.

  E. Now grasp the flesh of the chicken in one hand and the bone in the other hand and pull them apart. (There will always be a large and a small fillet that tend to separate from one another, through no fault of your own.)

• To use fresh mushrooms, select those with firm, closed caps (gills not showing) if possible. Store them in a paper bag in the refrigerator. Wash them just before using by shaking them in a plastic bag half full of water. Immediately pour off the water and dirt and wipe the mushrooms with a paper towel, removing any lingering dirt. If the cut end of the stem looks brown and dry, trim away a thin slice and discard. Position mushrooms on a cutting board with stems up, to slice, quarter, or halve them.

• Onions may be finely chopped in a flash using this method: Cut a slice off the top (opposite the root end); cut the onion in half through the root. Peel back the skin and one layer of the onion. Place the onion half, cut side down, on a cutting board. Make lengthwise incisions ⅛ to ¼ inch apart without cutting through at the root end. Then slice crosswise at ⅛- to ¼-inch intervals, slicing almost to the root end. Discard the root end.

• Garlic cloves can be quickly peeled as follows: Place a clove (one segment of a head of garlic) on a cutting board. Lay the flat of a knife on top and press down to flatten the garlic. This will loosen the skin, and it can then be pulled off.

• To section an orange, peel it deeply enough to remove all the white rind. Loosen each section by cutting down along the membranes on each side. Lift out the section in one piece and remove any seeds.

• If salad greens are limp and there is no time to crisp them in the refrigerator, place individual salads in the freezer for 5 minutes immediately before serving (before adding salad dressing).

MENU PLANNING

MENU-PLANNING PRINCIPLES
RECIPE DESCRIPTIONS
ALTERNATE MENUS

The three sections that follow offer information and ideas to help you plan rewarding menus.

Menu-Planning Principles is a guide to selecting recipes that are likely to work well together in a menu.

Recipe Descriptions gives a synopsis of the recipes in this book, to be used as a quick reference when planning your own menus. It's divided into four sections: starters, main dishes, sides dishes, and desserts.

Alternate Menus lists 20 additional menus made up of compatible recombinations of recipes in this book.

MENU-PLANNING PRINCIPLES

A recipe can only be appreciated to its fullest when the other dishes that accompany it combine to achieve a degree of perfection in the menu as a whole. It's sometimes difficult to know what food combinations are likely to work well together, particularly if you're preparing the recipes for the first time and aren't even sure how things will look and taste separately, much less together. The following principles can serve as a guide to help reduce the number of less-than-great combinations, although the ultimate test is to try a particular combination and see if it pleases you. The information below is primarily geared for three-course dinners, rather than lavish meals or buffets where many foods may be offered.

Principal ingredients. The most important point in planning a menu is to seek variety in the main ingredients. Try to avoid using the same major ingredients in more than one part of the menu. For example, if nuts are used in the dessert, don't use them in the appetizer or main course. An exception might be Middle Eastern meals where nuts are a very common ingredient and could appear in a menu more than once. The same with sour cream in Eastern European menus—a dollop of sour cream on the soup, as well as sour cream in the main dish, would be okay. But as a general rule avoid duplication.

A limit of one starchy dish is wise for most menus. There should be no more than one dish cooked in wine. One highly seasoned dish is usually a maximum too, although Mexican, Indian, and similar cuisines may have more than one.

Several fruits and vegetables can be used in a menu, but *similar* fruits and *similar* vegetables are best combined in one dish, rather than spread throughout the menu. For example, a mixture of root vegetables, say carrots and parsnips, would be a nice vegetable accompaniment for a pork roast, but it would not be as good to serve a carrot soup and then accompany the roast with parsnips—the vegetable accompaniment is then too similar to the main ingredient in the soup. *Dissimilar* fruits can be good in a menu. For instance, an orchard fruit (such as oranges or apples) might appear in the first course, and the dessert could still include berries or grapes. And of course *dissimilar* vegetables—a starchy one, a leafy green one, and an orange, yellow, or red one—are very appropriate in a menu to enhance variety and add color.

Color. There was a time when monochromatic menus were fashionable. Various shades of a single theme color would be used throughout the menu. Today, however, contrasting colors seem more appealing. Keep color in mind when planning a menu and avoid clashing colors (beets and tomatoes, perhaps) or the obvious boredom of the colorless chicken-in-cream-sauce, mashed-potato, and cauliflower menus.

Composition. The dishes that form the main course, when viewed together, should have good visual composition, like an aesthetically satisfying painting. This usually means combining colorful mixtures of foods with one-color accompaniments and avoiding similarly cut foods in the same course. An example of the latter would be to serve julienne-cut vegetables as an accompaniment to chicken with julienne dried fruit—it would be visually disconcerting.

Texture and Temperature. Contrast in textures and temperatures is also desirable. Try for a variety of textures, such as crisp, soft, chewy, liquid, tender, crumbly, etc., and some change in temperature—hot, warm, cool, cold, and frozen.

Flavor. Flavors in a menu need to be varied, yet compatible. One dish might contain spices, another herbs, another aromatics (onion, garlic, ginger, etc.), along with a plain dish and a sweet dessert. Strongly flavored dishes need to be balanced with bland ones, such as well seasoned Chinese stir-fry dishes with plain boiled rice.

Richness versus Lightness. Rich dishes are best accompanied by lighter dishes. Even the most avowed chocoholic would probably have difficulty swallowing a chocolate torte after a rich serving of cassoulet. Consider also compatibility with the season. Winter menus are appropriately richer and heartier than summer meals.

Theme. Another aspect of menu planning is what might be called the "theme." It's safest not to combine recipes with widely varying themes. For example, peasant-style dishes should not generally be combined with elegant, gourmet dishes, that is, *crepes suzette* is not an appropriate dessert after a hearty goulash. If a menu has a decidedly ethnic theme, stick with dishes that would not be jarringly out of place in that culture.

Cooking Methods. Variety in cooking methods is desirable. It is particularly important in Oriental menus. Cooking methods include boiling, braising, steaming, stir-frying, sautéing, deep-frying, baking, roasting, and broiling.

Nutrition. Take care to include the building blocks of a good diet in daily menus: protein foods; vitamin- and mineral-rich vegetables, fruits, grains, and dairy products; and foods that contain fiber.

RECIPE DESCRIPTIONS

Note: A wine suggestion is given for every menu (see featured menus), and two beverage recipes are included (Pineapple Yogurt Drink, page 62, and Irish Coffee, page 271).

STARTERS

Working Time	Other Time	Descriptions*	Page
APPETIZERS AND APPETIZER SALADS			
10	0	*Kipper Paté* (butter, lemon juice, served on crackers)	269
10	10	*Shrimp Spread* (butter, mace, nutmeg, served on crackers)	130
10	10	*Hot Ham Canapés* (buttered toast, cream cheese, sour cream, Parmesan cheese, paprika), 375°F oven	46
10	30	*Smoked-Oyster Appetizer Salad* (artichoke hearts, tomatoes, cucumbers, lettuce leaves, French dressing)	53
10	30	*Shrimp-Stuffed Avocado* (celery, mayonnaise, mustard, chives, lettuce leaves, lime wedges)	33

*Significant ingredients that are not obvious from recipe titles are given in parentheses.

GREEN SALADS

Working Time	Other Time	Description	Page
15	15	*Bulgur Yogurt* (beef or chicken broth, cracked wheat, egg yolk, mint)	195
15	15	*Ratatouille* (chicken broth, onions, garlic, eggplant, zucchini, tomatoes, basil, ground coriander)	149
15	20	*Chick Pea and Rice* (chicken broth, onions, garlic, ground coriander, curry powder, lemon juice, parsley)	60
15	40	*Lemon Barley* (chicken broth, cream, chopped tomatoes, egg yolk, lemon juice, parsley)	239
15	45	*Chilled Cantaloupe* (orange juice, lemon juice, sugar, mint)	182

MAIN DISHES

Working Time	Other Time	Description	Page

SEAFOOD

Working Time	Other Time	Description	Page
15	10	*Fish Fillets in Herbed Sour Cream* (butter, thyme, tarragon, lemon wedges)	46
15	25	*Sea Bass with Mushrooms and Tomatoes* (dill weed, green onions), 350°F oven	33
20	0	*Spicy Sole Fillets* (chili powder, cloves, cardamom, ground coriander, tarragon vinegar)	60
20	40	*Swordfish Kebabs* (oregano, garlic, paprika, lemon juice, olive oil), broiler	53
30	0	*Stir-Fried Scallops and Vegetables* (garlic, ginger, carrots, celery, snow peas, green onions, oyster sauce, soy sauce, sesame oil)	68

Working Time	Other Time	Description	Page
30	0	*Veal with Garden Vegetables* (cutlets, onion, yellow summer squash, zucchini, green peppers, tomatoes, white wine)	162
30	0	*Fillet of Beef Stroganoff* (mushrooms, Madeira wine, sour cream, A-1 Steak Sauce)	130
30	10	*Beef and Mushroom Brochettes with Rice, Snow Peas, and Papaya* (lemon, butter, mustard, chicken broth)	124
30	30	*Moussaka* (ground beef, onions, tomato paste, basil, oregano, cinnamon, eggplant, sour cream, cheese, eggs), 375°F oven	137
30	30	*Roast Beef and Crab Salad* (deli roast beef, butterhead lettuce, chick peas, artichoke hearts, alfalfa sprouts, avocado, tomatoes, black olives, Louis dressing)	144

LAMB

Working Time	Other Time	Description	Page
15	15	*Orange-Glazed Lamb Chops* (loin chops, mustard, brown sugar, lemon juice), broiler	188
25	40	*Rack of Lamb with Sherried Mushroom Sauce* (cream, green onion), 425°F oven	169
30	0	*Lamb Chops, Peppers, and Tomatoes in Spicy Sauce* (onions, brown sugar, curry powder, soy sauce, oyster sauce, catsup)	176
30	30	*Lamb-Chop Couscous* (shoulder chops, lemon juice, turmeric, ginger, red pepper, garlic, onions, chick peas, zucchini, tomatoes, couscous grain, butter)	183
30	50	*Lamb-Chop Oven Dinner* (shoulder chops, onions, garlic, mushrooms, green pepper, yellow summer squash, zucchini, tomatoes, oregano, thyme, lemon juice), 400°F oven	196

Working Time	Other Time	Description	Page
20	40	*Knockwurst with Red Cabbage* (onions, apples, sugar, red wine vinegar, cloves), 400°F oven	245

SIDE DISHES

Working Time	Other Time	Description	Page

GRAINS, BREADS, AND NOODLES

Working Time	Other Time	Description	Page
5	15	*Rosemary Rice* (chicken broth)	189
5	20	*Boiled Rice*	69, 211
5	25	*Saffron Risotto* (Arborio rice, chicken broth, Parmesan cheese)	110
5	55	*White and Wild Rice* (chicken broth)	131
5	50	*Pecan Wild Rice* (chicken broth)	89
5	60	*Brown Rice* (chicken broth)	177
10	10	*Skillet Cornbread* (egg, milk)	35
10	10	*Brussels Sprouts and Green Noodles* (thyme)	103
10	15	*Parmesan Corncakes* (chicken broth, cornmeal), 450°F oven	217
10	20	*Green Rice* (chicken broth, green onions, parsley)	54
10	25	*Irish Soda Bread* (buttermilk, golden raisins), 375°F oven	270
15	12	*Poppy Seed Biscuits* (milk, sour cream), 450°F oven	257
15	15	*Vegetable Pilaf* (chicken broth, onions, garlic, green beans, carrots, cinnamon stick)	83

Working Time	Other Time	Description	Page
20	0	*Vegetable Medley with Lemon Crumbs* (cauliflower, green beans, cherry tomatoes)	170
25	10	*Layered Spinach, Onions, Mushrooms, and Tomatoes* (garlic, nutmeg, lemon juice), 350°F oven	47

DESSERTS

Working Time	Other Time	Description	Page

ICE CREAM AND SHERBET DESSERTS

Working Time	Other Time	Description	Page
10	0	*Raspberry Liqueur Sundaes* (vanilla ice cream, hazelnuts, whipped cream)	171
10	0	*Pineapple Caramel Sundaes* (vanilla ice cream, butter)	177
10	0	*Kumquat Walnut Sundaes* (vanilla ice cream, sugar)	211
10	0	*Almond Ice Cream with Lychee Sauce* (butter, sugar, lemon juice)	69
10	0	*Kahlua Parfaits* (vanilla ice cream, chocolate cookie crumbs)	233
10	30	*Chocolate Ice Cream Chantilly with Raspberries* (sugar)	91
10	30	*Ice Cream with Galliano Peach Sauce* (vanilla ice cream, sugar, lemon juice)	112
10	60	*Strawberry Sherbet* (lemon juice, egg white, sugar)	133
10	60	*Brandied Apricot Sundaes* (vanilla ice cream, canned apricots, apricot preserves, apricot brandy, lemon juice)	84
10	150	*Lemon Gelato* (cream, egg)	252

Working Time	Other Time	Description	Page
15	60	*Brandied Cherry Sherbet Sundaes* (vanilla ice cream, frozen dark sweet cherries, cherry brandy, sugar, lemon juice, egg white)	48

BAKED DESSERTS

Working Time	Other Time	Description	Page
10	20	*Oven Pancakes with Lingonberries* (sour cream), 400°F oven	97
10	35	*Cointreau Custards*, 325°F oven	264
10	45	*Coconut Pecan "Pie,"* 350°F oven	205
15	20	*Gingerbread Oven Pancake with Banana Sauce* (sauce with brown sugar, cream, lemon juice), 400°F oven	247
15	30	*Lemon Puddings*, 350°F oven	271
15	40	*Deep-Dish Blueberry Pies* (sugar, lemon juice, pie crust with brown sugar and nutmeg, vanilla ice cream), 425°F oven	226
15	60	*Sugar-Topped Baked Apples with Cream* (sugar, cinnamon, lemon juice), 375°F oven	241
5	55	*Honey Almond Turnovers* (patty shell, egg yolk, sugar), 400°F oven	197
15	55	*Buttered Pear Tart* (patty shell, egg, sugar, powdered sugar), 375°F oven	104
15	85	*Chocolate Rum Custards* (with whipped cream), 325°F oven, served cold	125

OTHER FRUIT DESSERTS

Working Time	Other Time	Description	Page
5	30	*Winter Fruit and Cheese Dessert* (pineapple, grapes, Brie or Camembert)	77
10	30	*Strawberries with Grand Marnier Sauce* (cream cheese, egg yolk, cream, sugar)	42
10	30	*Cointreau Fruit Cup* (oranges, kiwi, pineapple, sugar)	145

Working Time	Other Time	Description	Page
10	60	*Melon and Peaches Anisette* (sugar, lemon juice, mint)	55
10	60	*Bananas and Strawberries in Port* (sugar, orange juice, lemon juice and peel)	157
15	0	*Bananas in Cardamom Orange Sauce* (butter, brown sugar, lemon juice, sour cream)	63
15	15	*Walnut Date Confections* (powdered sugar, butter, lemon juice)	138
15	20	*Buttered Rum Fruit Compote* (mixed dried fruit, orange slices, cinnamon, sugar, whipped cream)	258
15	20	*Pears in Red Wine with Whipped Cream* (ginger, lemon peel, sugar)	218
15	30	*Grapes in Honey Cream* (orange liqueur, sour cream, whipping cream, lemon juice, powdered sugar)	184
15	30	*Summer Fruit with Cassis* (peaches, strawberries, blueberries, sugar, whipped cream)	163
15	45	*Orange and Apple Dessert* (sugar, lemon peel and juice)	117
15	60	*Piña Colada Dessert* (pineapple, sugar, rum, cream of coconut, cream)	35
15	60	*Vanilla Mousse with Strawberries* (gelatin, sugar, cream, yogurt)	190
15	60	*Bananas with Raspberries and Whipped Cream* (sugar, lemon juice, vanilla)	151

ALTERNATE MENUS

*Substitute 1 small carrot, peeled and coarsely grated, for the tomato.

Working Time	Other Time	Description	Page
MENU 4			
15	40	*Onion, Cheese, and Walnut Pastry*	143
25	20	*Tuscan Chicken*	109
5	6	*Broccoli Florets*	132
15	20	*Pears in Red Wine with Whipped Cream*	218
──			
60			
MENU 5			
20	30	*Walnut Green Salad*	123
15	30	*Garlic Chicken and Vegetables* French Bread	116
5	30	*Winter Fruit and Cheese Dessert*	77
──			
40			
MENU 6			
10	10	*Shrimp Spread*	130
30	0	**Chicken with Garden Vegetables* Hot Rolls	116
15	60	*Vanilla Mousse with Strawberries*	190
──			
55			
MENU 7			
10	15	*Valencia Consommé*	169
20	0	*Veal Chops with Currants and Pine Nuts*	156

*Substitute boned chicken breasts in veal recipe.

Working Time	Other Time	Description	Page
10	5	Broccoli and Cherry Tomato Sauté French Bread	76
10	0	Pineapple Caramel Sundaes	177
50			

MENU 8

10	10	Hot Ham Canapés	46
30	30	Roast Beef and Crab Salad Fisherman's Wharf Bread	144
10	60	Bananas and Strawberries in Port	157
55			

MENU 9

10	30	Smoked-Oyster Appetizer Salad	53
15	0	Rib Steaks in Herbed Wine Sauce	149
20	0	Vegetable Medley with Lemon Crumbs	170
15	30	Grapes in Honey Cream	184
55			

MENU 10

10	0	Red Beet Soup	256
30	0	*Fillet of Beef Stroganoff	130
5	55	White and Wild Rice	131
5	10	Buttered Brussels Sprouts (recipe not included)	

*Serve main course dishes on one platter and garnish with orange slices.

Working Time	Other Time	Description	Page
10	0	Chocolate Ice Cream Chantilly with Raspberries	91
60			

MENU 11

15	45	Chilled Cantaloupe Soup	182
30	0	Lamb Chops, Peppers, and Tomatoes in Spicy Sauce	176
5	20	Boiled Rice	69
10	0	Almond Ice Cream with Lychee Sauce	69
60			

MENU 12

20	30	Middle Eastern Green Salad	137
15	15	Orange-Glazed Lamb Chops	188
5	55	Pecan Wild Rice	89
5	6	Buttered Green Beans (recipe not included)	
15	15	Honey Almond Turnovers	197
60			

MENU 13

15	30	Artichoke and Grapefruit Green Salad	75
30	30	Lamb-Chop Couscous	183

*Substitute ¼ tsp. orange extract for Cointreau.

Working Time	Other Time	Description	Page
MENU 17			
10	0	Caraway Mushroom Bouillon	245
20	10	Swiss Bratwurst with Winter Vegetables	239
15	30	Lemon Puddings	271
—			
45			
MENU 18			
15	10	Sardine and Bacon Canapés	109
20	25	Corned Beef and Cabbage Soup	269
		Hot Rolls	
15	40	Deep-Dish Blueberry Pies	226
—			
45			
MENU 19			
10	0	*Smoked Herring Paté	269
20	10	Kielbasa, Mushroom, Cabbage, and Tomato Sauté	256
		Rye Bread	
0	60	Brandied Apricot Sundaes	84
—			
45			
MENU 20			
20	30	Cucumber Green Salad with Hot Almonds	40

*Same as Kipper Paté.

Working Time	Other Time	Description	Page
15	30	*Roasted Italian Sausages, Potatoes, and Peppers* Italian Bread	251
15 — 50	45	*Orange and Apple Dessert*	117

SEAFOOD MENUS

Caribbean Menu
Continental Menu
Yugoslavian Menu
Mediterranean Menu
Indian Menu
Oriental American Menu

CARIBBEAN MENU

- **Shrimp-Stuffed Avocado**

- **Sea Bass with Mushrooms and Tomatoes**
- **Chard with Bacon**
- **Skillet Cornbread**
  California Chardonnay

- **Piña Colada Dessert**
  Coffee

Caribbean cuisine is at its most successful when native cooks use the abundant tropical fruits of the region or the fruits of the surrounding sea—shrimp, spiny lobster, endless varieties of fish.

The avocado is a native American fruit that grows on most of the more than 7,000 Caribbean Islands. It makes an easy and attractive first course when stuffed with a tasty shrimp salad.

Any variety of sea bass, as well as red snapper, rock cod, or halibut, can be used in the fish recipe given here. The fish is seasoned with red pepper and dill, topped with sliced mushrooms, tomatoes, and green onions, then baked. It turns out very moist and flavorful. Sautéed chard with bacon and skillet cornbread go well with the fish. Making the cornbread on top of the stove is convenient when the oven is in use at a temperature too low for breads.

"Wine" in the West Indies is more likely to mean orange, grapefruit, or rice wine, rather than grape wine. Nevertheless, this menu, being mildly seasoned compared to much of Caribbean cooking, lends itself to a true wine accompaniment. Try a dry, full-flavored white, such as a California Chardonnay.

A popular Puerto Rican drink, Piña Colada, is the inspiration for the fruit dessert that completes this meal. Fresh pineapple cubes are marinated in rum, then topped with whipped cream enriched with cream of coconut.

SHOPPING LIST FOR CARIBBEAN MENU

Seafood, Meat, Dairy, Eggs:

☐ ¼ lb. (1 cup) tiny cooked, peeled shrimp

☐ 1 lb. sea bass steaks or fillets (or red snapper, rock cod, or halibut)

☐ bacon (2 slices or 1½ ozs.)

☐ butter (1½ Tbsp. + butter to serve with cornbread)

☐ whipping cream (⅓ cup)

☐ milk (½ cup)

☐ eggs (1)

Produce:

☐ celery (¼ cup chopped)

☐ 1 medium-size avocado*

☐ red-leaf (or other) lettuce (about 4 leaves)

☐ 1 lime or lemon (need 2 wedges)

☐ chives (1 tsp. chopped), or use frozen

☐ 2 medium-size mushrooms

☐ 1 small (4-oz.) tomato

☐ green onions (1 Tbsp. minced)

☐ 1 lb. chard

☐ 1 pineapple (need 1½ cups)

Grocery:

☐ yellow cornmeal (½ cup)

☐ mayonnaise (¼ cup)

☐ frozen chives (1 tsp.), if not using fresh

Liquor:

☐ 1 bottle dry, full-flavored white wine, such as California Chardonnay

☐ light or golden rum (2 Tbsp.)

☐ Lopez cream of coconut (2 Tbsp.)

Check Staples:

☐ salt

☐ black pepper

☐ ground red pepper

☐ dried dill weed (¼ tsp.)

☐ sugar (1½ Tbsp.)

☐ baking powder (1 tsp.)

☐ salad (not olive) oil (½ Tbsp.)

☐ Dijon mustard (¼ tsp.)

☐ coffee

*May need to be purchased a few days ahead to allow time for ripening.

COUNTDOWNS FOR CARIBBEAN MENU

Last-Minute Countdown

Time in   *Activity*
Minutes

60 minutes ahead:
15   Chill wine; Steps 1–2 of dessert
10   Prepare appetizer.
10   Steps 1–2 of chard
15   Prepare sea bass.
10   Uncork wine; Steps 1–3 of corn-
      bread
‾‾
60

Serving:
Serve appetizer.
(5 minutes after serving appetizer, do
    Step 4 of cornbread and Step 3 of
    chard.)
Step 4 of chard
Serve sea bass, chard, cornbread, butter,
    and wine.
Make coffee.
Serve dessert (Step 3) and coffee.

Plan-Ahead Countdown

Time in   *Activity*
Minutes

One day ahead:
15   Chill wine; Steps 1–2 of dessert
10   Prepare appetizer.
 5   Step 2 of chard
‾‾
30

30 minutes ahead:
 5   Step 1 of chard
15   Prepare sea bass.
10   Uncork wine; Steps 1–3 of corn-
      bread
‾‾
30

Serving:
Serve appetizer.
(5 minutes after serving appetizer, do
    Step 4 of cornbread and Step 3 of
    chard.)
Step 4 of chard
Serve sea bass, chard, cornbread, butter,
    and wine.
Make coffee.
Serve dessert (Step 3) and coffee.

SHRIMP-STUFFED AVOCADO

Working Time: 10 minutes/Chilling Time: 30 minutes/Servings: 2

¼ cup finely chopped celery
¼ cup mayonnaise
Pinch of ground red pepper
¼ tsp. Dijon mustard
¼ lb. (1 cup) tiny shrimp (purchased cooked
  and peeled)

1 medium-size avocado (unpeeled)
4 red-leaf (or other) lettuce leaves
2 lime (or lemon) wedges
1 tsp. chopped fresh or frozen chives

    1.   Combine celery, mayonnaise, pepper, and mustard in a 3-cup bowl. Mix in shrimp. Cut avocado lengthwise around center, cutting all the way to seed. Twist halves apart. Impale seed on knife and twist out.

    2.   Fill avocado halves with shrimp mixture, mounding it high. Line individual salad bowls with lettuce leaves. Place avocado halves on top with a lime wedge to the side. Sprinkle shrimp with chives. Cover with plastic wrap and refrigerate at least 30 minutes.

To do ahead: Prepare up to 1 day ahead.

SEA BASS WITH MUSHROOMS AND TOMATOES

Working Time: 15 minutes/Baking Time: 25 minutes (350°F)/Servings: 2

1 lb. sea bass steaks or fillets, ¾ inch thick*
½ tsp. plus ⅛ tsp. salt
⅛ tsp. ground black pepper
Pinch (or more) of ground red pepper
¼ tsp. dried dill weed

2 medium-size mushrooms, sliced ¹⁄₁₆ inch
  thick
1 small (4-oz.) tomato, sliced ⅛ inch thick
1 Tbsp. minced green onion
1½ Tbsp. butter

    1.   Turn oven to 350°F. Season bass with ½ tsp. salt, the black pepper, red pepper, and dill weed. Place in a buttered gratin dish (10 inches long).

    2.   Cover bass with sliced mushrooms and top with slightly overlapping tomato slices. Sprinkle with minced green onion and ⅛ tsp. salt. Dot with butter.

3. Bake, uncovered, in center of oven, just until fish is opaque and flakes easily, about 25 minutes. Serve from gratin dish, spooning juices over fish.

*Sea bass includes black sea bass (black jewfish, giant sea bass, grouper bass, California black sea bass), white sea bass, and blackfish or common sea bass. This recipe is also good using red snapper, rock cod, or halibut.

To do ahead: Do Steps 1 and 2 up to 30 minutes ahead. Cover and leave at room temperature.

CHARD WITH BACON

Working Time: 15 minutes/Cooking Time: 10 minutes/Servings: 2

2 slices bacon (1½ ozs. total)   ¼ tsp. salt
l lb. chard

1. Cook bacon in a 10-inch skillet over medium heat until crisp. Drain on paper towels and crumble. (Reserve bacon fat.)

2. Cut off stems of chard even with base of leaf. Wash leaves, stack, and cut in ⅓-inch-wide shreds. Cut across shreds at 1-inch intervals. (Makes 4 to 5 cups.)

3. Add chard (with only the amount of water clinging to the leaves after washing) and salt to skillet. Cover and cook, stirring occasionally, until chard is wilted, about 5 minutes.

4. Uncover and cook until chard is tender when tasted and liquid in skillet has evaporated, about 3 minutes. Serve in a small bowl garnished with the crumbled bacon.

*Chard is a leafy green vegetable of the beet family. It's also known as Swiss chard and Italian spinach. Chard is in season from March through December, with May, June, and July the peak months.

To do ahead: Do Step 2 up to 1 day ahead. Refrigerate in a plastic bag.

SKILLET CORNBREAD

Working Time: 10 minutes/Cooking Time: 10 minutes/Servings: 2 to 3

½ cup milk
½ cup yellow cornmeal
½ tsp. salt

1 tsp. baking powder
½ Tbsp. salad (not olive) oil for frying
1 egg

1. Scald milk in a ¾-qt. saucepan over medium-high heat. In a 1-qt. bowl stir together cornmeal, salt, and baking powder.

2. Remove milk from burner and replace with a heavy 5-inch skillet containing the oil. Reduce heat to medium-low. Add milk to cornmeal mixture, beating with a fork until smooth (mixture will foam up).

3. Let mixture cool 1 minute. Add egg and beat again. Pour into hot skillet. Cover and cook until brown on bottom and just set enough around the edges to turn over, about 5 minutes.

4. Turn bread over with spatula. Cook, uncovered, until browned on second side, 3 to 4 minutes. Cut into wedges and serve with plenty of butter.

To do ahead: Do Step 1 up to 30 minutes ahead.

Note: Leftover wedges of cornbread are very good split, buttered, and toasted under the broiler.

PIÑA COLADA DESSERT

Working Time: 15 minutes/Chilling Time: 1 hour/Servings: 2

1½ cups fresh pineapple tidbits
1½ Tbsp. sugar
2 Tbsp. light or golden rum

⅓ cup whipping cream
2 Tbsp. Lopez cream of coconut*

1. In a 1-qt. bowl toss pineapple with sugar and rum. Cover and refrigerate.

   2.   In a 3-cup bowl whip cream with a rotary beater until stiff. Gently beat in cream of coconut. Cover and refrigerate.

   3.   To serve, divide pineapple and juices between 2 compotes. Mound the coconut whipped cream on top.

*Cream of coconut is a sweetened coconut concentrate available in 8½-oz. cans in most liquor stores. Stir before using. Unused coconut cream will keep several months stored in a glass jar in the refrigerator.

To do ahead: Do Step 1 up to 1 day ahead. Do Step 2 up to 2 hours ahead.

CONTINENTAL MENU

- **Cucumber Green Salad with Hot Almonds**

- **Herbed Salmon and Vegetable Sauté**
  Crusty French Bread
  Chablis

- **Strawberries with Grand Marnier Sauce**
  Grand Marnier Coffee

Judging by the restaurants people choose when they go out for an elegant meal, Continental food—that subtle, classic cuisine from the European continent—is a favorite. Try this menu for a lovely spring dinner.

Salads are now universally accepted as a first course, and the hot almonds in this one make it particularly appealing as a starter. The salad itself should be very simple—butterhead lettuce, sliced cucumbers, a sprinkling of minced shallots, and a vinaigrette dressing. At the last moment freshly pan-roasted, salted almonds are scattered on top.

The main course is a one-dish meal, a beautiful sauté of salmon steaks, new potatoes, mushrooms, asparagus, and cherry tomatoes. Oregano and tarragon are the complementary herbs. The salmon is very lightly sauced in a white wine reduction swirled with butter.

A fine accompaniment for this dish is a dry, crisp, white wine with a subtle, flinty character, such as Chablis.

The fruit and cheese of Continental menus consists, in this case, of sliced fresh strawberries with a sauce made by whirling cream cheese, sugar, an egg yolk, cream, and Grand Marnier in a blender. The Grand Marnier theme can be carried further by adding it to the coffee served with dessert.

SHOPPING LIST FOR CONTINENTAL MENU

Fish, Dairy, Eggs:

☐ 2 salmon steaks, about 1 inch thick (¾ to 1 lb. total)

☐ butter (3 Tbsp. + butter for bread)

☐ whipping cream (2 Tbsp.)

☐ 3-oz. pkg. cream cheese

☐ eggs (1 yolk)

Produce:

☐ 1 large head butterhead lettuce

☐ 1 small cucumber (need ½)

☐ 2 large (⅔ lb. total) new potatoes

☐ 6 medium-size (¼ lb.) mushrooms

☐ 6 cherry tomatoes

☐ ⅔ lb. (8 stalks) asparagus

☐ garlic (½ tsp. minced)

☐ shallots (1½ tsp. minced)

☐ 1-pt. basket strawberries

Grocery:

☐ whole blanched almonds (20)

☐ French dressing (oil and vinegar type), such as Trader Vic's (¼ cup)

Liquor:

☐ 1 bottle dry, crisp white wine, such as (French) Chablis (need ⅓ cup for cooking)

☐ Grand Marnier liqueur (1 Tbsp. + ¼ cup or more for coffee)

Check Staples:

☐ salt

☐ white pepper

☐ dried oregano (½ tsp.)

☐ dried tarragon (¼ tsp.)

☐ sugar (¼ cup)

☐ salad (not olive) oil (1 Tbsp.)

☐ olive oil (1 Tbsp.)

☐ coffee

☐ plastic wrap

COUNTDOWNS FOR CONTINENTAL MENU

Last-Minute Countdown

Time in   *Activity*
Minutes

60 minutes ahead:
15 Chill wine; Step 1 of salad (blanch almonds if necessary)
10 Steps 1-2 of dessert
20 Steps 1-4 of salmon
15 Oven to 200°F; Step 5 of salmon; uncork wine; put bread and salmon and potatoes in oven.
___
60

Serving:
Serve salad (Step 3).
Step 6 of salmon
Serve salmon (with vegetables), bread, butter, and wine.
Make coffee.
Serve dessert and coffee (Step 3).

Plan-Ahead Countdown

Time in   *Activity*
Minutes

One day ahead:
15 Chill wine; Step 1 of salad (blanch almonds if necessary)
 5 Step 1 of dessert
___
20

40 minutes ahead:
 5 Step 2 of dessert
20 Steps 1-4 of salmon
15 Oven to 200°F; Step 5 of salmon; uncork wine; put bread and salmon and potatoes in oven.
___
40

Serving:
Serve salad (Step 3).
Step 6 of salmon
Serve salmon (with vegetables), bread, butter, and wine.
Make coffee.
Serve dessert and coffee (Step 3).

CUCUMBER GREEN SALAD WITH HOT ALMONDS

Working Time: 20 minutes/Chilling Time: 30 minutes/Servings: 2

3½ cups bite-size pieces butterhead lettuce
½ small cucumber
1½ tsp. minced shallots*
20 whole blanched** almonds

1 Tbsp. salad (not olive) oil
⅛ tsp. salt
¼ cup bottled French dressing (oil and vine-gar type), such as Trader Vic's

1. Divide lettuce between two individual salad bowls. Peel cucumber, slice lengthwise, and remove seeds if large. Slice cucumber ⅛ inch thick and scatter over lettuce. Sprinkle with shallots. Cover with plastic wrap and refrigerate.

2. In a 5-inch skillet heat almonds in oil over medium-low heat, stirring frequently, until lightly (but thoroughly) browned, about 5 minutes. Drain on paper towels and sprinkle with salt. Let cool at least 2 minutes before serving.

3. To serve, drizzle French dressing over salads and top with the hot almonds.

*Shallots are a cousin of the onion and grow in clusters of two to six from a common base (somewhat like garlic). If shallots are unavailable, substitute 2 tsp. minced onion or white part of green onion.
**Blanched almonds are those that have the skin removed. If you cannot buy them already blanched, blanch them yourself as follows: Bring ½ inch of water to a boil in a ¾-qt. saucepan. Add almonds and boil until skins puff, about 1 minute. Drain and cool in cold water. Slip off skins and dry almonds on a paper towel.

To do ahead: Do Step 1 up to 1 day ahead.

HERBED SALMON AND VEGETABLE SAUTÉ

Working Time: 35 minutes/Cooking Time: 5 minutes more/Servings: 2

2 cups water
1⅝ tsp. salt, divided
2 large (⅔ lb. total) new potatoes, peeled,
   quartered
6 medium-size (¼ lb.) mushrooms, halved
½ tsp. minced garlic
3 Tbsp. butter, divided
2 salmon steaks, about 1 inch thick (¾ to 1
   lb. total)

6 cherry tomatoes
⅔ lb. (8 stalks) asparagus
⅛ tsp. ground white pepper
1 Tbsp. olive oil
½ tsp. dried oregano
¼ tsp. dried tarragon
⅓ cup dry white wine

1.   In a 1-qt. saucepan bring water to a rapid boil over high heat. Add potatoes and 1 tsp. salt. Lower heat and boil, covered, until potatoes are barely tender when tested with a toothpick, about 15 minutes.

2.   In a 10-inch skillet with a nonstick finish sauté mushrooms and garlic in 1 Tbsp. butter over medium-high heat until lightly browned, about 3 minutes. Set aside on a small plate.

3.   Scrape salmon skin with a knife to remove any scales. Halve cherry tomatoes. Break off butts of asparagus stalks as far from bud ends as they will snap easily. Slice tips diagonally ⅓ inch thick. (Makes about 1 cup slices.)

4.   When potatoes are done, remove from water with a slotted spoon and drain on paper towels. Turn heat to high and add asparagus to potato water. Boil 2 minutes. Drain in a colander.

5.   Season salmon with pepper and ½ tsp. salt. Brown salmon and potato quarters (in skillet used for mushrooms) in 1 Tbsp. each butter and oil over medium-high heat, about 8 minutes. Sprinkle with oregano and tarragon toward end of browning. Remove salmon and potatoes to a serving platter (reserve skillet).

6.   Add mushrooms, asparagus, and tomatoes to skillet and heat through over medium-high heat, 1 or 2 minutes. Sprinkle with ⅛ tsp. salt. Place around salmon.

Add wine to skillet and boil down to 1 Tbsp. over high heat, 3 minutes. Swirl in 1 Tbsp. butter and pour over salmon steaks.

*The best months for asparagus are March, April, and May. If not in season, substitute 1½ cups of small broccoli florets and boil for 4 minutes.
**Fresh salmon is generally available from April through October.

To do ahead: This is best if not prepared ahead, although salmon and potatoes may be held in a warm oven up to 15 minutes after completing Step 5. (Turn oven to 200°F before starting Step 5.)

STRAWBERRIES WITH GRAND MARNIER SAUCE

Working Time: 10 Minutes/Chilling Time: 30 minutes/Servings: 2

1 egg yolk	1 pkg. (3-oz.) cream cheese, cut in quarters
1 Tbsp. Grand Marnier*	2 Tbsp. whipping cream
¼ cup sugar	1 basket (1 pt.) strawberries

1.   Place all ingredients, except cream and strawberries, in blender. Blend just until smooth, stopping occasionally to scrape down sides of blender. Mix in cream and pour sauce into a 1-cup bowl, cover, and refrigerate.

2.   Rinse and dry strawberries and hull. Thickly slice enough strawberries to make 1½ cups. Divide between 2 compotes, cover with plastic wrap, and refrigerate.

3.   To serve, pour sauce over strawberries. Accompany with Grand Marnier coffee if desired (see Note).

*Grand Marnier is a French liqueur based on Cognac and flavored with orange peel. It's available in any liquor store.

To do ahead: Do Step 1 up to several days ahead. Do Step 2 up to 2 hours ahead.

Note: For Grand Marnier coffee, add 1 to 2 Tbsp. Grand Marnier (to taste and depending on strength of coffee) to each cup of strong, hot coffee.

YUGOSLAVIAN MENU

- Hot Ham Canapés

- Fish Fillets in Herbed Sour Cream
- Layered Spinach, Onions, Mushrooms, and Tomatoes
  Green Hungarian Wine

- Brandied Cherry Sherbet Sundaes
  Coffee

Yugoslavia has a magnificent abundance of fruits, vegetables, herbs, livestock, and fish, as well as a history of sophisticated cooking—a composite of Central European and Middle Eastern traditions. Here is a delectable meal drawn from this exciting blend of cultural influences.

The hot ham canapés are made by spreading toast triangles with a mixture of finely chopped ham, cream cheese, sour cream, and grated Parmesan cheese, then baking them in a hot oven.

Monkfish, an Atlantic and Mediterranean fish, or any other lean-fleshed fish, can be sautéed and served with this butter-and-sour-cream sauce flavored with green onions, thyme, and tarragon. The sauce is so easy there's enough time to prepare the exquisite vegetable accompaniment, a colorful example of the layered casseroles (usually containing meats) called *djuveč*, for which the Yugoslavs are famous. This *djuveč* has layers of spinach, sautéed onions and garlic, sliced tomatoes, and sautéed mushrooms.

A very nice wine to serve is a California Green Hungarian, such as that made by Weibel winery. It's crisp, fruity, and flavorful.

A fitting dessert for this menu is made by preparing a quick sherbet using frozen dark sweet cherries. Scoops of sherbet are served with scoops of vanilla ice cream, and brandied cherries are spooned over all.

SHOPPING LIST FOR YUGOSLAVIAN MENU

Meat, Fish, Dairy, Eggs:

☐ cooked sandwich ham (1 oz.)

☐ 2 fish fillets (¾ lb. total), such as monkfish or red snapper

☐ butter (9 Tbsp.)

☐ dairy sour cream (⅔ cup)

☐ whipping cream (2 Tbsp.)

☐ vanilla ice cream (2 scoops)

☐ Parmesan cheese (1 Tbsp. grated)

☐ cream cheese (1 oz.)

☐ eggs (1 white)

Produce:

☐ ⅛ lb. mushrooms

☐ 1 small (4-oz.) tomato

☐ 2 lemons (2 wedges plus 2½ Tbsp. juice)

☐ 1 large onion

☐ garlic (½ tsp. minced)

☐ green onions (1)

Grocery:

☐ good white bread (3 slices)

☐ 10-oz. pkg. frozen, chopped spinach

☐ 1 pkg. frozen, pitted, dark sweet cherries (need 8 oz.)

Liquor:

☐ 1 bottle Green Hungarian wine (Weibel winery)

☐ sweet, cherry-flavored brandy (2 Tbsp.)

Check Staples:

☐ salt

☐ ground white pepper

☐ ground nutmeg (a pinch)

☐ paprika (a pinch)

☐ dried tarragon (⅛ tsp.)

☐ dried thyme (⅛ tsp.)

☐ Dijon mustard (½ tsp.)

☐ flour (¼ cup)

☐ sugar (½ cup)

☐ coffee

COUNTDOWNS FOR YUGOSLAVIAN MENU

Last-Minute Countdown

Time in   *Activity*
Minutes

60 minutes ahead:

10   Chill wine; cream cheese out of refrigerator (for canapés); Steps 1–3 of dessert (squeeze 1 tsp. lemon juice for vegetables)

25   Steps 1–6 of vegetables

10   Steps 1–3 of canapés (oven to 375°F)

15   Uncork wine; Step 1 of fish; Step 4 of canapés; Step 7 of vegetables (oven to 350°F)

 —
60

Serving:

Serve canapés and wine.

(Step 4 of dessert; Step 3 of fish and keep warm)

Serve fish (Step 4), vegetable, and more wine.

Make coffee.

Serve dessert (Step 5) and coffee.

Plan-Ahead Countdown

Time in   *Activity*
Minutes

One day ahead:

10   Chill wine; cream cheese out of refrigerator (for canapés); Steps 1–3 of dessert (squeeze 1 tsp. lemon juice for vegetables)

25   Steps 1–6 of vegetables

10   Steps 1–3 of canapés
 —
45

25 minutes ahead:

—   Oven to 375°F.

15 minutes ahead:

15   Step 4 of dessert; uncork wine; Step 1 of fish; Step 4 of canapés; Step 7 of vegetables (oven to 350°F)

Serving:

Serve canapés and wine.

(Do Step 3 of fish and keep warm.)

Serve fish (Step 4), vegetable, and more wine.

Make coffee.

Serve dessert (Step 5) and coffee.

HOT HAM CANAPÉS

Working Time: 10 minutes/Baking Time: 10 minutes (375°F)/Servings: 2

3 slices good white bread
1 Tbsp. butter, melted
1 oz. (⅓ of a 3-oz. pkg.) cream cheese,
   softened
1 Tbsp. sour cream

1 Tbsp. freshly grated Parmesan cheese
3 Tbsp. finely chopped cooked ham (1-oz.
   slice sandwich ham)
Pinch of paprika

Chop celery 1 tbs
Chop onion 4

   1.   Turn oven to 375°F. Toast bread in toaster, then cut off crusts. Brush one side of bread slices with melted butter.

   2.   On a small plate, using a fork, blend together cream cheese, sour cream, Parmesan cheese, and ham. Spread mixture on buttered side of bread slices. Sprinkle with paprika.

Cut first

   3.   Cut each slice diagonally both ways to make 4 triangles. Place on a small baking sheet.

   4.   Bake in center of oven for 10 minutes. Serve hot as an hors d'oeuvre.

To do ahead: Do Steps 1–3 up to 1 day ahead. Cover and refrigerate.

FISH FILLETS IN HERBED SOUR CREAM

Working Time: 15 minutes/Cooking Time: 10 minutes/Servings: 2

HERBED SOUR CREAM SAUCE:
1 Tbsp. finely chopped green onion
3 Tbsp. butter
⅛ tsp. dried tarragon
⅛ tsp. dried thyme
⅛ tsp. salt
Pinch of ground white pepper
¼ tsp. sugar
½ cup dairy sour cream

FISH FILLETS:
2 fish fillets* (¾ lb. total)
¼ tsp. salt
2 Tbsp. (about) flour
1 Tbsp. butter
2 lemon wedges

1. In a ¾-qt. saucepan (not aluminum) cook onion in butter over medium heat for 1 minute. Remove pan from heat and add remaining sauce ingredients, mixing well.

2. Sprinkle fish with salt and dust with flour. In a 10-inch skillet with a non-stick surface brown fillets over medium-high heat in 1 Tbsp. butter, about 4 minutes on first side.

3. Turn fish and brown on second side, about 4 minutes. Do not overcook. Heat sour cream sauce over low heat just until hot (overheating may cause slight curdling).

4. Place fillets (and any juices) on a small platter. Pour sauce over them, leaving parts of fish showing. Garnish with lemon wedges and serve.

*Authentically this dish can be prepared using monkfish (also called angler, goose-fish, or lotte), a fish with lobster-like flesh, which is now available in the United States. The fillets (from the tail actually) are thick and should be cut in half horizontally to sauté. A good substitute for monkfish is rockfish, but sole or flounder are also delicious with this special sauce.

To do ahead: Do Step 1 up to 2 days ahead, if desired. Cover and refrigerate.

LAYERED SPINACH, ONIONS, MUSHROOMS, AND TOMATOES

Working and Cooking Time: 25 minutes/Baking Time: 10 minutes (350°F)/
Servings: 2 to 3

1 pkg. (10-oz.) frozen, chopped spinach	⅛ lb. (4 medium-size) mushrooms
2 Tbsp. water	¼ tsp. plus a pinch of salt
1 large onion, peeled and sliced ¹⁄₁₆ inch thick	Pinch of ground nutmeg
	2 Tbsp. whipping cream
½ tsp. minced garlic	1 small (4-oz.) tomato, sliced ⅛ inch thick
4 Tbsp. butter, divided	1 tsp. fresh lemon juice

1. Place spinach and water in an 8-inch skillet, cover, and cook over medium-high heat until spinach is completely thawed, about 15 minutes. Break up the frozen spinach with a fork and reduce heat as it thaws.

2. In a 10-inch skillet with a nonstick surface sauté onion and garlic in 2 Tbsp. butter over medium heat until onion is very tender, about 10 minutes. Set aside.

3. Wash and dry mushrooms and slice thinly.

4. Turn oven to 350°F. Drain spinach in a strainer, pressing out as much water as possible. Return to saucepan and add 1 Tbsp. butter, ¼ tsp. salt, the nutmeg, and cream. Mix well.

5. Remove onions to a small plate. In same skillet sauté mushrooms in 1 Tbsp. butter until lightly browned, 3 minutes.

6. Spread spinach in a gratin dish (10 inches long). Spread onion over spinach to within ¾ inch of edge. Place overlapping tomato slices over onion. Sprinkle with a pinch of salt. Pile mushrooms in center and sprinkle with lemon juice.

7. Heat in oven until mixture is hot, 10 to 15 minutes.

To do ahead: Prepare through Step 6 up to 1 day ahead. Cover and refrigerate. To serve, reheat, uncovered, in 350°F oven for 15 minutes.

BRANDIED CHERRY SHERBET SUNDAES

Working Time: 15 minutes/Freezing Time: 1 hour/Servings: 2

BRANDIED CHERRIES, ETC.;
8 *frozen, pitted, dark sweet cherries*
  (unsweetened)
2 *Tbsp. sugar*
1 *Tbsp. water*
2 *Tbsp. sweet, cherry-flavored brandy*
2 *scoops vanilla ice cream*

CHERRY SHERBET:
1 *cup frozen, pitted, dark sweet cherries*
  (unsweetened)
¼ *cup sugar*
2 *Tbsp. fresh lemon juice*
1 *egg white*

1. Put the 8 cherries, water, and 2 Tbsp. sugar in a ¾-qt. saucepan over medium heat.

2. Put all ingredients for cherry sherbet in blender and blend on high speed for 1 minute. Pour into freezer tray and put in freezer.

3. When the 8 cherries have simmered about 2 minutes, remove from heat and add cherry brandy. Pour into a 1-cup bowl, cover, and refrigerate.

4. When sherbet is frozen, pack into a jar and return to freezer.

5. To serve, place a scoop of vanilla ice cream and a scoop of cherry sherbet in each of two individual compotes. Spoon brandied cherries (with liquid) over all.

To do ahead: Do Steps 1–4 up to 4 days ahead.

MEDITERRANEAN MENU

- Smoked-Oyster Appetizer Salad

- Swordfish Kebabs
- Green Rice
- Roasted Red Peppers with Pine Nuts
  Sauvignon Blanc

- Melon and Peaches Anisette
  Coffee

There's something captivating about Mediterranean food. Perhaps it's the flavors—garlic, onions, peppers, tomatoes; perhaps it's the colors—bright yellow, red, or green peppers, shiny black olives, the soft hues of melons, peaches, and plums. Whatever these qualities, they seem inherent in this impressive menu that's drawn from four Mediterranean countries—Portugal, Spain, Italy, and Turkey.

To create an easy appetizer salad, Portuguese smoked oysters, marinated artichoke hearts, tomato wedges, and cucumber slices are arranged on lettuce leaves and drizzled with a vinaigrette dressing.

The swordfish kebabs are a Turkish dish known as *kilic sis*. The pieces of swordfish are marinated in olive oil, lemon juice, garlic, paprika, and oregano before being broiled in the oven or over charcoal. A dry Sauvignon blanc, full-bodied and fruity with a wholesome earthiness, is very good with the swordfish.

Green rice is white rice that gets its color from puréed parsley, which also provides a clean, fresh taste. The skewered swordfish is served with the rice and a side dish of roasted red peppers, prepared Italian-style with toasted pine nuts, and garlic.

The Spanish dessert is a fruit mixture delicately perfumed with anisette liqueur. Melon and peaches are especially compatible with the flavor of anise.

SHOPPING LIST FOR MEDITERRANEAN MENU

Fish, Dairy:

☐ 1 lb. swordfish (to be cut in 1x1½x1½-inch pieces)

☐ butter (1 Tbsp.)

Produce:

☐ 1 medium-size (6-oz.) tomato

☐ 1 small (½-lb.) cucumber (need half)

☐ 1 lemon (need 2½ Tbsp. juice)

☐ 1 small (2-lb.) honeydew or other melon*

☐ 1 large or 2 small (8 oz.) peaches*

☐ romaine, butterhead, or leaf lettuce (4 to 6 leaves)

☐ green onions (¼ cup chopped)

☐ parsley (¼ cup packed)

☐ garlic (1½ tsp. minced)

☐ fresh mint (2 sprigs), optional

Grocery:

☐ 3¾-oz. can smoked oysters

☐ 1 jar (6-oz.) marinated artichoke hearts

☐ 1 jar (7-oz.) roasted red peppers

☐ pine nuts (¾ oz. or 2 Tbsp.), or substitute slivered almonds

Liquor:

☐ dry white wine, such as Sauvignon blanc

☐ anisette (1 Tbsp.)

Check Staples:

☐ salt

☐ black pepper

☐ sugar (2 Tbsp.)

☐ paprika (¼ tsp.)

☐ dried oregano (½ tsp.)

☐ olive oil (¼ cup)

☐ long-grain white rice (½ cup)

☐ canned condensed chicken broth (1 cup)

☐ coffee

☐ plastic wrap

☐ paper towels

☐ 4 bamboo skewers (6 to 9 inches long)

☐ charcoal briquets (if using)

☐ lighter fluid (if using)

*May need to be purchased several days ahead to allow for ripening.

COUNTDOWNS FOR MEDITERRANEAN MENU

Last-Minute Countdown

Time in   *Activity*
Minutes

55 minutes ahead:

10   Chill wine; Step 2 of fish (mince 1 tsp. garlic for peppers and squeeze 1 Tbsp. lemon juice for dessert)
10   Step 1 of salad
5   Step 1 of fish
10   Prepare dessert.
10   Prepare peppers.
5   Step 1 of rice
<u>5</u>   Step 3 of fish; uncork wine.
55

Serving:

Serve salad (Step 2).

(5 minutes before finishing salad, do Step 4 of fish.)

Step 5 of fish; Step 2 of rice; reheat peppers.

Serve fish (Step 6), rice, peppers, and wine.

Serve dessert.

Make and serve coffee.

Plan-Ahead Countdown

Time in   *Activity*
Minutes

One day ahead:

10   Chill wine; prepare dessert (squeeze 1½ Tbsp. lemon juice for fish).
10   Prepare rice.
10   Prepare peppers (mince ½ tsp. garlic for fish).
10   Step 2 of fish
<u>10</u>   Step 1 of salad
50

40 minutes ahead:

10   Steps 1 and 3 of fish; salad out of refrigerator; uncork wine.

Serving:

Serve salad (Step 2).

(5 minutes before finishing salad, do Step 4 of fish and put rice on to reheat.)

Step 5 of fish; reheat peppers.

Serve fish (Step 6), rice, peppers, and wine.

Serve dessert.

Make and serve coffee.

SMOKED-OYSTER APPETIZER SALAD

Working Time: 10 minutes/Chilling Time: 30 minutes/Servings: 2

4 to 6 leaves romaine, butterhead, or leaf
    lettuce
1 can (3¾-oz.) smoked oysters, drained
½ small cucumber (¼ lb.), peeled and sliced
    ⅛ inch thick
1 jar (6-oz.) marinated artichoke hearts,
    drained

1 medium-size (6-oz.) tomato, cut in 10
    wedges
¼ cup (about) oil and vinegar-type French
    dressing, such as Trader Vic's

1.   Line two salad plates with lettuce leaves. Arrange separate mounds of oysters, cucumber slices, and artichoke hearts attractively on each plate. Garnish with tomato wedges. Cover with plastic wrap and refrigerate 30 minutes to chill slightly.

2.   Just before serving spoon dressing over salads.

To do ahead: Do Step 2 up to 1 day ahead. Cover and refrigerate. Remove from refrigerator about 30 minutes before serving.

Note: For best flavor this salad should be served only slightly chilled.

SWORDFISH KEBABS

Working Time: 20 minutes/Marinating Time: 30 minutes to 24 hours/Broiling Time: 10 minutes/Total Time: 1 hour/Servings: 2

½ tsp. salt (scant)
½ tsp. dried oregano
½ tsp. minced garlic
¼ tsp. paprika

1½ Tbsp. fresh lemon juice
3 Tbsp. olive oil
1 lb. swordfish*, cut in 1x1½x1½-inch
    pieces

1.   If charcoal broiling, set up grill and light charcoal.

2.   Combine all recipe ingredients, except swordfish, in a 1½-qt. bowl. Beat

together with a fork. Add swordfish, mixing well with marinade. Let stand at least 30 minutes.

3.   Thread swordfish on 4 bamboo skewers (6 to 9 inches long). Reserve marinade.

4.   Broil 2 inches from heat (if using an electric oven, keep door ajar so element stays red hot), basting once or twice, until lightly browned, about 5 minutes on first side.

5.   Turn fish and broil about 4 minutes on second side, basting once or twice.

6.   Serve fish on a small platter with the green rice and red peppers.

*Swordfish is generally available from April to September. If unavailable, shark is a good substitute.

To do ahead: Do Step 2 up to 1 day ahead. Cover and refrigerate.

GREEN RICE

Working Time: 10 minutes/Cooking Time: 20 minutes/Servings: 2

1 Tbsp. butter
¼ cup chopped green onions
½ cup long-grain white rice

1 cup canned condensed chicken broth, divided
¼ cup (packed) parsley leaves

1.   In a 1-qt. saucepan sauté onion and rice in butter over medium heat for 2 minutes. Add ¾ cup chicken broth and bring to a boil over high heat. Reduce heat to low, cover, and simmer until liquid is absorbed, about 15 minutes.

2.   Combine parsley and ¼ cup chicken broth in blender and whirl until parsley is puréed. Add to cooked rice, cover, and heat 5 minutes. Serve on same platter as fish.

To do ahead: Prepare up to 1 day ahead. Reheat over low heat about 8 minutes, stirring occasionally.

ROASTED RED PEPPERS WITH PINE NUTS

Working and Cooking Time: 10 minutes/Servings: 2

1 Tbsp. olive oil
2 Tbsp. pine nuts*

1 tsp. minced garlic
1 jar (7-oz.) roasted red peppers, drained

    1. In a 9-inch skillet sauté pine nuts in oil over medium-low heat, stirring frequently, until nuts are lightly browned, about 5 minutes.

    2. Remove any large pieces of charred skin from red peppers. Drain peppers on paper towels. If pieces of pepper are large, tear them into 1-inch-wide strips.

    3. When nuts are browned, remove skillet from heat, add garlic, and stir 1 minute. Add red peppers and heat through. Serve on same platter as fish.

*Pine nuts are the seeds of several varieties of pine trees. They have a soft texture and mild flavor. They are available in gourmet markets—be sure to buy them with the black shells already removed. If pine nuts are unavailable, substitute 1½ tablespoons slivered almonds.

To do ahead: Prepare up to 1 day ahead. Cover and refrigerate.

MELON AND PEACHES ANISETTE

Working Time: 10 minutes/Chilling Time: 1 hour/Servings: 2

2 Tbsp. sugar
1 Tbsp. fresh lemon juice
1 Tbsp. anisette*
1 small (2-lb.) honeydew melon**

1 large or 2 small (8 oz.) ripe peaches,
    peeled and sliced
2 sprigs fresh mint (optional)

    1. Combine sugar, lemon juice, and anisette in a 1½-qt. bowl. Halve melon and remove seeds. With a melon-ball cutter scoop out as many melon balls as possible. Gently mix melon balls and peach slices with anisette mixture.

2. Divide fruit and liquid between two compotes and garnish with mint, if using. Cover with plastic wrap and refrigerate at least 1 hour for flavor to mellow.

*Anisette is a sweet, anise-flavored liqueur. Spanish Anis del Mono, French Anisette de Bordeaux, or any domestic anisette may be used. Anisette is readily available in liquor stores.
**Cantaloupe, casaba, crenshaw, or Persian melon may be substituted. Fresh melons are most readily available from about May through October.

To do ahead: May be prepared up to 1 day ahead.

INDIAN MENU

- **Chick Pea and Rice Soup**

- **Spicy Sole Fillets**
- **Sherried Tomatoes**
- **Broccoli with Cashews and Sesame Seeds**
- **Pineapple Yogurt Drink**

- **Bananas in Cardamom Orange Sauce**
  Darjeeling Tea

Looking for a change of pace in quick cuisine? Indian cooking, with its exotic spicing, offers some wonderful possibilities. Here's a menu that's different, yet quite appealing to Western palates.

Dinner begins with a chick pea and rice soup, fragrant with onions and garlic, and lightly seasoned with curry powder and ground coriander. It's richly flavored and hearty, but not too filling for a first course.

The main course dishes are conveniently served all on one platter, the golden fried sole fillets in the center and, at each end, a sherried tomato with a serving of bright green broccoli. (It will be beautiful!)

The sole, while not fiery, is nicely spiced with ground chili, coriander, cloves, and cardamom, with a slight piquancy from tarragon vinegar. The tomatoes are fried whole with a slice cut from each end to allow the flavors of butter, turmeric, dill weed, and sherry to seep in. The broccoli is stir-fried with sesame and mustard seeds and tossed with cashews, a superb vegetable dish.

An easy and cooling beverage to balance these well-seasoned dishes is made by combining pineapple yogurt, pineapple juice, and crushed ice in a blender.

For dessert bananas are cooked in a sauce of butter, brown sugar, orange juice, grated orange peel, and ground cardamom. The bananas are served hot, topped with the sauce and a little sour cream.

SHOPPING LIST FOR INDIAN MENU

Fish, Dairy:

☐ ⅔ lb. fillet of sole (to be cut in 6 to 8 pieces)

☐ butter (4 Tbsp.)

☐ 1 carton (8-oz.) pineapple yogurt

☐ sour cream (3 Tbsp.)

Produce:

☐ 1 small onion (need ¼ cup chopped)

☐ garlic (¼ tsp. minced)

☐ 1 lemon (need 4 tsp. juice)

☐ 1 orange

☐ 2 medium-size tomatoes (¾ lb. total)

☐ ⅔ lb. broccoli

☐ 2 small bananas*

☐ parsley (1 tsp. chopped)

Grocery:

☐ 1 can (8½-oz.) chick peas

☐ 1 can (6-oz.) unsweetened pineapple juice

☐ roasted, salted cashews (¼ cup)

☐ ground turmeric (⅛ tsp.)

Liquor:

☐ medium (golden or oloroso) sherry (2 Tbsp.)

Check Staples:

☐ salt

☐ black pepper

☐ ground red pepper

☐ curry powder (½ tsp.), preferably Madras or Schilling's Indian curry powder

☐ chili powder (½ tsp.)

☐ ground coriander (½ tsp.)

☐ ground cardamom (⅜ tsp.)

☐ sesame seeds (2 tsp.)

☐ mustard seeds (½ tsp.)

☐ ground cloves (⅛ tsp.)

☐ dried dill weed (⅛ tsp.)

☐ sugar (1 Tbsp.)

☐ light brown sugar (2 Tbsp.)

☐ flour (2 Tbsp.)

☐ cornstarch (2 Tbsp.)

☐ salad (not olive) oil (6 Tbsp.)

☐ tarragon vinegar (1 Tbsp.)

☐ long-grain white rice (1½ Tbsp.)

☐ 1 can (10¾-oz.) condensed chicken broth

☐ ice cubes (8)

☐ tea (Darjeeling)

*May need to be purchased several days ahead to allow for ripening.

COUNTDOWNS FOR INDIAN MENU

Last-Minute Countdown

Time in   Activity
Minutes

55 minutes ahead:

10 Step 1 of dessert (squeeze 2 tsp.
      lemon juice for soup and broccoli)
10 Step 1 of sole
15 Steps 1–2 of soup and chop parsley.
 5 Step 1 of beverage and crush ice.
10 Steps 1–3 of broccoli
 5 Step 1 of tomatoes
55

Serving:

Serve soup (Step 3).
Step 2 of tomatoes; Step 2 of sole; Step 4
  of broccoli; Step 3 of tomatoes
Serve sole (Step 3), tomatoes, broccoli
  (Step 5), and beverage (Step 2).
Make tea; Step 2 of dessert
Serve dessert (Step 3) and tea.

Plan-Ahead Countdown

Time in   Activity
Minutes

One day ahead:

15 Steps 1–2 of soup
10 Step 1 of dessert
10 Steps 1–3 of broccoli
35

20 minutes ahead:

10 Chop parsley for soup; Step 1 of
      sole
 5 Step 1 of beverage and crush ice;
      put soup on to reheat.
 5 Step 1 of tomatoes
20

Serving:

Serve soup (Step 3).
Step 2 of tomatoes; Step 2 of sole; Step 4
  of broccoli; Step 3 of tomatoes
Serve sole (Step 3), tomatoes, broccoli
  (Step 5), and beverage (Step 2).
Make tea; Step 2 of dessert
Serve dessert (Step 3) and tea.

CHICK PEA AND RICE SOUP

Working Time: 15 minutes/Cooking Time: 20 minutes more/Servings: 2

¼ cup finely chopped onion
¼ tsp. minced garlic
½ tsp. curry powder*
¼ tsp. ground coriander
1 Tbsp. butter

1 can (8½-oz.) chick peas
1 can (10¾-oz.) condensed chicken broth
1½ Tbsp. long-grain white rice
1 tsp. fresh lemon juice
1 tsp. finely chopped parsley

1. In a 1½-qt. saucepan over medium heat sauté onion, garlic, curry powder, and coriander in butter for 4 minutes.

2. Put chick peas with their liquid and rice (raw) in blender. Blend to purée peas and break up rice. Add to onion mixture along with chicken broth. Bring to a boil over high heat, reduce heat to low, cover, and simmer 20 minutes.

3. Add lemon juice to soup, divide between 2 soup bowls, sprinkle with chopped parsley, and serve.

*Preferably Madras curry powder or Schilling's Indian curry powder.

To do ahead: Do Steps 1–2 up to 1 day ahead. Cool, cover, and refrigerate.

SPICY SOLE FILLETS

Working and Cooking Time: 20 minutes/Servings: 2

2 Tbsp. flour
2 Tbsp. cornstarch
¼ tsp. salt
¼ tsp. ground coriander
½ tsp. chili powder
⅛ tsp. ground black pepper

⅛ tsp. ground cloves
⅛ tsp. ground cardamom
1 Tbsp. tarragon vinegar
3 Tbsp. cold water
⅔ lb. fillet of sole, cut in 6 to 8 pieces
¼ cup salad (not olive) oil for frying

1.   In a 1-qt. bowl stir together all dry ingredients. With a whisk blend in vinegar and water. Dry sole fillets with paper towels and add to spice mixture, coating the pieces well.

2.   Heat oil over medium-high heat in a 10-inch skillet with a nonstick surface. Add half the pieces of sole to skillet, trying not to let them touch and keeping as much of the spice mixture on them as possible. Fry until brown on both sides, 5 minutes total. Repeat with remaining fillets.

3.   Arrange fillets in center of large platter. Place a tomato and a serving of broccoli at each end of platter.

To do ahead: Do Step 1 up to 1 hour ahead. Cover and refrigerate.

SHERRIED TOMATOES

Working Time: 10 minutes/Cooking Time: 10 minutes/Servings: 2

2 medium-size tomatoes (¾ lb. total)
⅛ tsp. salt
⅛ tsp. dried dill weed
⅛ tsp. ground turmeric*

Pinch of ground black pepper
1 Tbsp. butter
2 Tbsp. medium sherry (golden or oloroso)

1.   Cut a thin slice from tops and bottoms of tomatoes. Sprinkle cut surfaces with salt, dill weed, turmeric, and pepper.

2.   Heat butter in a 5-inch skillet over medium heat. Cook tomatoes about 5 minutes on each cut surface.

3.   Place tomatoes on serving platter with fish. Add sherry to skillet and boil down quickly to 1½ tablespoons liquid. Pour over tomatoes.

*Turmeric is the root of a tropical herb belonging to the ginger family. It has a bittersweet flavor, musty aroma, and yellow color. It's available in Indian grocery stores and many supermarkets. (Turmeric can stain, so keep it away from porous surfaces, including your fingernails.)

To do ahead: Do Step 1 up to 30 minutes ahead.

BROCCOLI WITH CASHEWS AND SESAME SEEDS

Working Time: 10 minutes/Cooking Time: 10 minutes/Servings: 2

2 tsp. sesame seeds	½ tsp. mustard seeds
2 Tbsp. salad (not olive) oil	2 Tbsp. water
⅔ lb. broccoli (2 medium-size stalks)	⅛ tsp. sugar
¼ tsp. salt	¼ cup roasted, salted cashews
Pinch of ground red pepper	1 tsp. fresh lemon juice

1. In a wok or a 9-inch skillet over medium heat toast sesame seeds in oil until golden, stirring occasionally, 5 minutes.

2. Discard about 1 inch from end of broccoli stalks. Slice remainder of stalks ¼ inch thick. Cut florets into bite-size pieces. (You should have about 3 cups.)

3. When sesame seeds are toasted, add salt and red pepper, then mustard seeds.

4. Add broccoli to hot wok or skillet and stir-fry 1 minute. Add water, cover, and steam until tender, 5 minutes.

5. Uncover, toss with sugar, and let any excess water evaporate. Add cashews. Place on same platter as fish, and sprinkle lemon juice over broccoli.

To do ahead: Do Steps 1–3 up to 1 day ahead. Cover and refrigerate broccoli; leave seed mixture at room temperature.

PINEAPPLE YOGURT DRINK

Working Time: 5 minutes/Servings: 2

1 carton (8-oz.) pineapple yogurt	1 Tbsp. sugar
1 can (6-oz.) unsweetened pineapple juice	1 cup crushed ice (about 8 ice cubes)

1. Mix yogurt, pineapple juice, and sugar in blender.

2.   Just before serving add crushed ice and blend.

To do ahead: Do Step 1 and crush ice (but do not add) up to 3 hours ahead. Refrigerate yogurt and freeze crushed ice.

BANANAS IN CARDAMOM ORANGE SAUCE

Working and Cooking Time: 15 minutes/Servings: 2

2 Tbsp. butter

2 Tbsp. light brown sugar

¼ tsp. ground cardamom

¼ tsp. grated orange peel

¼ cup strained fresh orange juice

2 tsp. fresh lemon juice

2 small, ripe bananas

3 Tbsp. sour cream

1.   In an 8-inch skillet (not uncoated aluminum) boil all ingredients, except bananas and sour cream, over medium-high heat until mixture is reduced to ⅓ cup and looks syrupy, about 4 minutes.

2.   Peel bananas and remove any strings. Cut in half crosswise, then lengthwise. Add to sauce, cut side up. Cook 1 minute, basting with sauce. Turn bananas over and cook, basting, until soft but not falling apart, about 1 minute.

3.   Transfer bananas to 2 rimmed serving plates, pour sauce over bananas, top with a dollop of sour cream, and serve.

To do ahead: Do Step 1 up to 1 day ahead. Cool, cover, and refrigerate.

ORIENTAL AMERICAN MENU

- Spinach, Mushroom, and Bean Sprout Salad

- Stir-Fried Scallops and Vegetables
- Boiled Rice
  Sake

- Almond Ice Cream with Lychee Sauce
  Tea

Many elements of Oriental cuisine have been absorbed into American menus. The diversity of tastes and textures that can be introduced into everyday meals by drawing from thousands of years of Oriental creativity can be exciting and rewarding. This menu is one example.

The tossed salad contains ingredients typical of the Orient, such as bean sprouts and sesame seeds. The dressing is made with Japanese rice vinegar, sugar, and sesame oil. This salad is a good addition to almost any menu that features a Japanese, Chinese, Korean, or Vietnamese style meat or fish dish.

When it comes to preparing seafood, Cantonese cooks are among the most artful in the world. In this dish, of Cantonese origin, scallops are stir-fried with garlic, ginger, sliced carrots and celery, snow peas, and green onions. The seasoning mixture contains oyster sauce, which has a subtle, meaty flavor that's complementary to the scallops. Scallops are among the easiest of shellfish to prepare because they are readily purchased free of their shells.

Boiled rice and warm sake are appropriate accompaniments with the stir-fried scallops.

Not to deny Westerners their just desserts, this menu includes a favorite American finale with an Oriental twist. A warm sauce made with lychees, a sweetly perfumed fruit native to Southeast Asia, is served over toasted almond ice cream.

SHOPPING LIST FOR ORIENTAL AMERICAN MENU

Seafood, Dairy:

☐ ½ lb. scallops

☐ toasted almond ice cream (⅔ pt.)

☐ butter (1 Tbsp.)

Produce:

☐ 1 bunch tender young spinach

☐ 2 medium-size mushrooms (about ½ cup sliced)

☐ 1½ oz. bean sprouts (⅔ cup)

☐ 1 small (3-oz.) carrot

☐ celery (1 stalk)

☐ ⅛ lb. (16 small) snow peas

☐ 1 bunch thin green onions

☐ garlic (½ tsp. minced)

☐ ginger (½ tsp. minced)

☐ 1 lemon (need 2 tsp. juice)

Grocery:

☐ Japanese rice vinegar (2 Tbsp.)

☐ Oriental sesame oil (½ Tbsp.)

☐ oyster sauce (1½ Tbsp.)

☐ 1 can (11-oz.) lychees (need half)

Liquor:

☐ 1 bottle sake

Check Staples:

☐ salt

☐ sugar (6¼ tsp.)

☐ cornstarch (2½ tsp.)

☐ sesame seeds (1 Tbsp.)

☐ soy sauce (1 Tbsp.)

☐ salad (not olive) oil (¼ cup)

☐ long-grain white rice (¾ cup)

☐ tea

☐ plastic wrap

COUNTDOWNS FOR ORIENTAL AMERICAN MENU

Last-Minute Countdown

Time in   Activity
Minutes

55 minutes ahead:
20   Steps 1–4 of salad
10   Steps 1–2 of dessert
20   Steps 1–2 of scallop dish
 5   Steps 1–2 of rice
55

Serving:
Serve salad (Step 5).
Step 3 of rice; heat sake; Steps 3–6 of
  scallop dish
Serve scallop dish, rice, and sake.
Make tea.
Serve dessert (Step 3) and tea.

Plan-Ahead Countdown

Time in   Activity
Minutes

One day ahead:
20   Steps 1–4 of salad
10   Steps 1–2 of dessert
30

25 minutes ahead:
20   Steps 1–2 of scallop dish
 5   Steps 1–2 of rice
25

Serving:
Serve salad (Step 5).
Step 3 of rice; heat sake; Steps 3–6 of
  scallop dish
Serve scallop dish, rice, and sake.
Make tea.
Serve dessert (Step 3) and tea.

SPINACH, MUSHROOM, AND BEAN SPROUT SALAD

Working Time: 20 minutes/Chilling Time: 30 minutes/Servings: 2

SALAD INGREDIENTS:
1 Tbsp. sesame seeds
1 bunch tender young spinach
2 medium-size mushrooms, very thinly
   sliced (about ½ cup)
⅔ cup (1½ oz.) fresh bean sprouts

SESAME DRESSING:
1½ tsp. sugar
¼ tsp. salt
2 Tbsp. Japanese rice vinegar*
2 Tbsp. salad (not olive) oil
1 tsp. Oriental sesame oil**

1. Place sesame seeds in a dry 5-inch skillet over medium heat. When they begin to brown, stir frequently until sesame seeds are toasted and fragrant.

2. Meanwhile, clean spinach and tear leaves into bite-size pieces, to make about 3 cups lightly packed.

3. Mix spinach, mushrooms, and bean sprouts in a 2-qt. salad bowl. Sprinkle with the toasted sesame seeds. Cover with plastic wrap and refrigerate at least 30 minutes.

4. For dressing, combine sugar, salt, and vinegar in a ½-pt. jar. Cover and shake until sugar dissolves. Add oils and shake again. Refrigerate.

5. At serving time toss salad with dressing.

*Japanese rice vinegar is available in Oriental markets and many supermarkets. Five teaspoons of cider vinegar can be substituted in this recipe.
**Oriental sesame oil is a brown oil extracted from toasted sesame seeds and used as a seasoning in Oriental dishes. It's available in bottles in Oriental markets. Omit if unavailable.

To do ahead: Prepare through Step 4 up to 1 day ahead.

STIR-FRIED SCALLOPS AND VEGETABLES

Working and Cooking Time: 30 minutes/Servings: 2

SCALLOPS AND VEGETABLES:

2 Tbsp. salad (not olive) oil, divided

½ lb. scallops (slice in half across the grain if large)

½ tsp. minced garlic

½ tsp. minced fresh ginger

1 small (3-oz.) carrot, peeled, sliced diagonally ⅛ inch thick

1 stalk celery, sliced diagonally ¼ inch thick (½ cup)

⅛ lb. (16 small) snow peas, tips and any strings removed

⅓ cup 1-inch pieces thin green onions (include part of tops)

2 Tbsp. water

SEASONING MIXTURE:

1½ tsp. cornstarch

¼ tsp. salt

¼ tsp. sugar

1 Tbsp. soy sauce

1½ Tbsp. oyster sauce*

3 Tbsp. water

½ tsp. Oriental sesame oil**

1. Cut and measure ingredients for scallops and vegetables as indicated.

2. In a 1-cup bowl blend together all ingredients for seasoning mixture.

3. Heat a wok or 10-inch skillet over medium-high to high heat. Add 1 tablespoon oil and immediately add scallops, garlic, and ginger. Stir-fry until scallops become opaque, about 2 minutes.

4. Remove scallops to a small bowl, add 1 tablespoon oil to wok, and immediately add carrot and celery slices. Stir-fry 30 seconds.

5. Add snow peas and green onions to wok and stir-fry 30 seconds. Add 2 tablespoons water, cover, and steam 2 minutes.

6. Return scallops (with liquid) to wok. Stir seasoning mixture and add to wok, pouring it down the side of the pan. Stir and cook until liquid thickens, 1 minute. Serve alongside rice on a small platter.

*Oyster sauce is a thick brown sauce made of oyster extractives and other ingredients. It's available in Oriental markets and many supermarkets. It comes in bottles and keeps indefinitely tightly covered.

**Oriental sesame oil is a brown oil extracted from toasted sesame seeds and used as a seasoning in Oriental dishes. It's available in bottles in Oriental markets. Omit if unavailable.

To do ahead: Prepare through Step 2 up to 1 hour ahead. Cover and leave at room temperature.

BOILED RICE

Working Time: 5 minutes/Cooking Time: 20 minutes/Servings: 2

¾ cup long-grain white rice   1¼ cups water

1.   Place rice in a 1-qt. saucepan. Wash rice in several changes of water, rubbing the grains between your fingers to remove excess starch. Pour off rinse water.

2.   Add 1¼ cups water to rice and bring to a boil over high heat. Reduce heat to medium and boil, uncovered, until no bubbles appear on surface of rice, about 10 minutes.

3.   Turn heat to very low, cover pan, and let steam 10 minutes more. Serve.

To do ahead: Step 1 can be done up to 1 hour ahead.

ALMOND ICE CREAM WITH LYCHEE SAUCE

Working Time: 10 minutes/Servings: 2

1 Tbsp. butter   2 tsp. fresh lemon juice
¼ cup liquid from canned lychees   6 to 8 lychees* (half of an 11-oz. can)
1½ Tbsp. sugar   2 servings (⅔ pt.) toasted almond ice cream
1 tsp. cornstarch

1.   In a ¾-qt. saucepan heat butter, ¼ cup lychee liquid, and the sugar over medium-high heat until mixture boils.

2.   In a ½-cup bowl mix cornstarch and lemon juice. Whisk into boiling mixture and boil until sauce thickens, 2 minutes. Add lychees and heat through.

3. Divide ice cream between 2 serving dishes. Spoon lychee sauce over ice cream and serve.

*Lychees (also spelled litchis) are the fruit of a large tropical tree native to southeastern Asia. Canned lychees are available in Oriental markets and some supermarkets.

To do ahead: Do Steps 1–2 up to 1 day ahead. Cool, cover, and refrigerate. Reheat sauce before proceeding with Step 3.

CHICKEN MENUS

Winter Menu
Greek Menu
Festive Menu
Scandinavian Menu
Oregon Menu
Northern Italian Menu
French Menu

WINTER MENU

- Grapefruit and Artichoke Green Salad

- Herb-Roasted Chicken and Potatoes
- Broccoli and Cherry Tomato Sauté
  Gamay Beaujolais

- Winter Fruit and Cheese Dessert
  Coffee

It's fun to cook in the wintertime when the cold and dampness outside are no competition for a warm, cozy kitchen and the fragrance of wonderful food. Here's a menu to celebrate the season.

Take advantage of a good winter crop—Florida grapefruit—and begin this meal beautifully with a salad that's a palette of pastel colors—pink grapefruit sections and pale green artichoke hearts against multicolored red-leaf lettuce.

The aroma of chicken brushed with herb butter and roasting in the oven is irresistible. And the chicken need not be stuffed to be elegant and tasty. Half a lemon and two green onions in the chicken cavity will insure juiciness and flavor. Quartered potatoes are roasted along with the chicken and brushed with the herb butter too. An excellent accompaniment for the chicken and potatoes is a sauté of broccoli florets and cherry tomatoes with garlic.

A light-bodied red wine is best with wintertime roasted chicken. A Gamay Beaujolais, just slightly chilled, would be very nice. There are many California wineries making good Gamays—Mondavi, Inglenook, Sebastiani, Sterling, and Pedroncelli, for example.

An elegant and easy dessert matches juicy winter fruit—fresh pineapple and grapes—with creamy Brie or Camembert cheese.

SHOPPING LIST FOR WINTER MENU

Poultry, Dairy:

☐ 1 whole chicken, 2 to 2½ lbs.

☐ butter (7 Tbsp.)

☐ 4 oz. Brie or Camembert cheese

Produce:

☐ 1 pineapple (need 1 cup chunks)

☐ ½ lb. grapes, such as red (Emperor), black (Ribier), or seedless green grapes

☐ 1 red or pink grapefruit

☐ 1 lemon (need ½)

☐ 1 head red-leaf lettuce

☐ parsley (1 Tbsp. chopped)

☐ green onions (2)

☐ 2 medium-size baking potatoes (⅔ lb. total)

☐ broccoli (2 cups florets)

☐ cherry tomatoes (12 small)

☐ garlic (¼ tsp. minced)

Grocery:

☐ 1 jar (6-oz.) marinated artichoke hearts

☐ French dressing (oil and vinegar type), such as Trader Vic's (¼ cup)

Liquor:

☐ 1 bottle Gamay Beaujolais

Check Staples:

☐ salt

☐ white pepper

☐ dried thyme (¼ tsp.)

☐ dried tarragon (½ tsp.)

☐ paprika (½ tsp.)

☐ coffee

☐ plastic wrap

☐ paper towels

☐ white string

COUNTDOWNS FOR WINTER MENU

Last-Minute Countdown

Time in　　　*Activity*
Minutes

60 minutes ahead:

25　Steps 1–4 of chicken (oven to
　　400°F)
15　Step 1 of salad
10　Chill wine; baste chicken; Steps
　　1–2 of broccoli and tomatoes
10　Step 1 of dessert; uncork wine; Step
　　5 of chicken
___
60

Serving:
Serve salad (Step 2).
When chicken is done, do Step 6; Step
　3 of broccoli and tomatoes
Serve chicken and potatoes, broccoli
　and tomatoes, and wine.
Make coffee.
Serve dessert (Step 2) and coffee.

Plan-Ahead Countdown

Time in　　　*Activity*
Minutes

One day ahead:

15　Step 1 of salad
15　Steps 1–2 of chicken (don't turn on
　　oven)
___
30

45 minutes ahead:

10　Oven to 400°F; Steps 3–4 of
　　chicken
10　Chill wine; Steps 1–2 of broccoli
　　and tomatoes
___
20

20 minutes ahead:
—　Baste chicken.

10 minutes ahead:

10　Step 1 of dessert; uncork wine; Step
　　5 of chicken

Serving:
Serve salad (Step 2).
When chicken is done, do Step 6; Step
　3 of broccoli and tomatoes
Serve chicken and potatoes, broccoli
　and tomatoes, and wine.
Make coffee.
Serve dessert (Step 2) and coffee.

GRAPEFRUIT AND ARTICHOKE GREEN SALAD

Working Time: 15 minutes/Chilling Time: 30 minutes/Servings: 2

1 head red-leaf lettuce, torn in bite-size
    pieces (3 to 4 cups)
1 red or pink grapefruit, sectioned

1 jar (6-oz.) marinated artichoke hearts,
    drained
¼ cup bottled French dressing (oil and vine-
    gar type), such as Trader Vic's

1. Combine lettuce, grapefruit sections, and artichoke hearts in 2 salad bowls. Cover with plastic wrap and refrigerate.

2. Just before serving pour French dressing over salads.

To do ahead: Do Step 1 up to 1 day ahead.

HERB-ROASTED CHICKEN AND POTATOES

Working Time: 25 minutes/Roasting and Resting Time: 55 minutes (400°F)/
Servings: 2 large

4 Tbsp. butter
1 Tbsp. finely chopped parsley
¼ tsp. ground white pepper
¼ tsp. dried thyme
½ tsp. dried tarragon
½ tsp. paprika
1¼ tsp. salt, divided

1 whole chicken (2 to 2½ lbs.), giblets and
    fat removed from cavity
½ lemon
2 green onions, trimmed
2 medium-size (⅔ lb. total) baking potatoes,
    peeled and quartered.

1. Turn oven to 400°F. Melt butter in a 1-cup metal measuring cup. Remove from heat and add parsley, pepper, thyme, tarragon, paprika, and 1 tsp. salt.

2. Dry chicken with paper towels. Squeeze juice from lemon half over skin of chicken. Sprinkle cavity with ¼ tsp. salt. Insert lemon half and green onions. Close opening with a metal skewer and tie legs together with white string.

3. Dry potatoes with a paper towel and brush all over with the herb butter. Place at one end of a large gratin dish (12 inches long). Brush chicken all over with remaining herb butter and place on its side next to the potatoes.

4. Roast in center of oven, basting chicken and potatoes with pan juices after 15 minutes.

5. After 30 minutes (total) turn chicken on its other side and baste chicken and potatoes. Roast 20 minutes more, or until chicken and potatoes are browned and potatoes are tender.

6. Let chicken rest at least 5 minutes. Serve chicken, potatoes, and pan juices directly from gratin dish. Chicken may be halved with poultry shears for easy serving. (Discard lemon and onions.)

To do ahead: Do Steps 1–2 up to 1 day ahead. Cover and refrigerate herb butter and chicken separately. Remelt herb butter before proceeding to Step 3.

BROCCOLI AND CHERRY TOMATO SAUTÉ

Working Time: 10 minutes/Cooking Time: 5 minutes more/Servings: 2

2 cups (packed) broccoli florets	3 Tbsp. butter
¼ cup water	12 small cherry tomatoes
¼ tsp. minced garlic	¼ tsp. salt

1. Place broccoli florets and water in an 8-inch skillet. Bring water to a boil over medium-high heat, cover, and steam broccoli until crisp tender, 5 minutes. Remove broccoli to a colander.

2. In same skillet sauté garlic in butter over low heat for 2 minutes without letting garlic brown.

3. Add broccoli to skillet and sauté 2 minutes over medium-high heat. Add cherry tomatoes and heat through, 2 minutes. Sprinkle with salt. Serve in a small vegetable dish.

To do ahead: Do Steps 1 and 2 up to 30 minutes ahead. Leave at room temperature.

WINTER FRUIT AND CHEESE DESSERT

Working Time: 5 minutes/Warming and Chilling Time: 30 minutes/Servings: 2

4 oz. Brie* or Camembert**
1 cup fresh pineapple chunks

2 small bunches (about ½ lb. total) grapes, such as red (Emperor), black (Ribier), or seedless green grapes

1. Allow at least 30 minutes to bring cheese almost to room temperature and to chill lightly the prepared fruit.

2. To serve, place a wedge of cheese, a small bunch of grapes, and half the pineapple chunks on each dessert plate.

*Brie is a delicate, rich, creamy, fruity French cheese made from cow's milk. It can be purchased by the wedge at cheese shops and supermarkets. The soft rind is edible. American versions of Brie are good too.
**Camembert is a tangy, rich, creamy French cheese made from cow's milk. There are many varieties with varying flavors, almost all of them good when purchased at the optimum peak of ripeness. (The rind is edible.)

To do ahead: Do Step 1 up to 2 hours ahead.

GREEK MENU

- Spinach, Tomato, and Feta Salad
- Lemon Broiled Chicken with Walnut Honey Glaze
- Vegetable Pilaf
  White Demestica

- Brandied Apricot Sundaes
  Coffee

Much of Greece is beautiful and sunny, and everywhere it's pleasant and relaxing. Food plays a key role in the easygoing pageant of Greek life, and this equally easygoing menu might well win center stage.

The salad combines tender, young spinach leaves with tomato wedges and crumbled feta cheese. It has an oil and vinegar dressing generously flavored with oregano, a favorite Greek herb.

For the lemon broiled chicken, a small, whole chicken is butterflied, and a lemon marinade is spooned beneath the chicken skin. Placing the marinade underneath the skin is quick and simple to do and greatly speeds penetration. After broiling, a mixture of buttered walnuts and honey is spread over the chicken, balancing its lemon flavor and producing a lovely glaze.

All that's needed by way of accompaniment is rice with fresh green beans and carrots, starch and vegetable in one dish. The rice is cooked in chicken broth with a cinnamon stick and is flavored with garlic and onion.

For the beverage a pleasant Greek white wine, such as Demestica, would be appropriate.

To make dessert, apricot halves are steeped in apricot brandy blended with apricot preserves. At serving time the mixture is heated, flamed, and served over vanilla ice cream. Delicious, elegant, and easy!

SHOPPING LIST FOR GREEK MENU

Poultry, Dairy:

☐ 2½-lb. whole chicken

☐ feta cheese (2 Tbsp. crumbled)

☐ butter (2½ Tbsp.)

☐ vanilla ice cream (⅔ pt.)

Produce:

☐ 1 large bunch young spinach

☐ 1 medium-size (6-oz.) tomato

☐ 1 large or 2 small lemons

☐ ¼ lb. green beans

☐ 1 medium-size (4-oz.) carrot

☐ 1 small (4-oz.) onion

☐ garlic (½ tsp. minced)

☐ parsley or watercress for garnish

Grocery:

☐ walnuts (2 Tbsp. chopped)

☐ mild honey, such as orange blossom (¼ cup)

☐ 1 can (8¾-oz.) apricot halves in heavy syrup

☐ apricot preserves (2 Tbsp.)

Liquor:

☐ 1 bottle unresinated Greek white wine, such as Demestica

☐ apricot brandy (2½ Tbsp.)

Check Staples:

☐ salt

☐ black pepper

☐ dried oregano (½ tsp.)

☐ cinnamon (1 stick)

☐ Dijon mustard (½ tsp.)

☐ red wine vinegar (1 Tbsp.)

☐ olive oil (6 Tbsp.)

☐ long-grain white rice (½ cup)

☐ canned condensed chicken broth (¾ cup)

☐ coffee

☐ plastic wrap

☐ matches

☐ toothpicks

COUNTDOWNS FOR GREEK MENU

Last-Minute Countdown

Time in   Activity
Minutes

55 minutes ahead:
10 Chill wine; Step 1 of chicken
 5 Step 2 of salad
15 Turn on broiler; Step 1 of salad
 5 Step 1 of dessert
15 Step 3 of chicken; Steps 1–3 of pilaf
 5 Steps 4 and 2 of chicken; uncork
     wine.
___
55

Serving:
Serve salad (Step 3).
(Baste chicken 5 minutes after serving
  salad.)
Step 4 of pilaf; Steps 5–6 of chicken
Serve chicken, pilaf, and wine.
Serve dessert (Step 2).
Make coffee and serve.

Plan-Ahead Countdown

Time in   Activity
Minutes

One day ahead:
20 Steps 1–2 of salad
10 Chill wine; Step 1 of chicken
 5 Step 1 of dessert
___
35

30 minutes ahead:
 5 Turn on broiler; Step 2 of chicken;
     uncork wine.

15 minutes ahead:
15 Step 3 of chicken; Steps 1–3 of pi-
     laf; Step 4 of chicken

Serving:
Serve salad (Step 3).
(Baste chicken 10 minutes after serving
  salad.)
Step 4 of pilaf; Steps 5–6 of chicken
Serve chicken, pilaf, and wine.
Serve dessert (Step 2).
Make coffee and serve.

SPINACH, TOMATO, AND FETA SALAD

Working Time: 20 minutes/Servings: 2

SALAD INGREDIENTS:

3½ cups (lightly packed) tender, young spinach leaves, torn in bite-size pieces
1 medium-size (6-oz.) tomato, cut in 10
   wedges
2 Tbsp. crumbled feta cheese*

OREGANO DRESSING:

¼ tsp. salt
½ tsp. dried oregano
⅛ tsp. ground black pepper
½ tsp. fresh lemon juice
½ tsp. Dijon mustard
1 Tbsp. red wine vinegar
¼ cup olive oil

1. Put spinach in individual salad bowls. Arrange tomato wedges on top in a spoke pattern. Pile cheese in center. Cover with plastic wrap and refrigerate.

2. Put all ingredients for dressing, except oil, in a ½-pt. jar. Cover and shake until salt is dissolved. Add oil and shake again.

3. Just before serving shake dressing and pour over salads.

*Feta cheese is a crumbly white sheep- or goat-milk cheese imported from Greece. It has a tart, salty flavor. Feta can be found in specialty cheese shops and delicatessens. Domestically produced feta can be substituted and is available in some supermarkets.

To do ahead: Prepare through Step 2 up to 1 day ahead. Refrigerate.

LEMON BROILED CHICKEN WITH WALNUT HONEY GLAZE

Working Time: 20 minutes/Marinating Time: 20 minutes to 24 hours/Broiling Time: 30 minutes/Total Time: 1 hour and 10 minutes/Servings: 2 large

CHICKEN:
1½ tsp. salt
¼ tsp. ground black pepper
3 Tbsp. fresh lemon juice
2 Tbsp. olive oil
2½-lb. whole chicken (minimum 2 lbs. without giblets and neck), butterflied (see Note)

GLAZE AND GARNISH:
1 Tbsp. butter
2 Tbsp. finely chopped walnuts
¼ cup (scant) mild honey, such as orange blossom
Parsley sprigs or watercress

1. Combine salt, pepper, lemon juice, and oil in a 4-oz. jar; shake to mix. With your fingers loosen skin of butterflied chicken (see Note) over each side of breast and down over thigh and leg. Try not to tear skin. Spoon half of marinade under skin, distributing it fairly evenly. Coat outside of chicken with remaining marinade and let stand at least 20 minutes at room temperature.

2. In a 1-cup metal measuring cup melt butter over medium heat. Add walnuts and toast lightly, about 3 minutes. Mix in honey and set aside.

3. Preheat broiler. Place chicken, skin-side down, on a rack in a broiling pan. Broil 6 inches from heat for 15 minutes.

4. Turn chicken by grasping the legs (ankles) with 2 pairs of tongs and flipping it over. Broil about 15 minutes more, basting once with pan drippings, until chicken is browned and juices clear (not tinged with pink) when thigh is pierced.

5. Place chicken on a small platter. Reheat glaze, if necessary, and spoon over chicken. Garnish with parsley or watercress.

6. Pour drippings from broiler pan into a small pitcher. Let settle a minute, then pour off most of fat, leaving juices (to be served with the chicken). At the table cut the chicken in half, which will be easy since there are no bones in the way.

To do ahead: Do Step 1 up to 1 day ahead. Bring chicken to room temperature before broiling.

Note: To butterfly chicken, rinse chicken and dry with paper towels. Cut all the way down one side of backbone with a knife or poultry shears. Spread chicken out on a flat surface, skin-side up, legs toward you. Press down against breastbone with your thumbs, and pull wings and shoulders of chicken toward you until breastbone pops out. Remove breastbone and cut through the bones just above it, including wishbone. (When chicken is butterflied, rather than cut in half, the breast meat is protected and stays juicy during broiling.)

VEGETABLE PILAF

Working Time: 15 minutes/Cooking Time: 15 minutes more/Servings: 2

1 qt. water
¼ lb. green beans
1¼ tsp. salt, divided
1 medium-size (4-oz.) carrot, peeled, sliced
  crosswise ⅛ inch thick
¼ cup finely chopped onion

½ tsp. minced garlic
1½ Tbsp. butter
½ cup long-grain white rice
¾ cup canned, condensed chicken broth
1 stick cinnamon

1. Bring water to a rapid boil in a 1½-qt. saucepan. Break tips off beans. Cut beans in 1-inch lengths and add to boiling water. Add 1 tsp. salt. Boil, uncovered, until beans are tender when pierced with a toothpick, about 6 minutes. Drain.

2. In same saucepan, over medium heat, sauté carrot, onion, and garlic in butter until softened, about 5 minutes.

3. Add rice to pan. Raise heat, add chicken broth, ¼ tsp. salt, and cinnamon stick. Bring liquid to a boil, reduce heat, cover, and simmer 15 minutes or until rice is tender and liquid absorbed.

4. Remove cinnamon stick. Stir cooked green beans into rice mixture. Heat a minute or two and serve.

To do ahead: Do Steps 1–2 up to 1 hour ahead. Set aside at room temperature.

Note: Leftover canned chicken broth may be frozen for future use.

BRANDIED APRICOT SUNDAES

Working Time: 10 minutes/Standing Time: 1 hour/Servings: 2

2 Tbsp. apricot preserves
½ tsp. fresh lemon juice
2½ Tbsp. apricot brandy, divided

1 can (8¾-oz.) apricot halves in heavy
　syrup, drained
2 servings (about ⅔ pt.) vanilla ice cream

1.　In a ¾-qt. saucepan (not aluminum) combine preserves, lemon juice, and ½ Tbsp. brandy. Stir in apricots and let stand 1 hour at room temperature, or overnight in refrigerator.

2.　To serve, heat apricot mixture to boiling. Divide ice cream between 2 heat-proof compotes. In a 1-cup metal measuring cup heat 2 Tbsp. brandy to boiling. Quickly flame and add to apricot mixture, shaking pan. Spoon mixture over ice cream and serve.

To do ahead: Do Step 1 up to 1 day ahead. Cover and refrigerate.

FESTIVE MENU

- Zucchini Bisque

- Cointreau Chicken with Carrots and Grapes
- Pecan Wild Rice
- Buttered Romaine
  Champagne

- Chocolate Ice Cream Chantilly with Raspberries
  Coffee

The world turns, bringing holidays, important milestones, and special interludes for two. If you're approaching just such an occasion and haven't much time to prepare, here are some ideas.

A delicate zucchini bisque is a sophisticated beginning for this dinner. A touch of onion, nutmeg, and cream gives the soup its pleasing flavor.

Cointreau chicken consists of large strips of boned chicken breast, sautéed and glazed with a reduction of chicken broth and Cointreau. Butter adds body and flavor to the sauce. Carrots and green grapes are wonderful served around the chicken, similarly glazed.

To further the festive theme, wild rice is superb, especially when combined with butter-toasted pecans. For an unusual cooked vegetable try the French-inspired lettuce dish—it's similar to spinach, but with a little more bite. (Conveniently, lettuce is also easier to wash and chop than spinach.)

For the champagne choose one labeled "extra dry," for in spite of the name, it will be just slightly sweet, and will match the Cointreau chicken. In California Paul Masson and Korbel are reliable producers of extra dry champagne. Have the champagne well chilled for serving.

The final decadence for this glamorous dinner is dark, rich chocolate ice cream, topped with whipped cream and sweetened raspberries. (You don't need fresh raspberries for this to be great.)

SHOPPING LIST FOR FESTIVE MENU

Poultry, Dairy, Eggs:

☐ 2 large chicken breasts (1⅓ lbs. total), or ⅔ lb. skinned and boned breasts

☐ butter (7½ Tbsp.)

☐ whipping cream (⅔ cup)

☐ dark, rich chocolate ice cream (⅔ pt.)

Produce:

☐ 1 small onion (need ¼ cup chopped)

☐ 1 medium-size (⅓-lb.) zucchini

☐ 2 small carrots (⅓ lb. total)

☐ 1 large or 2 small heads romaine

☐ ½ lb. seedless green grapes

☐ raspberries (½ cup), or use frozen

☐ 1 orange (need ½ tsp. grated peel)

Grocery:

☐ frozen, whole, unsweetened raspberries (½ cup), if not using fresh

☐ pecans (¼ cup chopped)

☐ wild rice (3 oz. or ½ cup)

Liquor:

☐ 1 bottle extra dry champagne, such as Paul Masson or Korbel

☐ Cointreau (¼ cup)

Check Staples:

☐ salt

☐ white pepper

☐ ground nutmeg (⅛ tsp.)

☐ sugar (1 Tbsp.)

☐ flour (1½ Tbsp.)

☐ 2 cans (10¾-oz. each) condensed chicken broth

☐ coffee

☐ paper towels

COUNTDOWNS FOR FESTIVE MENU

Last-Minute Countdown

Time in   Activity
Minutes

65 minutes ahead:

15 Chill champagne; Steps 1–2 of soup
10 Steps 1–3 of romaine; Steps 1–2 of wild rice; Step 4 of romaine
5 Take soup off stove; Steps 1–2 of dessert
30 Steps 1–5 of chicken
5 Oven to 350°F; Step 3 of soup
65

Serving:

Serve soup.

Put chicken in oven; Step 3 of wild rice; Step 6 of chicken; Step 5 of romaine; open champagne.

Serve chicken, wild rice, romaine, and champagne.

Make coffee.

Serve dessert (Step 3) and coffee.

Plan-Ahead Countdown

Time in   Activity
Minutes

One day ahead:

5 Chill champagne; Steps 1–2 of wild rice
15 Steps 1–2 of soup
10 Steps 1–4 of romaine; Step 3 of soup
30 (Plus 30 minutes more cooking time for wild rice, then do Step 3.)

40 minutes ahead:

5 Steps 1–2 of dessert
30 Steps 1–5 of chicken;
    Oven to 350°F;
    soup on to reheat
35

Serving:

Serve soup.

Reheat wild rice; chicken in oven and do Step 6; Step 5 of romaine; open champagne.

Serve chicken, wild rice, romaine, and champagne.

Make coffee.

Serve dessert (Step 3) and coffee.

ZUCCHINI BISQUE

Working Time: 15 minutes/Cooking Time: 10 minutes/Servings: 2

1½ Tbsp. butter
¼ cup finely chopped onion
1 medium-size (⅓-lb.) zucchini, sliced ⅛
   inch thick
1 can (10¾-oz.) condensed chicken broth

Pinch of ground white pepper
Pinch of ground nutmeg
⅓ cup whipping cream
(few slices cooked zucchini for garnish)
Dash of nutmeg

    1. In a 1½-qt. saucepan over medium heat sauté onion in butter for 2 minutes. Add zucchini slices and sauté 3 minutes.

    2. Add chicken broth, pepper, and nutmeg to saucepan and bring to a boil over high heat. Cover, reduce heat, and simmer until zucchini is just tender, 10 minutes.

    3. Reserve a few slices of cooked zucchini for garnish and pour remaining soup into blender. Purée soup and return to saucepan. Add cream.

    4. Reheat soup, if necessary. Serve in individual bowls topped with zucchini slices and a dusting of nutmeg.

To do ahead: Do Steps 1–3 up to 2 days ahead. Cover and refrigerate soup and zucchini slices for garnish separately.

COINTREAU CHICKEN WITH CARROTS AND GRAPES

Working and Cooking Time: 30 minutes/Servings: 2

1½ cups water
1 tsp. salt, divided
2 small carrots (⅓ lb. total), peeled and
   sliced diagonally ⅓ inch thick
2 large chicken breasts (1⅓ lbs. total), or ⅔
   lb. skinned and boned breasts
1½ Tbsp. flour

⅛ tsp. ground white pepper
4 Tbsp. butter, divided
¼ cup Cointreau*
½ tsp. grated orange peel
¼ cup canned, condensed chicken broth
1 cup seedless green grapes

1. In a ¾-qt. saucepan, bring water to a boil over high heat. Add ½ tsp. salt and the carrots. Cover, reduce heat, and simmer until carrots are tender, 10 to 15 minutes. Drain.

2. Skin and bone chicken breasts, if necessary. Separate small fillet from each breast, and cut large fillets lengthwise into 2 strips each. Dry with paper towels.

3. Mix flour, ½ tsp. salt, and the pepper in a bag. Measure out other remaining ingredients.

4. In a 10-inch skillet with a nonstick surface heat 2 Tbsp. butter over medium-high heat. Add chicken to bag with flour and shake to coat the pieces. Brown in butter, about 2 minutes on each side.

5. Pour Cointreau over chicken. Turn strips to glaze them. Arrange down center of a warm gratin dish (12 inches long.) Add chicken broth and orange peel to juices remaining in skillet and boil down to 3 Tbsp. Add 2 Tbsp. butter.

6. Reduce heat to medium. Add carrots and heat 1 minute. Add grapes and heat through, 1 minute more. Spoon carrots and grapes around chicken, drizzle remaining sauce over chicken, and serve.

*Cointreau is a clear, orange-flavored liqueur of excellent quality, produced in France and available in any liquor store.

To do ahead: May be prepared through Step 5 up to 30 minutes ahead. Leave everything at room temperature. Reheat chicken in 350°F oven about 5 minutes before completing Step 6.

Note:
1. One 10¾-oz. can of chicken broth is enough for this recipe and the wild rice.

PECAN WILD RICE

Working Time: 5 minutes/Cooking Time: 50 minutes/Servings: 2

1 Tbsp. butter
¼ cup chopped pecans
½ cup (3 oz.) wild rice*

1 cup canned condensed chicken broth (see note)

1. Heat butter in a 5-inch skillet over medium heat. Add pecans and cook until butter is browned and pecans toasted, about 4 minutes. Set aside.

2. Place wild rice in a 1-qt. saucepan and wash in several changes of water. Drain. Add chicken broth and bring to a boil over high heat. Reduce heat to low, cover, and simmer 50 minutes.

3. After 50 minutes uncover wild rice and boil away any broth that was not absorbed. Mix in buttered pecans and serve.

*Wild rice is not a true rice, but an aquatic grass with long, brownish-black grains. It is expensive, but widely available in supermarkets and gourmet food stores in small packages of 4 or 6 ounces.

To do ahead: Prepare up to 1 day ahead. Cool, cover, and refrigerate. To serve, reheat over low heat (covered) for 10 minutes, stirring occasionally.

Note: One 10¾-oz. can of chicken broth is enough for this recipe and the Cointreau chicken.

BUTTERED ROMAINE

Working Time: 5 minutes/Cooking Time: 5 minutes/Servings: 2

1 qt. water	2 tsp. salt
1 large or 2 small heads romaine lettuce (4 cups packed)	1 Tbsp. butter

1. Bring water to a boil in a 2-qt. saucepan over high heat.

2. Remove coarse outer leaves of romaine. Rinse heads under running water. Cut crosswise in 1-inch slices to within 3 inches of stem end. Cut across lettuce to make 1-inch squares.

3. Add lettuce to boiling water. Add salt. Cook, uncovered, until lettuce is tender but still somewhat crunchy, about 5 minutes.

4. Drain lettuce in a sieve, pressing out as much water as possible.

5. When ready to serve, reheat lettuce in butter in same saucepan. Serve in a small, warm bowl.

To do ahead: Steps 1–4 may be done up to 1 day ahead. Rinse in cold water, press dry, cover, and refrigerate.

CHOCOLATE ICE CREAM CHANTILLY WITH RASPBERRIES

Working Time: 10 minutes/Thawing Time: 30 minutes/Servings: 2

1 Tbsp. sugar
½ cup fresh or frozen whole unsweetened raspberries

⅓ cup whipping cream
2 servings dark, rich chocolate ice cream (⅔ pt.)

1. Mix sugar and raspberries in a 1-cup bowl. Cover and refrigerate. (If using frozen raspberries and planning to serve within an hour, leave at room temperature.)

2. With a rotary beater whip cream in a 3-cup bowl until stiff. Cover and refrigerate.

3. To serve, place ice cream in compotes, mound with whipped cream, and spoon raspberries with juices over and around whipped cream.

To do ahead: Do Steps 1–2 up to 3 hours ahead.

Note: There are now good ice creams being sold through supermarket chains in many areas.

SCANDINAVIAN MENU

- **Danish Green Salad**

- **Chicken with Julienne Dried Fruit**
- **Dilled Potatoes and Green Beans**
  Vouvray

- **Oven Pancakes with Lingonberries**
  Coffee

The simple, down-to-earth cooking of Scandinavia lends itself easily to quick cuisine. Simple doesn't mean boring, however, and the dishes in this menu are good-tasting, attractive, and creative.

The salad contains tiny shrimp, cherry tomatoes, and alfalfa sprouts on a bed of red-leaf and butterhead lettuce leaves. The dressing is a Danish blue cheese vinaigrette.

For the chicken dish, large strips of breast meat are quickly sautéed, then topped with a sweet-and-sour mixture of julienne dried fruit. The fruit has a lovely glazed look with contrasting colors of bright orange apricots, dark prunes, and pale pears.

Potatoes accompany practically every Scandinavian meal, and this one combines them with whole green beans and adds shallots and dill for flavor. The vegetables are prepared together, but served side by side for better visual appeal.

A light, fruity and flowery white wine with a touch of sweetness, such as Vouvray, makes a good accompaniment for the main course.

Many types of pancakes are served in Scandinavia, from heart-shaped waffles to French crêpes. The easiest are the oven pancakes, which can be made large and cut up for serving, or in individual sizes, as suggested here. A favorite topping is sour cream and Swedish preserved lingonberries.

SHOPPING LIST FOR SCANDINAVIAN MENU

Poultry, Seafood, Dairy, and Eggs:

☐ 2 large chicken breasts (1⅓ lbs. total) or ⅔ lb. skinned and boned chicken breasts

☐ ¼ lb. (⅔ cup) tiny, cooked, peeled shrimp

☐ Danish blue cheese (2 Tbsp. crumbled)

☐ sour cream (¼ cup)

☐ milk (½ cup)

☐ butter (5 Tbsp.)

Produce:

☐ butterhead lettuce (1½ cups)

☐ red-leaf lettuce (1½ cups)

☐ alfalfa sprouts (½ cup)

☐ cherry tomatoes (6)

☐ 2 medium-size new potatoes (⅔ lb. total)

☐ ⅓ lb. small, tender green beans

☐ 1 lemon (need 1 tsp. grated peel and 1 Tbsp. juice)

☐ shallots (1 Tbsp. minced)

☐ fresh dill weed (2 tsp. chopped), or use dried

Grocery:

☐ 1 pkg. mixed dried fruit (need 2 pear halves and 4 each apricot halves and prunes)

☐ Swedish preserved lingonberries, or wholeberry cranberry sauce (⅓ cup)

Liquor:

☐ 1 bottle light, fruity white wine, such as white Vouvray

Check Staples:

☐ salt

☐ white pepper

☐ dried dill weed (½ tsp.), if not using fresh

☐ Dijon mustard (½ tsp.)

☐ white wine vinegar (1½ Tbsp.)

☐ salad oil (¼ cup)

☐ sugar (3 Tbsp.)

☐ flour (½ cup)

☐ coffee

☐ aluminum foil

☐ toothpicks

COUNTDOWNS FOR SCANDINAVIAN MENU

Last-Minute Countdown

Time in   Activity
Minutes

60 minutes ahead:
20 Chill wine; Steps 1–2 of salad
10 Steps 2 and 4 of dessert
20 Oven to 200°F; prepare chicken
     and put in oven.
10 Step 1 of vegetables, mince shal-
     lots, and chop dill; uncork wine;
     Step 2 of vegetables
___
60

Serving:
Serve salad (Step 3).
Oven to 400°F; Step 3 of vegetables
Serve chicken, vegetables, and wine.
(25 minutes before serving dessert do
    Steps 1 and 3.)
Make coffee; Step 5 of dessert
Serve dessert and coffee.

Plan-Ahead Countdown

Time in   Activity
Minutes

One day ahead:
20 Chill wine; Steps 1–2 of salad
 5 Step 2 of dessert
___
25

35 minutes ahead:
 5 Step 4 of dessert
20 Oven to 200°F; prepare chicken
     and put in oven.
10 Step 1 of vegetables, mince shal-
     lots, and chop dill; uncork wine;
     Step 2 of vegetables
___
35

Serving:
Serve salad (Step 3).
Oven to 400°F; Step 3 of vegetables
Serve chicken, vegetables, and wine.
(25 minutes before serving dessert do
    Steps 1 and 3.)
Make coffee; Step 5 of dessert
Serve dessert and coffee.

DANISH GREEN SALAD

Working Time: 20 minutes/Chilling Time: 30 minutes/Servings: 2

SALAD INGREDIENTS:
1½ cups (lightly packed) bite-size pieces
   butterhead lettuce
1½ cups (lightly packed) bite-size pieces red-
   leaf lettuce
½ cup alfalfa sprouts*
¼ lb. (⅔ cup) tiny shrimp, purchased
   cooked and peeled
6 cherry tomatoes, halved

BLUE CHEESE DRESSING:
¼ tsp. salt
⅛ tsp. ground white pepper
½ tsp. Dijon mustard
1½ Tbsp. white wine vinegar
2 Tbsp. crumbled Danish blue cheese
¼ cup salad oil

1. Mix salad greens and alfalfa sprouts and divide between 2 salad plates. Pile shrimp in center of lettuce and garnish with cherry tomatoes. Cover with plastic wrap and refrigerate.

2. Put all dressing ingredients, except cheese and oil, in a ½-pt. jar. Cover and shake until salt dissolves. Add cheese and oil and shake again. Refrigerate.

3. To serve, shake dressing and spoon over salads.

*If alfalfa sprouts are not available, they may be omitted.

To do ahead: Do Steps 1–2 up to 1 day ahead.

CHICKEN WITH JULIENNE DRIED FRUIT

Working and Cooking Time: 20 minutes/Servings: 2

2 dried pear halves
4 dried apricot halves
4 prunes, pitted
2 large chicken breasts (1⅓ lbs. total) or ⅔
   lb. if purchased skinned and boned
2 Tbsp. flour
½ tsp. salt

⅛ tsp. ground white pepper
2 Tbsp. butter, divided
⅓ cup water
1 tsp. grated lemon peel
1 Tbsp. sugar
1 Tbsp. fresh lemon juice

1. Cut dried fruit into strips about ⅛ inch wide.

2. Skin and bone chicken breasts, if necessary. Separate small fillet from each breast, and cut large fillets lengthwise into 2 strips each.

3. Mix flour, salt, and pepper in a bag. Add chicken strips and shake to coat them.

4. In a 10-inch skillet over medium-high heat brown chicken lightly in 1 Tbsp. butter, about 2 minutes on each side. Arrange on one end of a large warm platter.

5. Add water, dried fruit, lemon peel, sugar, and lemon juice to skillet. Boil liquid down to a few tablespoons, about 2 minutes.

6. To serve, spoon fruit mixture over chicken. Serve vegetables on the same platter.

To do ahead: Prepare through Step 5 up to 30 minutes ahead. Cover chicken with aluminum foil and keep warm in a 300°F oven. Reheat fruit in skillet, adding a little water if mixture is dry, before proceeding to Step 6.

Note: For the dried fruit, it is probably easiest to purchase a box or package of mixed dried fruit (soft pack) and select the pieces you want to use.

DILLED POTATOES AND GREEN BEANS

Working Time: 15 minutes/Cooking Time: 10 minutes more/Servings: 2

4 cups water	2 Tbsp. butter
2 tsp. salt	1 Tbsp. minced shallots**
2 medium-size new potatoes (⅔ lb. total)	2 tsp. chopped fresh or frozen dill weed, or
⅓ lb. green beans*	½ tsp. dried

1. Put water and salt in a wide 2-qt. saucepan over high heat. Peel and quarter potatoes and add to pan. Bring to a boil, reduce heat to low, cover, and simmer 8 minutes.

2. Break off stem ends of green beans and add to saucepan with potatoes. Cook, uncovered, until potatoes and beans are tender, 6 to 8 minutes.

3. Drain vegetables in a colander. Melt butter in same saucepan over medium heat. Add shallots and cook 2 minutes without browning. Add potatoes and beans and toss to coat with butter. Arrange beans and potatoes separately on same platter as chicken.

*Select small green beans that feel tender and crisp, rather than fibrous.
**Shallots are a cousin of the onion and grow in clusters of two to six from a common base (somewhat like garlic). If shallots are unavailable, substitute 1 tablespoon minced onion or white part of green onion plus ¼ teaspoon minced garlic.

To do ahead: Best to do at the last minute.

OVEN PANCAKES WITH LINGONBERRIES

Working Time: 10 minutes/Baking Time: 20 minutes (400°F)/Servings: 2

PANCAKES:
1 Tbsp. butter
½ cup milk
⅓ cup all-purpose white flour (do not sift)
1 Tbsp. sugar
¼ tsp. salt
1 egg

TOPPING:
¼ cup sour cream
2 tsp. sugar
¼ to ⅓ cup preserved lingonberries* or
    wholeberry cranberry sauce

1. Turn oven to 400°F. Put ½ Tbsp. butter in each of two 4-inch pie pans. Set on a baking sheet and put in center of oven.

2. Place ingredients for pancakes (except butter) in blender and blend until combined.

3. When butter has melted, reblend batter a few seconds, if necessary, and pour over butter in pans. Bake until brown and puffed, about 20 minutes.

4. Mix sour cream with 2 tsp. sugar and set aside at room temperature.

5. When pancakes are done, remove from pans and place on dessert plates. (Pancakes will sink some, but this is okay.) Spread with sour cream mixture and top with lingonberries. Serve at once.

*Lingonberries preserved in sugar are imported from Sweden and are available in gourmet markets and delicatessens. They are similar to cranberries but smaller in size (and much more expensive). Leftover lingonberries will keep indefinitely refrigerated and can be used like any other preserves. (Leftover cranberry sauce will keep 6 weeks in a jar in the refrigerator.)

To do ahead: Do Step 2 up to 1 day ahead. Refrigerate, covered, in blender.

OREGON MENU

- Spiced Pimiento Soup

- Chicken Breasts in Pecan Cream
- Brussels Sprouts and Green Noodles
- Lemon Carrots
  White (Johannesberg) Riesling

- Buttered Pear Tart
  Coffee

This appealing dinner from Oregon can be served any time of year, but it is especially appropriate from autumn through early spring.

The meal begins with a bright red soup, made with chicken broth, tomato juice, and pimientos, and flavored with allspice. Served with a swirl of cream and a sprinkling of chopped parsley, it's tasty and very pretty.

The few ingredients needed for chicken breasts in pecan cream result in a surprisingly flavorful dish. Boned chicken breasts are sautéed, then served in a sauce of cream cheese thinned with milk and flavored with pecans. The toasted pecans have a rich delicious taste that makes this dish special.

To accompany the chicken, brussels sprouts and green noodles are tossed with butter and thyme, and tender carrots are cloaked in a lemon and sugar glaze.

A Johannesberg Riesling goes well with this menu, and Oregon is producing some very good ones, although in small quantities. If you lack the authentic bottle, a California Riesling will do nicely.

A fresh fruit tart made in fifteen minutes? It's true—and it's delicious. A patty shell, rolled thin, forms the crust for this 6-inch tart, and the filling takes a single sliced pear, butter, sugar, an egg, and a little flour. The pears from Oregon's Willamette Valley are delicious, but the flavor secret here is browning the butter to a rich, nutty color.

SHOPPING LIST FOR OREGON MENU

Meat, Dairy:

☐ 2 large chicken breasts (1⅓ lbs. total) or ⅔ lb. skinned and boned chicken breasts

☐ milk (⅔ cup)

☐ whipping cream (2 Tbsp.)

☐ 1 pkg. (3-oz.) cream cheese

☐ butter (9 Tbsp.)

☐ eggs (1)

Produce:

☐ ¼ lb. (about 8) brussels sprouts, or use frozen

☐ 2 medium-size carrots (½ lb. total)

☐ 1 medium-size (⅓-lb.) pear*

☐ parsley (½ tsp. chopped)

☐ 1 lemon (need 2 tsp. juice)

Grocery:

☐ 1 pkg. (10-oz.) frozen brussels sprouts (need ½), if not using fresh

☐ Pepperidge Farm frozen patty shells (1 each)

☐ 1¼ oz. shelled pecans (⅓ cup)

☐ 1 can (6-oz.) tomato juice

☐ 1 jar (4-oz.) pimientos

☐ dark green noodles (2 oz.)

☐ 1 can (8½-oz.) pears, if not using fresh

Liquor:

☐ 1 bottle light, fruity white wine, such as white (Johannesberg) Riesling

Check Staples:

☐ salt

☐ white pepper

☐ ground allspice (a pinch)

☐ paprika (⅛ tsp.)

☐ dried thyme (⅛ tsp.)

☐ powdered sugar (1 tsp.)

☐ sugar (½ cup)

☐ flour (⅓ cup)

☐ 1 can (10¾-oz.) condensed chicken broth

☐ coffee

☐ paper towels

*May need to be purchased several days ahead to allow for ripening.

COUNTDOWNS FOR OREGON MENU

Last-Minute Countdown

Time in   *Activity*
Minutes

75 minutes ahead:
— Chill wine; patty shell out of freezer (for dessert)

65 minutes ahead:
20 Prepare chicken according to do-ahead instructions.
15 Steps 1–5 of dessert (oven to 375°F)
10 Step 1 of soup and chop parsley.
15 Step 1 of sprouts; Step 1 of carrots; Step 2 of sprouts; Step 2 of carrots (leave in saucepan); Step 3 of sprouts
5 Uncork wine; dessert out of oven; chicken in oven (reduce heat to 350°F); Step 4 of sprouts (leave in saucepan)
___
65

Serving:
Serve soup (Step 2).
Reheat sprouts; reheat carrots.
Serve chicken, sprouts, carrots, and wine.
Make coffee.
Serve dessert (Step 6) and coffee.

Plan-Ahead Countdown

Time in   *Activity*
Minutes

One day ahead:
20 Transfer patty shell (in plastic wrap) to refrigerator (for dessert); chill wine; Steps 1–6 of chicken
5 Step 1 of soup
___
25

50 minutes ahead:
15 Steps 1–5 of dessert (oven to 375°F)
10 Step 1 of sprouts; Step 1 of carrots; Step 2 of sprouts
10 Step 2 of carrots (leave in saucepan); Step 3 of sprouts; uncork wine; Step 4 of sprouts (leave in saucepan)
5 Heat soup and chop parsley; dessert out of oven; chicken in oven (reduce heat 350°F)
___
40

Serving:
Serve soup (Step 2).
Reheat sprouts; reheat carrots.
Serve chicken, sprouts, carrots, and wine.
Make coffee.
Serve dessert (Step 6) and coffee.

SPICED PIMIENTO SOUP

Working Time: 10 minutes/Cooking Time: 15 minutes/Servings: 2

1 jar (4-oz.) pimientos
1 can (6-oz.) tomato juice
1 can (10¾-oz.) condensed chicken broth
Pinch of ground allspice

⅛ tsp. sugar
2 Tbsp. whipping cream
½ tsp. finely chopped parsley

1. Purée all ingredients, except cream and parsley, in blender. Pour into a 1-qt. saucepan and bring to a boil over high heat. Cover, reduce heat, and simmer 15 minutes.

2. To serve, pour into individual soup bowls, drizzle 1 Tbsp. cream into each serving, and swirl slightly. Sprinkle with chopped parsley.

To do ahead: Do Step 1 up to 1 day ahead. Cool, cover, and refrigerate.

CHICKEN BREASTS IN PECAN CREAM

Working and Cooking Time: 20 minutes/Servings: 2

⅓ cup coarsely chopped pecans
2 Tbsp. butter, divided
2 large chicken breasts (1⅓ lbs. total) or ⅔ lb. skinned and boned chicken breasts
2 Tbsp. flour

½ tsp. salt
⅛ tsp. ground white pepper
1 pkg. (3-oz.) cream cheese — *Heffurtt*
½ cup (about) milk

1. In a 10-inch skillet over low heat slowly sauté pecans in 1 Tbsp. butter, stirring frequently, until pecans are well toasted, about 6 minutes. Remove to a small plate.

2. Meanwhile skin and bone chicken breasts, if necessary. Separate small fillet from each breast, and cut large fillets lengthwise into 2 strips each.

3. Mix flour, salt, and pepper in a bag. Add chicken strips and shake to coat them.

4. Add 1 Tbsp. butter to skillet, turn heat to medium-high and lightly brown chicken, about 2 minutes on each side. Remove to a heated gratin dish (12 inches long).

5. Add cream cheese and milk to skillet. Mash cheese and let it warm. Boil mixture and whisk until cheese blends into a smooth sauce. (Add more milk if sauce gets too thick.)

6. Add all but 2 Tbsp. pecans to sauce. Pour sauce over chicken and sprinkle with remaining pecans. Serve.

To do ahead: Prepare through Step 6 up to 1 day ahead, using enough milk in Step 4 to make a thin sauce (no need to heat gratin dish if preparing ahead). Cover and refrigerate. To serve, reheat, uncovered, in a 350°F oven for 20 minutes (or 10 minutes if chicken has not been refrigerated).

BRUSSELS SPROUTS AND GREEN NOODLES

nest noodles w/poly 2 min boil/soli.

Working Time: 10 minutes/Cooking Time: 10 minutes/Servings: 2

6 cups water
2 tsp. salt
¼ lb. brussels sprouts (about 8)

2 ozs. dark green noodles (2 cups)
2 Tbsp. butter
⅛ tsp. dried thyme

1. In a 3-qt. saucepan bring water and salt to a rapid boil.

2. Trim and halve brussels sprouts. Add to boiling water, and boil, uncovered, for 5 minutes.

nest noodles 2 min

3. Add noodles to saucepan with brussels sprouts and boil just until tender, 3 to 5 minutes.

4. Drain brussels sprouts and noodles in a colander. Melt butter in saucepan and mix in brussels sprouts, noodles, and thyme. Serve in a small dish.

lots of parsley

To do ahead: Prepare up to 1 hour ahead and set aside. Reheat to serve.

✓ LEMON CARROTS

Working Time: 10 minutes/Cooking Time: 15 minutes/Servings: 2

2 cups water
½ tsp. salt
2 medium-size carrots (½ lb. total)
1 Tbsp. butter

1½ tsp. sugar
⅛ tsp. paprika
2 tsp. fresh lemon juice

1. In a 1-qt. saucepan over high heat bring water and salt to a boil. Peel carrots and slice diagonally ¼ inch thick. Add to boiling water, cover, reduce heat, and simmer until carrots are tender, about 10 minutes. Drain.

2. In same saucepan combine butter, sugar, paprika, and lemon juice. Mix in carrots. Simmer, uncovered, until liquid has mostly evaporated and carrots are glazed, about 5 minutes. Serve in a small dish.

To do ahead: Prepare up to 1 hour ahead and set aside. (In Step 2 don't boil away all the liquid.) Reheat to serve.

BUTTERED PEAR TART

place pears w/ Ladyfir

Thawing Time: 30 minutes/Working Time: 15 minutes/Baking Time: 25 minutes (375°F)/Servings: 3

4 Tbsp. butter
2 Tbsp. flour plus more for rolling out patty
    shell
1 frozen patty shell*, thawed

1 medium-size (⅓-lb.) ripe pear**
⅓ cup sugar
1 egg
1 tsp. powdered sugar

1. Turn oven to 375°F. Heat butter in a 1-qt. saucepan over medium heat until it turns a nutty brown. Stir and watch carefully once it starts to brown. Cool.

2. Meanwhile, on a lightly floured surface roll out patty shell large enough to line a 6-inch pie plate (see Note). (Keep rolling—it's possible!) Fit into pie plate and trim off overhang.

3. Peel pear, quarter lengthwise, and core. Slice crosswise ¼ inch thick. Place in pastry-lined pie plate.

4. Whisk sugar and egg into browned butter, then whisk in 2 Tbsp. flour until smooth. Pour over pears.

5. Bake in lower third of oven until puffed and brown, 20 to 25 minutes.

6. Dust with powdered sugar pressed through a sieve. Serve warm or at room temperature.

*Patty shells are made by Pepperidge Farm and can be found in the frozen dessert section of most grocery stores.
**An 8-oz. can of sliced pears, drained, may be substituted for the fresh pear.

To do ahead: May be prepared up to 2 hours ahead.

Note: "Six-inch" pie plates are really 5 inches at the base and 7 inches across the top.

NORTHERN ITALIAN MENU

- Sardine and Bacon Canapés

- Tuscan Chicken
- Saffron Risotto
- Sautéed Zucchini
  Verdicchio

- Ice Cream with Galliano Peach Sauce
  Espresso

Since Italian cooking is characteristically a pure and straightforward cuisine, it lends itself easily to quick meals. You can prepare this five-dish menu in an hour.

The hot canapés consist of bacon-wrapped sardines, broiled until the bacon is crisp, then served on crackers. Using sardines that are packed in mustard sauce gives this hors d'oeuvre an extra tang.

Tuscan chicken is a sauté of chicken thighs, mushrooms, and tomato chunks, steeped in the essences of rosemary, garlic, and white wine. It's a delicious, classic dish.

A risotto in the style of Milan accompanies the chicken. Risotto is the Italian version of rice pilaf and uses the thick-grained Arborio rice (if available). Risottos are typically creamy in consistency rather than fluffy. Milan-style indicates the addition of saffron (for a soft yellow color) and Parmesan cheese.

For the vegetable, zucchini sautéed in olive oil with garlic is quite appropriate. For the wine try an earthy, robust white, such as a Verdicchio from the Marches region of Italy.

Dessert is vanilla ice cream, topped with a sauce of peaches and Galliano liqueur, made in minutes in a blender. Espresso would be especially nice after this meal, but any good strong coffee will suffice.

SHOPPING LIST FOR NORTHERN ITALIAN MENU

Meat, Dairy:

- ☐ 4 small chicken thighs (1 lb. total)
- ☐ bacon (6 thin slices)
- ☐ butter (3½ Tbsp.)
- ☐ Parmesan cheese (¼ cup grated)
- ☐ vanilla ice cream (⅔ pt.)

Produce:

- ☐ 1 lemon (need 1 Tbsp. juice)
- ☐ 6 medium-size mushrooms (3 oz.)
- ☐ 1 small (4-oz.) tomato
- ☐ 2 small zucchini (½ lb. total)
- ☐ 1 medium-size (5-oz.) peach, or use frozen peaches*
- ☐ garlic (1 tsp. minced)
- ☐ rosemary (3 or 4 sprigs), or use dried

Grocery:

- ☐ 1 can (3¾-oz.) large sardines in mustard sauce (6 to 12 per can)
- ☐ rectangular crackers (12), such as Waverly Wafers
- ☐ Arborio rice (½ cup), or use long-grain white rice
- ☐ frozen, whole, unsweetened peaches (1 cup), if not using fresh

- ☐ tomato paste (½ Tbsp.)
- ☐ powdered saffron (a pinch), or substitute ground turmeric

Liquor:

- ☐ 1 bottle dry, full-bodied white Italian wine, such as Verdicchio (need ½ cup for cooking)
- ☐ Galliano liqueur (2 Tbsp.)

Check Staples:

- ☐ salt
- ☐ black pepper
- ☐ dried rosemary (¼ tsp.), if not using fresh
- ☐ sugar (3 Tbsp.)
- ☐ olive oil (1 Tbsp.)
- ☐ 1 can (14½-oz.) single-strength chicken broth
- ☐ long-grain white rice (½ cup), if not using Arborio
- ☐ coffee (espresso)
- ☐ aluminum foil
- ☐ paper towels

*May need to be purchased several days ahead to allow for ripening.

COUNTDOWNS FOR NORTHERN ITALIAN MENU

Last-Minute Countdown

Time in   Activity
Minutes

60 minutes ahead:
5   Chill wine; Step 1 of dessert
10 Steps 1–2 of risotto and grate
    cheese
10 Step 1 of canapés
15 Turn off risotto if using long-grain
    rice; Steps 1–2 of chicken
10 Turn off risotto if using arborio rice;
    Step 2 of canapés; Steps 3–4 of
    chicken (uncork wine and mince ½
    tsp. garlic for zucchini)
10 Step 3 of canapés; Step 1 of zuc-
    chini; turn chicken and baste; put
    risotto on stove to reheat.
___
60

Serving:
Serve canapés (Step 4).
Step 3 of risotto; Step 5 of chicken; Step
  2 of zucchini
Serve chicken, risotto, zucchini, and
  wine.
Make espresso.
Serve dessert (Step 2) and espresso.

Plan-Ahead Countdown

Time in   Activity
Minutes

One day ahead:
10 Chill wine; prepare risotto.
5   Step 1 of dessert
10 Step 1 of canapés
___
25 (plus 10 minutes more cooking time
    for risotto if using arborio rice)

35 minutes ahead:
15 Steps 1–2 of chicken
10 Step 2 of canapés; Steps 3–4 of
    chicken (uncork wine and mince ½
    tsp. garlic for zucchini)
10 Step 3 of canapés; Step 1 of zuc-
    chini; turn chicken and baste; add
    2 Tbsp. water to risotto and heat.
___
35

Serving:
Serve canapés (Step 4).
Step 5 of chicken; Step 2 of zucchini
Serve chicken, risotto, zucchini, and
  wine.
Make espresso.
Serve dessert (Step 2) and espresso.

SARDINE AND BACON CANAPÉS

Working Time: 10 minutes/Broiling Time: 20 minutes/Servings: 2 to 3

1 can (3¾-oz.) sardines in mustard sauce (6
to 12 per can)
3 to 6 thin slices bacon, halved

6 to 12 crackers (1¼ inches x2½ inches),
such as Waverly Wafers

1. Drain sardines of excess oil (don't remove mustard). Wrap a piece of bacon loosely around each sardine and place on a foil-lined baking pan.

2. Broil sardines about 5 inches from heat (in unpreheated broiler) until bacon is crisp on top, 10 to 12 minutes.

3. Drain fat from pan and turn sardines over. Broil 5–7 minutes more.

4. Drain sardines on paper towels, then place each on a cracker. Serve on small plates.

To do ahead: Do Step 1 up to 1 day ahead. Cover and refrigerate.

Note: The amount of bacon and crackers needed depends on the number of sardines in the can. For proper broiling do not use thick-sliced bacon.

TUSCAN CHICKEN

Working Time: 25 minutes/Cooking Time: 20 minutes more/Servings: 2

6 medium-size mushrooms (3 oz.), quartered
2 Tbsp. butter, divided
4 small chicken thighs (1 lb. total)
½ tsp. salt
⅛ tsp. ground black pepper
½ tsp. minced garlic

1 tsp. finely chopped fresh rosemary, or ¼
tsp. dried
½ cup dry white wine
½ Tbsp. tomato paste
1 small (4-oz.) tomato, cut in ¾ inch
chunks
rosemary sprigs for garnish (if available)

1. In a 10-inch skillet with a nonstick surface sauté mushrooms in 1 Tbsp. butter over medium-high heat until lightly browned, 3 minutes. Remove to a plate.

2. Season chicken with salt and pepper. Add 1 Tbsp. butter to skillet and brown chicken, 3 minutes on each side.

3. Reduce heat to low. Add garlic and rosemary to skillet and turn chicken to mix with seasonings. Remove chicken and drippings to plate with mushrooms. Add wine and tomato paste to skillet. Boil down to ¼ cup.

4. Return chicken (not mushrooms) to skillet and coat with sauce. Cover and cook over low heat until flesh is no longer pink near bone, about 20 minutes. Turn chicken after 10 minutes and spoon pan sauce over.

5. Add mushrooms, with any juices, and chopped tomato to skillet. Heat through, about 2 minutes. Serve on a small platter, garnished with rosemary sprigs.

To do ahead: Prepare through Step 3 up to 1 hour ahead. Cover and leave at room temperature.

SAFFRON RISOTTO

Working Time: 10 minutes/Cooking Time: 25 minutes/Servings: 2

1½ Tbsp. butter, divided
½ cup Arborio rice*
1 can (14½-oz.) single-strength chicken broth

Pinch of powdered saffron** or ground turmeric***
¼ cup freshly grated Parmesan cheese

1. In a heavy 1½-qt. saucepan melt ½ Tbsp. butter over medium heat. Add rice and stir to coat with butter. Add chicken broth and bring to a boil over high heat.

2. Return heat to medium and simmer, uncovered, stirring occasionally, until most of liquid evaporates, about 25 minutes.

3. Stir saffron into rice until well blended. Stir in cheese and 1 Tbsp. butter. Serve in a small vegetable dish.

*Arborio is an Italian rice that has a thick grain and sturdy texture. It's available in Italian delicatessens and markets and is the authentic grain for risottos. It's possible, however, to substitute long-grain white rice—it won't turn to mush when you stir it. Cook at a rapid boil for 15 minutes only.

**Saffron comes from the dried, orange-colored stigmas of an autumn-blooming crocus. It's available in gourmet markets, ethnic grocery stores, and some supermarkets. It's expensive, so you may wish to substitute turmeric.

***Turmeric is the root of a tropical herb belonging to the ginger family. A small amount will impart the same delicate yellow to the rice that saffron does. Turmeric is available in Indian grocery stores and some supermarkets.

To do ahead: Prepare up to 1 day ahead. Cool, cover, and refrigerate. When reheating, add a few tablespoons water to restore creaminess.

SAUTÉED ZUCCHINI

Working and Cooking Time: 10 minutes/Servings: 2

1 Tbsp. olive oil
½ tsp. minced garlic
2 small zucchini (½ lb. total), sliced crosswise ¼ inch thick

¼ tsp. salt
Pinch of ground black pepper

1. Heat oil in an 8-inch skillet over medium-high heat. Add garlic and zucchini. Stir thoroughly to coat all zucchini slices with oil. Cook, stirring frequently, until zucchini is barely tender, about 5 minutes.

2. Season with salt and pepper. Serve in a small vegetable dish.

To do ahead: This is best prepared at the last minute, but can be set aside 5 minutes or so between Steps 1 and 2.

ICE CREAM WITH GALLIANO PEACH SAUCE

Working Time: 10 minutes/Chilling Time: 30 minutes/Servings: 2

1 cup fresh or frozen unsweetened peach
   chunks (1 medium-size fresh peach—no
   need to peel)
3 Tbsp. sugar

1 Tbsp. fresh lemon juice
2 Tbsp. Galliano*
2 servings vanilla ice cream (⅔ pt. total)

1. Put aside 6 bite-size peach chunks in a 1-cup bowl. Put remainder of peach in blender with sugar, lemon juice, and Galliano. Blend until smooth. Pour over peach chunks, cover, and refrigerate at least 30 minutes.

2. To serve, spoon 2 Tbsp. peach sauce into bottom of 2 compotes. Add ice cream. Spoon remaining sauce and peach chunks over ice cream.

*Galliano is a soft, sweet, yellow, Italian liqueur based on angelica and other herbs. It's available in any liquor store.

To do ahead: Do Step 1 up to 1 day ahead.

FRENCH MENU

- **Cream of Broccoli Soup**
- **Garlic Chicken with Vegetables**
  French Bread
  Macon Blanc
- **Orange and Apple Dessert**
  Coffee

French food can be as elaborate and delicious as a Filet de Boeuf Wellington or as simple and delicious as this menu that you can prepare from start to finish in only forty-five minutes.

The broccoli soup is made with just the florets, cooked in a creamy chicken broth base. The florets give the soup an attractive speckled green color; lemon juice sparks the soup's flavor.

Garlic chicken with vegetables is an easy one-dish meal. Chicken thighs are browned, then cooked with new potatoes, carrots, and whole cloves of garlic, with green peas added toward the end of the cooking time. Basil adds flavor and aroma to the dish. Eight large cloves of garlic might seem extravagant for two servings, but as they cook and soften, they become very mild-tasting. At the table the garlic is squeezed from its skin and spread on buttered French bread for a special treat.

To drink, a country French white wine, such as a Macon Blanc, is quite pleasant with this menu.

The orange and apple dessert is a great sweet course after rich or garlicky food. It's simply orange sections and raw apple slices with lemon juice, sugar, and lemon peel. You won't feel overstuffed after eating it, and your tastebuds will feel refreshed.

SHOPPING LIST FOR FRENCH MENU

Poultry, Dairy, Eggs:

☐ 4 small (1 lb. total) chicken thighs

☐ butter (3 Tbsp. + butter for bread)

☐ half and half (1 cup), or ⅔ cup milk + ⅓ cup whipping cream

Produce:

☐ broccoli (1 cup tightly packed florets)

☐ 1 head garlic (8 large cloves + 1 small clove)

☐ 2 small red-skinned potatoes (½ lb. total)

☐ 2 medium-size carrots (½ lb. total)

☐ 2 oranges

☐ 1 medium-size red apple

☐ 1 lemon (need ¼ tsp. grated peel + 1 Tbsp. juice)

Grocery:

☐ frozen green peas (½ cup)

☐ French bread

Liquor:

☐ 1 bottle dry white wine, such as Macon Blanc

Check Staples:

☐ salt

☐ black pepper

☐ white pepper

☐ dried basil (½ tsp.)

☐ sugar (2 Tbsp.)

☐ Worcestershire sauce (½ tsp.)

☐ flour (2 Tbsp.)

☐ 1 can (10¾-oz.) condensed chicken broth

☐ coffee

☐ plastic wrap

COUNTDOWNS FOR FRENCH MENU

Last-Minute Countdown

Time in   *Activity*
Minutes

45 minutes ahead:

15   Chill wine; Steps 1–2 of soup
15   Steps 1–4 of chicken and vegetables
15   Step 3 of soup; Step 1 of dessert;
___   reheat soup.
45

Serving:

Serve soup (Step 4).
Step 5 of chicken and vegetables; un-
   cork wine.
Serve chicken and vegetables, bread,
   butter, and wine.
Make coffee.
Serve dessert (Step 2) and coffee.

Plan-Ahead Countdown

Time in   *Activity*
Minutes

One day ahead:

20   Chill wine; Steps 1–2 of soup
15   Step 1 of dessert; Step 3 of soup
35

30 minutes ahead:

15   Steps 1–4 of chicken and vege-
      tables; reheat soup.

Serving:

Serve soup (Step 4).
Step 5 of chicken and vegetables; un-
   cork wine.
Serve chicken and vegetables, bread,
   butter, and wine.
Make coffee.
Serve dessert (Step 2) and coffee.

CREAM OF BROCCOLI SOUP

Working Time: 15 minutes/Cooking Time: 10 minutes/Servings: 2

¼ tsp. minced garlic
2 Tbsp. butter
5 tsp. flour
1 cup canned, condensed chicken broth
Pinch of ground white pepper

½ tsp. Worcestershire sauce
1 cup half and half (or ⅔ cup milk plus ⅓
   cup whipping cream)
1 cup (packed) broccoli florets
1½ tsp. fresh lemon juice

1.   In a 1½-qt. saucepan sauté garlic in butter over medium heat for 1 minute without browning. Whisk in flour and cook 2 minutes. Whisk in chicken broth and bring to a boil over medium-high heat, adding pepper and Worcestershire.

2.   Whisk in half and half and bring to a boil again. Add broccoli. Reduce heat and simmer, uncovered, stirring occasionally, until broccoli is tender, 10 minutes.

3.   Purée soup in blender and return to saucepan.

4.   Just before serving stir lemon juice into hot soup and pour into individual soup bowls.

To do ahead: Do Steps 1–3 up to 1 day ahead. Cool, cover, and refrigerate.

GARLIC CHICKEN WITH VEGETABLES

Working Time: 15 minutes/Cooking Time: 30 minutes/Servings: 2

4 small (1 lb. total) chicken thighs   *breast*
1 tsp. salt, divided
¼ tsp. ground black pepper, divided
1 Tbsp. butter   *sml turnip*
2 small red-skinned potatoes (½ lb. total)
2 medium-size carrots (½ lb. total)
Zucchini

8 large cloves garlic
½ tsp. dried basil
¼ cup chicken broth or water   *+ add more*
½ cup frozen green peas
French bread and butter   *pita*
thicken w/ cornstarch too
Serve over rice

mixed add P's after cooked

1.   Sprinkle chicken with ½ tsp. salt and ⅛ tsp. pepper. Brown in butter in a 10-inch skillet over medium-high heat, skin side first, about 8 minutes total.

2.   Meanwhile, quarter potatoes, peel carrots, and slice carrots on the diagonal ½-inch thick. Separate garlic cloves, but do not peel.

3.   Remove chicken to a plate. Add potatoes, carrots, and garlic to skillet and coat with fat. Sprinkle with ½ tsp. salt, ⅛ tsp. pepper, and the basil. Stir.

4.   Place chicken on top of vegetables in skillet. Add chicken broth or water, cover, and cook over low heat until vegetables are tender, 25 minutes.

5.   Add peas to skillet, cover, and cook 5 minutes. Serve chicken and vegetables on a small platter with the pan juices. To eat the garlic, squeeze cloves to remove skin, then spread garlic on buttered French bread.

To do ahead: Best if not prepared ahead.

ORANGE AND APPLE DESSERT

Working Time: 15 minutes/Chilling Time: 45 minutes/Servings: 2

2 oranges   1½ tsp. fresh lemon juice
1 red apple, peeled and cut in bite-size pieces   2 Tbsp. sugar
¼ tsp. grated lemon peel

1.   Peel and section oranges over a 1-qt. bowl, catching juices. (Discard peel.) Mix remaining ingredients with orange sections, cover, and refrigerate.

2.   To serve, divide fruit and liquid between 2 compotes.

To do ahead: Prepare up to 2 days ahead.

BEEF AND VEAL MENUS

Eclectic Menu
Minnesota Menu
Middle Eastern Menu
California Menu
Hearty Menu
Iberian Menu
Summer Menu

ECLECTIC MENU

- **Walnut Green Salad**
- **Beef and Mushroom Brochettes with Snow Peas, Rice, and Papaya**
  Cabernet Sauvignon
- **Chocolate Rum Custards**
  Coffee

For this menu ideas were gathered from diverse cuisines and combined into an exciting and unusual meal. The components seem made for each other in spite of their disparate sources.

The salad is a mixture of soft lettuces (butterhead and red-leaf) with watercress and walnuts. A creamy vinaigrette dressing is the perfect bond between the delicate lettuce and the more assertive watercress and walnuts.

Continental style beef and mushroom brochettes are basted with mustard butter and served on a bed of lightly cooked snow peas surrounded by rice, and garnished with papaya slices. The snow peas are an inspired Oriental contribution to the meal and taste wonderful bathed in the lemon butter sauce that's spooned over the brochettes. The elegant finishing touch that decorates the platter is borrowed from the tropics—golden slices of fresh, ripe papaya.

A well-aged California Cabernet Sauvignon would be excellent with this menu. If you cannot purchase (and don't have) one ten years or older, then choose a mellower, blended version, such as the Cabernets made by Sebastiani or Christian Brothers.

For dessert, chocolate custard is updated and made even richer by the addition of dark rum and a topping of rum-laced whipped cream. Since only the yolks of the eggs are used to thicken the custard, it is satin-smooth.

SHOPPING LIST FOR ECLECTIC MENU

Meat, Dairy, Eggs:

- ☐ 1 lb. fillet of beef (to be cut in 8 chunks)
- ☐ butter (4 Tbsp.)
- ☐ half and half (⅔ cup), or ½ cup milk + 3 Tbsp. whipping cream
- ☐ whipping cream (6 Tbsp.)
- ☐ eggs (3 yolks)

Produce:

- ☐ butterhead lettuce (1 cup bite-size pieces)
- ☐ red-leaf lettuce (1 cup bite-size pieces)
- ☐ watercress (1 cup leaves)
- ☐ ⅓ lb. snow peas
- ☐ 8 firm mushrooms, 1½ inches in diameter (about ⅓ lb.)
- ☐ 1 lemon (need 2 Tbsp. juice)
- ☐ 1 small (½-lb.) papaya*
- ☐ garlic (1 small clove)

Grocery:

- ☐ semi-sweet chocolate chips (¼ cup or 1½ oz.)
- ☐ walnuts (2 Tbsp. chopped)

Liquor:

- ☐ 1 bottle Cabernet Sauvignon
- ☐ Myers's dark rum (4 tsp.)

Check Staples:

- ☐ salt
- ☐ black pepper
- ☐ white pepper
- ☐ ground red pepper
- ☐ tarragon vinegar (1 Tbsp.)
- ☐ sugar (¼ cup)
- ☐ olive oil (¼ cup)
- ☐ Dijon mustard (2½ tsp.)
- ☐ 1 can (10¾-oz.) condensed chicken broth
- ☐ long-grain, white rice (⅔ cup)
- ☐ coffee
- ☐ 9-inch wooden skewers (4)
- ☐ plastic wrap

*May need to be purchased several days ahead to allow for ripening.

COUNTDOWNS FOR ECLECTIC MENU

Last-Minute Countdown

Time in   Activity
Minutes

65 minutes ahead:
15   Uncork wine; Steps 1–3 and 5 of
     dessert
20   Steps 1–2 of salad
15   Steps 1–2 of beef
15   Step 4 of dessert; Steps 3–5 of beef
___   and slice papaya.
65

Serving:
Serve salad (Step 3).
(5 minutes after serving salad do Step 6
     of beef.)
Step 7 of beef
Serve beef with rice, snow peas, and pa-
     paya (Step 8), and wine.
Make coffee.
Serve dessert (Step 6) and coffee.

Plan-Ahead Countdown

Time in   Activity
Minutes

One day ahead:
10   Steps 1–3 of dessert (skip freezer
     chilling)
25   Steps 1–3 and 5 of beef
20   Step 1 of salad; Step 4 of dessert;
___   Step 2 of salad
55

60 minutes ahead:
5   Uncork wine; Step 5 of dessert

5 minutes ahead:
5   Step 4 of beef and slice papaya; rice
     on stove to reheat

Serving:
Serve salad (Step 3).
(5 minutes after serving salad do Step 6
     of beef.)
Step 7 of beef
Serve beef with rice, snow peas, and pa-
     paya (Step 8), and wine.
Make coffee.
Serve dessert (Step 6) and coffee.

WALNUT GREEN SALAD

Working Time: 20 minutes/Chilling Time: 30 minutes/Servings: 2

CREAMY VINAIGRETTE DRESSING:
¼ tsp. salt
Pinch of ground white pepper
½ tsp. Dijon mustard
1 small clove garlic, peeled
1 Tbsp. tarragon vinegar
1 egg yolk (raw)
2 Tbsp. whipping cream
2 Tbsp. olive oil

SALAD INGREDIENTS:
1 cup (lightly packed) bite-size pieces
  butterhead lettuce
1 cup (lightly packed) bite-size pieces red-
  leaf lettuce
1 cup (lightly packed) watercress, large
  stems removed
2 Tbsp. chopped walnuts

1. Combine all ingredients for dressing, except olive oil, in a ½-pt. jar. Cover and shake until salt dissolves. Add olive oil and shake again. Refrigerate.

2. Divide lettuces and watercress between 2 salad bowls. Sprinkle with walnuts. Cover with plastic wrap and refrigerate.

3. Just before serving pour desired amount of dressing over salads. (Remove garlic clove.)

To do ahead: Do Steps 1–2 up to 2 days ahead.

BEEF AND MUSHROOM BROCHETTES
WITH RICE, SNOW PEAS, AND PAPAYA

Working Time: 30 minutes/Broiling Time: 10 minutes/Servings: 2

BEEF, ETC.:

2 cups water

⅓ lb. snow peas*, tips and any strings removed

1 tsp. salt

8 firm mushrooms, 1½ inches in diameter (about ⅓ lb.)

1 lb. fillet of beef, fat removed, cut in 8 equal chunks

1 can (10¾-oz.) condensed chicken broth

⅔ cup long-grain white rice

1 small (½-lb.) papaya**, peeled, seeded, sliced lengthwise ½ inch thick

BASTING SAUCE:

2 Tbsp. butter

2 Tbsp. olive oil

½ tsp. salt

Pinch of ground black pepper

Pinch of ground red pepper

2 tsp. Dijon mustard

SERVING SAUCE:

2 Tbsp. butter

2 Tbsp. fresh lemon juice

1. Bring water to a boil in a 1-qt. saucepan over high heat. Add snow peas and 1 tsp. salt. Cook 2 minutes. Drain in a colander.

2. Slice off stems of mushrooms even with caps. Alternate mushroom caps with beef on 4 wooden skewers (9 inches long).

3. For Basting Sauce melt butter in a 1-cup metal measuring cup. Remove from heat and add remaining ingredients.

4. For Serving Sauce melt butter in a ½-cup metal measuring cup. Remove from heat and add lemon juice.

5. In same pan used for snow peas heat chicken broth to boiling over high heat. Add rice, turn heat to low, cover, and simmer 15 minutes, or until rice is tender and liquid is absorbed.

6. Turn on broiler. Brush brochettes on all sides with basting sauce. Place on rack 1 inch from heat source. Broil 4 minutes, or until lightly browned (leave oven door partly open for electric broilers).

7.   Baste brochettes with sauce, turn them over, and baste again. Broil 4 minutes longer, or until browned.

8.   To serve, run hottest tap water over snow peas to rewarm them. Reheat serving sauce over low heat. Make a circle of rice on an oval serving platter, fill with snow peas, and top with brochettes. Pour serving sauce over brochettes and snow peas. Garnish ends of platter with papaya slices.

*The peak season for snow peas is May through September, although they can be found all year in Oriental markets. Select small pods with undeveloped peas.
**Select a papaya that is almost all yellow, unbruised, with no signs of shriveling. Papayas are available all year round, but may be difficult to obtain in some areas. A large, fresh peach may be substituted.

To do ahead: Do Steps 1–3 and 5 up to 1 day ahead. Cover and refrigerate items separately. Peel, seed, and slice papaya up to 1 hour ahead. Leave at room temperature.

CHOCOLATE RUM CUSTARDS

Working Time: 15 minutes/Baking Time: 35 minutes (325°F)/Chilling Time: 50 minutes/Servings: 2

CHOCOLATE RUM CUSTARD:	TOPPING:
⅔ cup half and half, or ½ cup milk plus 3 Tbsp. whipping cream	¼ cup whipping cream
¼ cup (1½ oz.) semi-sweet chocolate chips	1 tsp. sugar
3 Tbsp. sugar	1 tsp. Myers's dark rum*
1 Tbsp. Myers's dark rum*	
2 egg yolks	

1.   Turn oven to 325°F. Bring half and half to a boil in a ¾-qt. saucepan. Put chocolate chips in a blender and add about ⅓ cup of the half and half. Cover and blend at high speed for 1 minute.

2.   Add sugar, rum, and egg yolks, and blend again. Blend in remaining half and half and pour into two 6-oz. soufflé dishes or custard cups.

3. Half fill an 8- or 9-inch cake pan with hottest tap water and place in center of oven. Set custards in water and bake 35 minutes. (Custard will still feel quite soft to the touch but will firm on cooling.)

4. Carefully remove custards from oven. Tip pan to drain off some of the water. Remove custards and place in freezer until cold, but not frozen, 50 minutes. Remove to refrigerator.

5. In a 3-cup bowl whip cream until stiff with a rotary beater. Beat in sugar. Gently fold in rum. Cover and chill.

6. Serve custards topped with whipped cream.

*Myers's rum is a richly flavored Jamaican rum available in any liquor store. Other dark rums may be substituted.

To do ahead: Do Steps 1–4 up to 2 days ahead. (Flavor improves on standing, so make ahead, if possible.) Do Step 5 up to 3 hours ahead.

MINNESOTA MENU

- Shrimp Spread

- Fillet of Beef Stroganoff
- White and Wild Rice
- Broccoli Florets
- Spiced Apricots
  Zinfandel

- Strawberry Sherbet
  Hazelnut Cookies
  Coffee

Here's a three-star menu suitable for a special occasion when you want to serve something memorable.

The shrimp spread, a sort of paté to be served with crackers, evolved from the English "potted shrimp." The shrimp are finely chopped and blended with melted butter, mace, and nutmeg for a fascinating flavor—delicate, yet not bland. The spread makes a superb hors d'oeuvre or first course.

Minnesota is famous for wild rice and quality dairy products. It's only natural that these items would find many uses in Minnesota cooking, and one of the best is this elegant version of beef stroganoff. The recipe calls for beef fillet, mushrooms, Madeira wine, and of course sour cream. The stroganoff, juxtaposed with wild rice, is fabulous. Add spiced apricots and quickly cooked, lemon-sparked broccoli florets, and you have a winning combination.

A young, zestful, ruby-hued Zinfandel from California is a good choice to accompany the main course.

You don't need an ice cream freezer to make luscious fruit sherbets like this strawberry one. It's made in minutes in a blender and put in the freezer until serving time. The strawberry flavor is fresh and lively. Crisp cookies, especially those with nuts, complement the sherbet.

SHOPPING LIST FOR MINNESOTA MENU

Seafood, Meat, Dairy, Eggs:

☐ ¼ lb. (⅔ cup) tiny cooked, peeled shrimp

☐ 1 lb. beef fillet steaks (to be cut in ½x1x2-inch pieces)

☐ butter (10 Tbsp.)

☐ sour cream (½ cup)

☐ eggs (1 egg white)

Produce:

☐ lettuce (2 to 4 leaves)

☐ ¼ lb. medium-size mushrooms

☐ 1 bunch broccoli (need 2½ cups florets)

☐ 1 lemon

Grocery:

☐ crisp cookies, such as Pepperidge Farm Hazelnut

☐ plain crackers, such as Nabisco Waverly Wafers (need 16 to 20)

☐ wild rice (1½ oz.)

☐ 1 can (8¾-oz.) apricot halves in heavy syrup

☐ frozen unsweetened whole strawberries (4 oz.)

Liquor:

☐ 1 bottle young red wine, such as Zinfandel

☐ dry Madeira wine (⅓ cup)

Check Staples:

☐ salt

☐ black pepper

☐ ground mace (¼ tsp.)

☐ ground nutmeg (⅛ tsp.)

☐ cinnamon (1 stick)

☐ allspice (6 whole)

☐ flour (1 Tbsp.)

☐ salad oil (1 Tbsp.)

☐ A-1 Steak Sauce (½ tsp.)

☐ cider vinegar (2 Tbsp.)

☐ sugar (⅓ cup)

☐ long-grain white rice (⅓ cup)

☐ 1 can (10¾-oz.) condensed chicken broth

☐ coffee

COUNTDOWNS FOR MINNESOTA MENU

Last-Minute Countdown

Time in   *Activity*
Minutes

65 minutes ahead:

10 Steps 1–2 of sherbet (squeeze 2 tsp. lemon juice for broccoli)

5 Uncork wine; Step 1 of apricots

10 Sour cream out of refrigerator; Steps 1–2 of shrimp

5 Step 1 of rice

5 Step 2 of apricots; Step 1 of broccoli

30 Steps 1–4 of stroganoff; Step 2 of rice
___
65

Serving:

Serve shrimp and crackers (Step 3).

Steps 5–6 of stroganoff; Step 3 of rice; Step 2 of broccoli

Serve stroganoff, rice, broccoli, apricots, and wine.

Make coffee.

Serve sherbet and cookies (Step 3) and coffee.

Plan-Ahead Countdown

Time in   *Activity*
Minutes

One day ahead;

5 Step 1 of rice

5 Step 1 of apricots

10 Steps 1–2 of sherbet

10 Steps 1–2 of shrimp; Step 2 of apricots
___
30 Plus 25 more minutes cooking time for rice. (After 10 minutes do Step 2 of rice.)

35 minutes ahead:

5 Sour cream, shrimp out of refrigerator; Step 1 of broccoli; uncork wine.

30 Steps 1–4 of stroganoff
___
35

Serving:

Serve shrimp and crackers (Step 3).

Reheat rice; Steps 5–6 of stroganoff; Step 3 of rice; Step 2 of broccoli

Serve stroganoff, rice, broccoli, apricots, and wine.

Make coffee.

Serve sherbet and cookies (Step 3) and coffee.

SHRIMP SPREAD

Working Time: 10 minutes/Cooling Time: 10 minutes/Servings: 2

4 Tbsp. butter
¼ tsp. ground mace
⅛ tsp. ground nutmeg
⅛ tsp. salt

⅔ cup (¼ lb.) tiny shrimp, purchased
   cooked and peeled
16 to 20 plain crackers, such as Waverly
   Wafers
2 to 4 lettuce leaves for garnish

1.   Heat butter in a 1-cup metal measuring cup over medium heat just until melted. Remove from heat. Add mace, nutmeg, and salt. Cool.

2.   Chop shrimp very finely and place in a 3-cup bowl. Add butter mixture and blend well. Pack into 2 small crocks (or Oriental teacups). Let cool until firm, about 10 minutes.

3.   To serve, line two small plates with lettuce leaves. Arrange shrimp crocks and crackers on top. Provide individual butter knives to spread shrimp mixture onto crackers.

To do ahead: Prepare through Step 2 up to 1 day ahead. Cover and refrigerate. Remove from refrigerator 30 minutes before serving so mixture will be spreadable.

Note: Don't be tempted to add lemon juice to the shrimp mixture—it obscures the delicate spiciness that's the highlight of the dish.

FILLET OF BEEF STROGANOFF

Working and Cooking Time: 30 minutes/Servings: 2

1 lb. beef fillet steaks
¼ lb. medium-size mushrooms
2 Tbsp. butter, divided
1 Tbsp. flour
½ tsp. salt

⅛ tsp. ground black pepper
1 Tbsp. salad oil
⅓ cup dry Madeira wine*
½ tsp. A-1 Steak Sauce
½ cup sour cream, at room temperature

1.   Trim steak of all fat and membranes. Slice meat into ½x1x2-inch pieces. Wash, dry, and halve mushrooms.

2.   In a 10-inch skillet with a nonstick surface, sauté mushrooms in 1 Tbsp. butter over medium-high heat until lightly browned, 3 minutes. Remove to a 1-qt. bowl.

3.   Mix flour, salt, and pepper in a bag. Add steak and shake to coat with flour. In same skillet, brown steak in 1 Tbsp. each butter and oil over medium-high to high heat, about 5 minutes. Remove to bowl with mushrooms.

4.   Add Madeira and A-1 sauce to skillet. Boil down to 3 Tbsp.

5.   Return steak and mushrooms to skillet and heat until steak is hot, but still pink inside. Lower heat, push steak to one side, and stir sour cream into pan juices. Don't let mixture boil.

6.   Blend sauce with steak and mushrooms. Place on a large platter with rice and broccoli. Garnish with the spiced apricots and serve.

*Either a Portuguese Madeira or a domestic Madeira, such as Paul Masson (California), may be used.

To do ahead: Prepare through Step 4 up to 1 hour ahead. Cover and leave at room temperature.

WILD AND WHITE RICE

Working Time: 5 minutes/Cooking Time: 50 minutes/Servings: 2

¼ cup wild rice*   ⅓ cup long-grain white rice
1 can (10¾-oz.) condensed chicken broth   2 Tbsp. butter

1.   Place wild rice in a 1-qt. saucepan. Rinse rice in several changes of water and drain. Add chicken broth and bring to a boil over high heat. Lower heat, cover, and simmer 35 minutes.

2.   Add white rice to saucepan, bring to a boil again, cover, and simmer 15 minutes, or until both rices are tender and liquid is absorbed.

3. Add butter, cover, and heat until melted. Fluff rice, blending in butter, and serve.

*Wild rice is not a true rice, but an aquatic grass that grows wild in Minnesota. It's expensive, but flavorful enough to be extended with white rice and still be delicious (maybe even better for the combination). Wild rice is available in supermarkets and gourmet food stores.

To do ahead: Prepare through Step 2 up to 1 day ahead. Cool, cover, and refrigerate. Reheat over low heat and complete Step 3.

BROCCOLI FLORETS

Working Time: 5 minutes/Cooking Time: 6 minutes/Servings: 2

1 qt. water.

2½ cups broccoli florets*, in about 1½ inch
  pieces

1⅛ tsp. salt, divided

2 Tbsp. butter

2 tsp. fresh lemon juice

1. In a 2-qt. saucepan bring water to a boil over high heat. Add broccoli, then 1 tsp. salt. Boil, uncovered, until broccoli is just tender, about 6 minutes. Drain in a colander.

2. Melt butter in same saucepan over low heat. Mix in broccoli and ⅛ tsp. salt. When broccoli is hot, remove from heat and add lemon juice.

*Broccoli stems can be saved for another use, such as in a Chinese stir-fry dish.

To do ahead: Do Step 1 up to 1 hour ahead. Run cold water over broccoli to stop the cooking process.

SPICED APRICOTS

Working Time: 5 minutes/Cooking and Standing Time: 45 minutes/Servings: 2

1 can (8¾-oz.) apricot halves in heavy
  syrup

1 stick cinnamon

6 whole allspice

2 Tbsp. cider vinegar

1.   Drain syrup from apricots into a ¾-qt. saucepan. Add spices and vinegar and simmer, covered, for 15 minutes.

2.   Add apricots to saucepan and coat with syrup. Remove from heat and let stand at least 30 minutes, or until serving time. Drain and serve warm or cold.

To do ahead: Prepare up to 3 days ahead. Cover and refrigerate.

STRAWBERRY SHERBET

Working Time: 10 minutes/Freezing Time: 1 hour/Servings: 2

1 cup (4 oz.) frozen, unsweetened whole
  strawberries
⅓ cup sugar
2 Tbsp. fresh lemon juice

1 egg white
Crisp nut cookies, such as Pepperidge Farm
  Hazelnut

1.   Combine all ingredients in blender. Blend on high speed until puréed, about 2 minutes, stopping several times to stir mixture and rest blender motor.

2.   Transfer to freezer tray and freeze until firm, at least 1 hour. Pack into a freezer container for storage.

3.   Serve in small compotes, accompanied by cookies.

To do ahead: May be prepared up to 1 week ahead.

MIDDLE EASTERN MENU

- Middle Eastern Green Salad

- Moussaka
  Sesame Seed Rolls
  Greek Red Demestica

- Walnut Date Confections
  Coffee

Even the subtly exotic, colorful, and spicy cookery of the Middle East can be captured in a quick and easy menu. Put together a minty tossed salad, a simplified (but very good) moussaka, bakery sesame rolls, and walnut-stuffed dates with lemon frosting, and you have a terrific meal that can be prepared in an hour (and entirely ahead of time, if you wish).

Typically Middle Eastern, the salad contains lettuce, chopped tomato, grated carrot, chopped green pepper, and fresh or dried mint in an oil and vinegar dressing. The sweetness of the raw carrot is a pleasant counterpoint to the flavors of the other ingredients.

Moussaka is a Greek or Turkish gratin of sliced eggplant and ground beef or lamb, topped with a fluffy cheese custard. In this version the eggplant is broiled, eliminating the usual steps of salting, drying, and frying the slices. The meat used is beef, which is browned and mixed with tomato paste, cinnamon, and herbs. The cheese layer requires no precooking, just the mixing of cottage cheese, sour cream, eggs, and grated Kasseri or Kefalotyri (or Parmesan) cheese. You can assemble this dish ahead and bake it when you're ready.

Sesame seed rolls (hard rolls if you can get them) make a good accompaniment for the moussaka, as does an unresinated Greek wine, such as a red Demestica.

Lemon-frosted, walnut-stuffed dates make a delightful confection to nibble while sipping tiny cups of rich, strong coffee.

SHOPPING LIST FOR MIDDLE EASTERN MENU

Meat, Dairy, Eggs:

☐ ½ lb. lean ground beef

☐ Kasseri, Kefalotyri, or Parmesan cheese (¼ cup grated)

☐ 1 carton (8-oz.) cottage cheese

☐ sour cream (⅔ cup)

☐ butter (4½ Tbsp. + butter for rolls)

☐ eggs (2)

Produce:

☐ 1 head green-leaf (or other) lettuce

☐ 1 medium-size (6-oz.) tomato

☐ 1 small (4-oz.) carrot

☐ 1 small green pepper (need ¼ cup chopped)

☐ fresh mint (1 Tbsp.), or use dried

☐ 1 small onion (need ¼ cup chopped)

☐ 1 medium-size (1-lb.) eggplant (need ½)

☐ 1 lemon (need 1½ tsp. juice)

Grocery:

☐ French dressing (oil and vinegar type), such as Trader Vic's (¼ cup)

☐ tomato paste (3 Tbsp.)

☐ packaged, pitted dates (10)

☐ walnut halves (5)

Liquor:

☐ 1 bottle unresinated Greek wine, such as red Demestica

Check Staples:

☐ salt

☐ white pepper

☐ ground cinnamon (⅛ tsp.)

☐ dried basil (¼ tsp.)

☐ dried oregano (⅛ tsp.)

☐ dried mint (1 tsp.), if not using fresh

☐ powdered sugar (½ cup)

☐ plastic wrap

☐ coffee

COUNTDOWNS FOR MIDDLE EASTERN MENU

Last-Minute Countdown

Time in   *Activity*
Minutes

60 minutes ahead:

30   Uncork wine; Steps 1–7 of moussaka (oven to 375°F)

15   Step 1 of salad

15   Steps 1–3 of dessert; place salads in freezer for 5 minutes; moussaka out of oven

__

60

Serving:
Serve salad (Step 2).
(Heat rolls in oven, if desired.)
Serve moussaka, rolls, butter, and wine.
Make coffee.
Serve dessert and coffee.

Plan-Ahead Countdown

Time in   *Activity*
Minutes

One day ahead:

30   Steps 1–6 of moussaka (turn oven off after Step 4)

15   Step 1 of salad

15   Steps 1–3 of dessert

60

50 minutes ahead:
—   Oven to 375°F; uncork wine.

35 minutes ahead:
—   Step 7 of moussaka

1 minute ahead:
—   Moussaka out of oven.

Serving:
Serve salad (Step 2).
(Heat rolls in oven, if desired.)
Serve moussaka, rolls, butter, and wine.
Make coffee.
Serve dessert and coffee.

MIDDLE EASTERN GREEN SALAD

Working Time: 15 minutes/Chilling Time: 30 minutes/Servings: 2

3 cups bite-size pieces green-leaf (or other)
    lettuce leaves

1 medium-size (6-oz.) tomato, seeded and
    chopped

1 small (4-oz.) carrot, peeled and coarsely
    grated

¼ cup chopped green pepper

1 Tbsp. chopped fresh mint, or 1 tsp. dried

¼ cup French dressing (oil and vinegar
    type), such as Trader Vic's

1.   Combine all ingredients except dressing in a 2-qt. salad bowl. Cover with plastic wrap and refrigerate.

2.   Just before serving, toss with dressing and serve in individual salad bowls.

To do ahead: Do Step 1 up to 1 day ahead.

MOUSSAKA

Working Time: 30 minutes/Baking Time: 30 minutes (375°F)/Settling Time: 10 Minutes/Servings: 2 large

EGGPLANT:

1 medium-size (1-lb.) eggplant (need half)

2 Tbsp. butter, melted

MEAT MIXTURE:

¼ cup finely chopped onion

½ Tbsp. butter

½ lb. lean ground beef

3 Tbsp. tomato paste

¼ tsp. salt

⅛ tsp. ground cinnamon

⅛ tsp. dried oregano

¼ tsp. dried basil

CHEESE LAYER:

¼ cup grated Kasseri* or Kefalotyri*
    cheese, divided

1 carton (8-oz.) cottage cheese

⅔ cup sour cream

2 eggs

½ tsp. salt

¼ tsp. ground white pepper

1. Turn broiler on. Cut eggplant in half lengthwise. Slice one of the halves crosswise into ½-inch-thick slices, discarding ends. (Save other half for another use.)

2. Put eggplant on a baking sheet and brush on both sides with melted butter, using all the butter. Broil 3 inches from heat for 3 to 5 minutes on each side, or until browned. Set oven to bake at 375°F.

3. In a 10-inch skillet sauté onion in ½ Tbsp. butter over medium heat until wilted, 3 minutes. Raise heat to medium-high and add beef. Cook, breaking up the meat and stirring occasionally, until meat is well browned, about 8 minutes.

4. Remove from heat and mix in tomato paste, salt, cinnamon, oregano, and basil.

5. For cheese layer, reserve 2 Tbsp. grated cheese for topping, and combine remaining ingredients in a 2-qt. bowl, blending well with a whisk.

6. Arrange eggplant slices in two gratin dishes (8 inches long). Spread with meat mixture, top with cheese mixture, and sprinkle with the reserved grated cheese.

7. Bake in upper third of oven until puffed and golden, 30 minutes. Let settle 10 minutes before serving.

*These are mild cheeses made from sheep's milk (or cow's milk in the United States). If not available, substitute freshly grated Parmesan cheese.

To do ahead: Prepare through Step 6 (except turn off oven after Step 4) up to 1 day ahead. Cover tightly and refrigerate. Bake straight from refrigerator at 375°F until puffed and brown, about 35 minutes. Any leftovers are good reheated too.

WALNUT DATE CONFECTIONS

Working Time: 15 minutes/Chilling Time: 15 minutes/Servings: 2

2 Tbsp. butter
½ cup (unsifted) powdered sugar
1½ tsp. fresh lemon juice

8 or 10 pitted dates
4 or 5 walnut halves

1. Melt butter in a 1-cup metal measuring cup over low heat. Remove from heat and blend in sugar until smooth. Add lemon juice. (Enough frosting for 8 to 10 dates.)

2. Break walnut halves in half lengthwise. Slit each date lengthwise and insert a walnut piece.

3. With a small metal spatula coat one side of stuffed dates with frosting and place, coated side down, on a wire rack. Then coat top sides with frosting. Refrigerate until firm, about 15 minutes. Serve chilled.

To do ahead: May be prepared up to 2 days ahead. Refrigerate airtight.

CALIFORNIA MENU

- **Onion, Cheese, and Walnut Pastry**
  Medium Sherry

- **Roast Beef and Crab Salad**
- **Sourdough Bread**
  Zinfandel Rosé

- **Cointreau Fruit Cup**
  Coffee

California's greatest contributions to the culinary world are its incredible array of fresh foods and its fine wines to accompany them. This menu includes quite a few California products, from the walnuts in the pastry hors d'oeuvre to the kiwi fruit in the dessert compote.

The hors d'oeuvre is easily made by topping a rolled-out puff patty shell with sautéed onions, a few anchovies, walnuts, and Gruyère cheese, and baking it until golden and puffy. This goes beautifully with small glasses of a nutty-flavored medium sherry, such as Almaden Golden or Ingelnook Vintage sherry.

California is America's salad bowl, and this hearty salad makes a great main course. Lettuce-lined plates are filled with rolled slices of rare roast beef, chunks of fresh Dungeness crabmeat, mounds of marinated artichoke hearts, garbanzo beans (chick peas), alfalfa sprouts, avocado slices, tomato wedges, and black olives. (You will not go hungry!) The salad has a Louis dressing that probably originated in Washington State, but is an institution in San Francisco, as is sourdough bread, the natural accompaniment for this meal.

To drink you might try a Zinfandel rosé on the dry side, such as those made by Pedroncelli or Concannon wineries.

For a simple, light, and refreshing dessert, California-grown kiwis and oranges are combined with pineapple and Cointreau and served in stemmed goblets.

SHOPPING LIST FOR CALIFORNIA MENU

Meat, Seafood, Dairy:

☐ ⅓ lb. thinly sliced rare roast beef (from delicatessen)

☐ ¼ lb. lump Dungeness crabmeat, or use Alaskan king crab or tiny, cooked, shelled shrimp

☐ butter (1 Tbsp. + butter for bread)

☐ Gruyère cheese (¼ cup grated)

☐ whipping cream (3 Tbsp.)

Produce:

☐ 1 large onion

☐ 1 lemon (need 1½ Tbsp. juice)

☐ 2 heads butterhead lettuce

☐ alfalfa sprouts (½ cup)

☐ 1 medium-size avocado (need half)*

☐ 1 medium-size (6-oz.) tomato

☐ 1 large orange

☐ 1 large kiwi fruit,* or use ½ cup seedless green grapes

☐ pineapple (need heaping ½ cup chunks), or use canned

Grocery:

☐ frozen Pepperidge Farm patty shells (1)

☐ 1 can anchovy fillets (need 3)

☐ walnuts (1 Tbsp. chopped)

☐ 1 can (8½-oz.) chick peas

☐ 1 jar (6-oz.) marinated artichoke hearts

☐ 1 small can black olives (need 12)

☐ 1 can (8-oz.) pineapple chunks, if not using fresh

☐ bottled chili sauce (3 Tbsp.)

☐ sourdough bread

Liquor:

☐ 1 bottle Zinfandel rosé, such as Pedroncelli or Concannon

☐ Amontillado sherry, such as Almaden Golden or Inglenook Vintage California sherry

☐ Cointreau (2 Tbsp.)

Check Staples:

☐ salt

☐ black pepper

☐ sugar (2 Tbsp.)

☐ flour (2 Tbsp.)

☐ Worcestershire sauce (1 tsp.)

☐ mayonnaise (¾ cup)

☐ coffee

☐ paper towels

☐ plastic wrap

*May need to be purchased several days ahead to allow for ripening.

COUNTDOWNS FOR CALIFORNIA MENU

Last-Minute Countdown

Time in   Activity
Minutes

60 minutes ahead:
35 Chill wine; patty shell out of freezer
    (for hors d'oeuvre); prepare salad.
15 Oven to 425°F; prepare hors
    d'oeuvre.
10 Step 1 of dessert; uncork wine;
    oven to 400°F; bread in oven to
___ warm
60

Serving:
Serve hors d'oeuvre and sherry.
Serve salad, bread, butter, and wine.
Make coffee.
Serve dessert (Step 2) and coffee.

Plan-Ahead Countdown

Time in   Activity
Minutes

One day ahead:
35 Chill wine; patty shell in refrigera-
    tor (in plastic wrap) for hors
    d'oeuvre; prepare salad.

25 minutes ahead:
15 Oven to 425°F; prepare hors
    d'oeuvre.
10 Step 1 of dessert; uncork wine;
    oven to 400°F; bread in oven to
___ warm
25

Serving:
Serve hors d'oeuvre and sherry.
Serve salad, bread, butter, and wine.
Make coffee.
Serve dessert (Step 2) and coffee.

ONION, CHEESE, AND WALNUT PASTRY

Thawing Time: 30 minutes/Working Time: 15 minutes/Baking Time: 10 minutes (425°F)/Servings: 2

1 Tbsp. butter

1 large onion, peeled, halved, and sliced ⅛ inch thick

1 frozen patty shell*, thawed

2 Tbsp. (about) flour for rolling out pastry

3 canned anchovy fillets, drained on a paper towel

1 Tbsp. chopped walnuts

¼ cup grated Gruyère cheese

1. Turn oven to 425°F. Sauté onions in butter in a 10-inch skillet over medium heat until soft, about 8 minutes.

2. On a lightly floured surface roll out patty shell to a 7-inch circle. Spread with the sautéed onions to within ¾ inch of edge. Lay anchovies on top and sprinkle walnuts and cheese over all.

3. Bake in center of oven until puffed and brown, about 10 minutes. Cut into wedges and serve hot.

*Patty shells are made by Pepperidge Farm and can be found in the frozen dessert section of most grocery stores. They come in 10-oz. packages containing 6 shells.

To do ahead: Onions can be sautéed and other ingredients readied up to 1 hour ahead. (Don't roll out patty shell because it might dry out.)

ROAST BEEF AND CRAB SALAD

Working Time: 30 minutes/Chilling Time: 30 minutes/Servings: 2

LOUIS DRESSING:
¾ cup mayonnaise
3 Tbsp. whipping cream
3 Tbsp. bottled chili sauce
1½ Tbsp. fresh lemon juice
1 tsp. Worcestershire sauce

SALAD INGREDIENTS:
2 heads butterhead lettuce
⅓ lb. thinly sliced rare roast beef (from delicatessen)
¼ lb. lump Dungeness crabmeat*

1 can (8½-oz.) chick peas
1 jar (6-oz.) marinated artichoke hearts, drained
½ cup alfalfa sprouts
½ medium-size avocado, peeled, thinly sliced lengthwise
1 medium-size (6-oz.) tomato, cut in 10 wedges
1 dozen black olives (canned)
Freshly ground black pepper

1.   In a 1-qt. bowl whisk together all ingredients for dressing. Transfer to sauceboat, cover, and refrigerate at least 45 minutes to blend flavors.

2.   Line 2 dinner plates with large lettuce leaves. Tear remaining lettuce into bite-size pieces and place in center of plates. Roll up roast beef slices and arrange over lettuce.

3.   Place mounds of crabmeat, drained chick peas, artichoke hearts, alfalfa sprouts, and avocado slices artfully atop lettuce. Garnish with tomato wedges and olives. Cover tightly with plastic wrap and refrigerate at least 30 minutes.

4.   Serve with dressing on the side and pass pepper mill.

*The Dungeness is a Pacific Coast crab, in season from October to May. Alaskan king crab or tiny cooked, shelled shrimp may be substituted.

To do ahead: May be prepared up to 1 day ahead if crabmeat is very fresh.

COINTREAU FRUIT CUP

Working Time: 10 minutes/Chilling Time: 30 minutes/Servings: 2

1 large orange, sectioned
1 large kiwi fruit*, peeled and thinly sliced
½ cup (heaping) fresh pineapple chunks or 1
    can (8 oz.)

2 Tbsp. sugar
2 Tbsp. Cointreau**

1.   In a 1½-qt. bowl toss fruit gently with sugar and Cointreau. Cover and refrigerate at least 30 minutes.

2.   To serve, stir again gently and divide fruit and liquid between 2 compotes.

*A kiwi is an oval-shaped fruit about 3 inches long and 2 inches in diameter with fuzzy brown skin. The flesh, which has a refreshing sweet-tart flavor, is brilliant green with a sunburst pattern of tiny, black, edible seeds. Kiwis are available from June through March. Ripen them at room temperature until soft as a ripe peach. If unavailable, substitute ½ cup seedless green grapes.
**Cointreau is a clear, orange-flavored liqueur of excellent quality, produced in France and available in any liquor store.

To do ahead: Prepare up to 1 day ahead.

HEARTY MENU

- **Ratatouille Soup**
- **Rib Steaks in Herbed Wine Sauce**
- **Cheddar Baked Potato Strips**
  Burgundy
- **Bananas with Raspberries and Whipped Cream**
  Coffee

Here's a hearty menu for cool weather that's a pleasant variation on the popular meat and potatoes meal.

A savory Mediterranean dish is the basis for ratatouille (ra-ta-tooy) soup. Traditionally, ratatouille is a mélange of vegetables, such as eggplant, onions, zucchini, and tomatoes, cooked with garlic and herbs. Here, with the addition of chicken broth, it becomes a delicious soup.

Rib steaks are tender and juicy and ready in fifteen minutes when pan-broiled and served with an herbed garlic and wine sauce. The herbs are thyme, tarragon, and marjoram, along with a generous amount of chopped chives.

Luscious cheddar potato strips make an excellent accompaniment to the beef and can bake unattended while you prepare the rest of the dinner. The potatoes are cut as for French fries, piled in a gratin dish, topped with butter, grated cheese, and whipping cream, then baked. No green vegetable is necessary if you use the herbs with the meat and don't omit the soup.

A hearty French burgundy is the natural accompaniment here and can be used in making the wine sauce as well.

While peaches and raspberries are a classic combination, bananas and raspberries are equally delicious and very easy too. Whipped cream tops off this dessert prettily.

146

SHOPPING LIST FOR HEARTY MENU

Meat, Dairy:

☐ 2 small beef rib steaks (1½ to 2 lbs. total)

☐ butter (5 Tbsp.)

☐ whipping cream (⅔ cup)

☐ sharp Cheddar cheese (⅓ cup grated)

Produce:

☐ 1 small (4-oz.) tomato

☐ 1 lemon (need 1 Tbsp. juice)

☐ 2 medium-size baking potatoes (⅔ lb. total)

☐ 1 small onion (need ¼ cup chopped)

☐ 1 small eggplant (need 1 cup diced)

☐ 1 small (3-oz.) zucchini

☐ 2 small bananas*

☐ chives (2 Tbsp. chopped), or use frozen

☐ garlic (1½ tsp. minced)

Grocery:

☐ frozen chives (2 Tbsp.), if not using fresh

☐ frozen whole, unsweetened raspberries (1 cup)

Liquor:

☐ 1 bottle hearty red wine, such as Burgundy (need ½ cup for cooking)

Check Staples:

☐ salt

☐ black pepper

☐ white pepper

☐ ground coriander (¼ tsp.)

☐ dried thyme (⅛ tsp.)

☐ dried tarragon (¼ tsp.)

☐ dried marjoram (¼ tsp.)

☐ dried basil (¼ tsp.)

☐ vanilla extract (¼ tsp.)

☐ sugar (¼ cup)

☐ olive oil (1 Tbsp.)

☐ red wine vinegar (1 Tbsp.)

☐ 1 can (10¾-oz.) condensed chicken broth

☐ coffee

☐ paper towels

☐ aluminum foil

*May need to be purchased several days ahead to allow for ripening.

COUNTDOWNS FOR HEARTY MENU

Last-Minute Countdown
Time in   Activity
Minutes

55 minutes ahead:
15   Uncork wine; Steps 1–2 of potatoes
     (oven to 450°F)
10   Steps 1–2 of dessert
15   Steps 1–2 of soup and chop tomato.
15   Steps 1–4 of steaks; Step 3 of pota-
     toes (250°F oven); place steak plat-
     ter in oven.
___
55

Serving:
Serve soup (Step 3).
Serve steaks (Step 5), potatoes, and
  wine.
Make coffee; Step 3 of dessert
Serve dessert and coffee.

Plan-Ahead Countdown
Time in   Activity
Minutes

One day ahead:
20   Steps 1–2 of soup

60 minutes ahead:
15   Uncork wine; Steps 1–2 of potatoes
     (oven to 450°F)
10   Steps 1–2 of dessert
___
25

20 minutes ahead:
15   Chop tomato for soup; Steps 1–4 of
     steaks; reheat soup; Step 3 of pota-
     toes; place steak platter in oven.

Serving:
Serve soup (Step 3).
Serve steaks (Step 5), potatoes, and
  wine.
Make coffee; Step 3 of dessert
Serve dessert and coffee.

RATATOUILLE SOUP

Working Time: 15 minutes/Cooking Time: 15 minutes/Servings: 2 to 3

¼ cup chopped onion
½ tsp. minced garlic
1 Tbsp. olive oil
1 cup peeled, diced eggplant
1 small (3-oz.) zucchini, sliced ⅛ inch thick

1 can (10¾-oz.) condensed chicken broth
¼ tsp. ground coriander
¼ tsp. dried basil
Pinch of ground white pepper
1 small (4-oz.) tomato, seeded and chopped

1. In a 1½-qt. saucepan over medium heat sauté onion and garlic in oil 3 minutes.

2. Add remaining ingredients, except chopped tomato, to saucepan. Cover and simmer 15 minutes, or until vegetables are tender.

3. Add chopped tomato, heat 1 minute, and serve.

To do ahead: Do Steps 1–2 up to 2 days ahead. Cool, cover, and refrigerate.

RIB STEAKS IN HERBED WINE SAUCE

Working and Cooking Time: 15 minutes/Servings: 2

2 small beef rib steaks (1½ to 2 lbs. total)
½ tsp. salt
⅛ tsp. ground black pepper
3 Tbsp. butter, divided
1 tsp. minced garlic
½ cup dry red wine

1 Tbsp. red wine vinegar
⅛ tsp. dried thyme
¼ tsp. dried tarragon
¼ tsp. dried marjoram
2 Tbsp. chopped fresh or frozen chives

1. Trim steaks of excess fat. Dry meat with a paper towel. Season with salt and pepper. Warm a large serving platter. Heat a 12-inch electric frying pan or skillet over medium-high heat.

2. Add 1½ Tbsp. butter to pan. Sauté steaks 2 minutes on each side or until lightly browned, but still pink inside. Transfer to warm platter and keep warm.

3.   Lower heat, add garlic to pan, and sauté 1 minute. Add wine and wine vin-egar and turn heat to high. Add thyme, tarragon, and marjoram. Boil until mixture is reduced to ¼ cup (5 minutes), lowering heat after 3 minutes.

4.   Turn off heat and swirl 1½ Tbsp. butter into wine mixture. Pour sauce over steaks.

5.   Sprinkle steaks with chives and serve.

To do ahead: May be prepared through Step 4 and kept warm in a 250°F oven for 15 minutes or so.

CHEDDAR BAKED POTATO STRIPS

Working Time: 15 minutes/Baking Time: 55 minutes (450°F then 250°F)/ Servings: 2

2 medium-size baking potatoes (⅔ lb. total)   ⅓ cup grated sharp Cheddar cheese
½ tsp. salt   ⅓ cup whipping cream
2 Tbsp. butter

1.   Turn oven to 450°F. Peel potatoes and cut into ⅓x⅓x3-inch strips. Pile potato strips in a small gratin dish (8 inches long, preferably rimmed).

2.   Sprinkle potatoes with salt, dot with butter, and sprinkle with cheese. Pour cream over potatoes. Cover tightly with aluminum foil. Bake in upper third of oven for 40 minutes.

3.   Reduce heat to 250°F and continue baking 15 minutes longer. Remove foil to serve.

To do ahead: Potatoes may be prepared ahead and kept warm up to 15 minutes in a 250°F oven.

BANANAS WITH RASPBERRIES AND WHIPPED CREAM

Working Time: 15 minutes/Thawing Time: 1 hour/Servings: 2

1 cup frozen, whole, unsweetened raspberries
3 Tbsp. plus 1 tsp. sugar
1 Tbsp. fresh lemon juice

⅓ cup whipping cream
¼ tsp. vanilla extract
2 small bananas

1. In a 1-qt. bowl mix raspberries, 3 Tbsp. sugar, and lemon juice. Set aside to thaw.

2. In a 3-cup bowl whip cream with a rotary beater until thick. Beat in sugar and vanilla. Cover and refrigerate.

3. At serving time, peel bananas and slice ½ inch thick. Add to raspberries and mix gently. Place in 2 compotes and top with whipped cream.

To do ahead: Prepare through Step 2 up to 2 hours ahead.

IBERIAN MENU

- Asparagus Appetizer Salad
- Veal Chops with Currants and Pine Nuts
- Orange-Garnished Chard
  Viña Esmeralda

- Bananas and Strawberries in Port
  Coffee

Here's an elegant menu that's drawn from the cuisines of Iberia, the European peninsula comprised of Spain and Portugal.

The appetizer is a beautiful salad composed of asparagus (or broccoli when asparagus is not in season) garnished with sliced tomatoes, sliced mushrooms, quartered hard-cooked eggs, and anchovy fillets, and served with a vinaigrette dressing.

The exquisite Spanish entrée consists of sautéed veal chops and pine nuts in a rich cream sauce. Dried currants add a sweet-tart flavor accent to the sauce, and thyme and marjoram give it a sophisticated character.

Orange-garnished chard provides a colorful vegetable accompaniment for the veal. Fresh, coarsely chopped chard is sautéed in olive oil with garlic and served surrounded by an edible garnish of orange slices.

For the wine an interesting choice would be Viña Esmeralda, a medium-dry, very flavorful white wine, produced by Miquel Torres in the Penedés region of Spain.

The port wines of Portugal are a magnificent contribution to the world, and the Portuguese contribution to this menu is a light and lovely fruit dessert. Almost any fruit steeped in port is wonderful, and this combination of bananas and strawberries, with lemon and orange flavors, is especially pleasing.

SHOPPING LIST FOR IBERIAN MENU

Meat, Dairy, Eggs:

☐ 2 veal chops (about 1 lb. total)

☐ butter (1 Tbsp.)

☐ whipping cream (⅔ cup)

☐ eggs (1)

Produce:

☐ 1 lb. asparagus

☐ 1 medium-size (6-oz.) tomato

☐ 2 medium-size mushrooms

☐ garlic (1 tsp. minced)

☐ 1 lb. chard

☐ 2 oranges (need 3 slices + ¼ cup juice)

☐ 1 lemon (need ½ tsp. grated peel + 2 tsp. juice)

☐ 1 large banana*

☐ strawberries (⅔ cup sliced)

Grocery:

☐ anchovy fillets (4)

☐ French dressing (oil and vinegar type), such as Trader Vic's (⅓ cup)

☐ pine nuts (2 Tbsp.), or use slivered almonds

☐ dried currants (¼ cup), or use dark raisins

Liquor:

☐ 1 bottle medium-dry white wine, such as Viña Esmeralda

☐ tawny or ruby port (2 Tbsp.)

Check Staples:

☐ salt

☐ white pepper

☐ dried thyme (⅛ tsp.)

☐ dried marjoram (⅛ tsp.)

☐ olive oil (2½ Tbsp.)

☐ flour (1 Tbsp.)

☐ sugar (2 Tbsp.)

☐ coffee

☐ plastic wrap

☐ toothpicks

☐ paper towels

*May need to be purchased several days ahead to allow for ripening.

COUNTDOWNS FOR IBERIAN MENU

Last-Minute Countdown

Time in   *Activity*
Minutes

65 minutes ahead:

10 Chill wine; Steps 1–2 of salad and ready remaining ingredients.

20 Step 1 of dessert; Steps 3–4 of salad

15 Steps 1–3 of chard

20 Steps 1–3 of veal (oven to 200°F); put veal in oven.

—

65

Serving:

Serve salad (Step 5).

Reheat chard; uncork wine.

Serve veal (Step 4), chard (Step 3), and wine.

Make coffee.

Serve dessert (Step 2) and coffee.

Plan-Ahead Countdown

Time in   *Activity*
Minutes

One day ahead:

10 Chill wine; Steps 1–2 of salad and ready remaining ingredients.

10 Steps 1–2 of chard

15 Step 3 of salad; Step 3 of chard; Step 4 of salad

—

35

30 minutes ahead:

10 Step 1 of dessert

20 Steps 1–3 of veal (oven to 200°F); put veal in oven.

—

30

Serving:

Serve salad (Step 5).

Reheat chard; uncork wine.

Serve veal (Step 4), chard (Step 3), and wine.

Make coffee.

Serve dessert (Step 2) and coffee.

ASPARAGUS APPETIZER SALAD

Working Time: 20 minutes/Cooking Time: 10 minutes/Chilling Time: 30 minutes/Servings: 2

2 qts. water
1 egg
1 lb. asparagus*
2 tsp. salt
1 medium-size (6-oz.) tomato, sliced ¼ inch thick

2 medium-size mushrooms, sliced ⅛ inch thick
4 anchovy fillets
⅓ cup (about) French dressing (oil and vinegar type), such as Trader Vic's

1. Put water and egg in a wide 3-qt. saucepan (not aluminum) and bring to a boil over high heat. Break off butts of asparagus stalks as far from bud ends as they will snap easily.

2. Add asparagus to boiling water. Add 2 teaspoons salt. Boil, uncovered, until tender when pierced with a toothpick, about 6 minutes.

3. Lift asparagus from water and drain on paper towels. Let egg simmer 4 minutes longer, then peel immediately under cold running water.

4. Divide asparagus spears between 2 salad plates. Arrange tomato and mushroom slices partially over the asparagus. Cut egg into 4 wedges. Garnish salads with egg wedges and crisscrossed anchovy fillets. Cover with plastic wrap and refrigerate.

5. To serve, spoon dressing over salads.

*The best months for asparagus are March, April, and May. If it's not in season, substitute ⅔ lb. (2 stalks) of broccoli, prepared as described in the note below.

To do ahead: Prepare through Step 4 up to 1 day ahead.

Note: To prepare fresh broccoli, cut 1 inch off the stems and remove the leaves. Peel the stalks with a knife by cutting into the stem at the base and pulling the peel toward the head until it pulls off. Split the broccoli in half lengthwise and boil as for asparagus.

VEAL CHOPS WITH CURRANTS AND PINE NUTS

Working and Cooking Time: 20 minutes/Servings: 2

2 veal chops (about 1 lb. total)
½ tsp. plus ⅛ tsp. salt
⅛ tsp. ground white pepper
1 Tbsp. (about) flour
1 Tbsp. butter
½ Tbsp. olive oil
2 Tbsp. pine nuts*

½ tsp. minced garlic
¼ cup dried currants, or chopped dark raisins
⅔ cup whipping cream
⅛ tsp. dried thyme
⅛ tsp. dried marjoram

1.   Dry veal with paper towels. Sprinkle with ½ tsp. salt and the pepper. Dust with flour. In a 10-inch skillet over medium to medium-high heat brown chops in butter and oil, cooking just until veal is no longer pink near bone, about 5 minutes on each side. Remove to a warm platter (or 12-inch gratin dish if preparing ahead).

2.   Add pine nuts to skillet and cook over low heat until lightly browned, 2 minutes. Add garlic and currants and cook 1 minute.

3.   Add cream, thyme, marjoram, and ⅛ tsp. salt. Raise heat to medium-high and boil down until sauce thickens, 2 minutes.

4.   Pour hot sauce over veal and serve.

*Pine nuts are the seeds of several varieties of pine trees. They have a soft texture and mild flavor. They are available in gourmet markets. Slivered almonds (1½ Tbsp.) may be substituted.

To do ahead: Do Steps 1–3 up to 30 minutes ahead. Keep veal warm in a 200°F oven. To serve, reheat sauce and pour over veal. Add a little water to sauce if it becomes too thick.

ORANGE-GARNISHED CHARD

Working and Cooking Time: 15 minutes/Servings: 2

1 lb. chard*
2 Tbsp. olive oil
½ tsp. minced garlic

¼ tsp. salt
3 orange slices, ¼ inch thick, halved

1. Cut off stems of chard at base of leaf and wash leaves thoroughly. Stack leaves and slice lengthwise, then crosswise at 1-inch intervals. (Makes about 5 cups packed.)

2. In a 9-inch skillet over medium heat sauté garlic in oil a few minutes without letting it brown. Mix in chard, with the water that clings to leaves, and salt. Cover and steam 5 minutes, stirring once.

3. Uncover and cook over medium-high heat until moisture evaporates, about 2 minutes. Taste for salt (it may need more).

4. Serve in a small vegetable dish, encircled by the halved orange slices.

*Chard is a leafy green vegetable of the beet family. It's also known as Swiss chard and Italian spinach. Chard is in season from March through December.

To do ahead: Do Steps 1–3 up to 1 day ahead. Cover and refrigerate. Reheat to serve.

BANANAS AND STRAWBERRIES IN PORT

Working Time: 10 minutes/Chilling Time: 1 hour/Servings: 2

2 Tbsp. sugar
½ tsp. grated lemon peel
2 tsp. fresh lemon juice
¼ cup fresh orange juice

2 Tbsp. tawny or ruby port wine
1 large banana, peeled, sliced ⅓ inch thick
⅔ cup thickly sliced strawberries*

1.   In a 1½-qt. bowl combine sugar, lemon peel and juice, orange juice, and port. Stir until sugar dissolves. Gently mix in banana and strawberries. Cover and refrigerate for 1 to 2 hours, stirring occasionally.

2.   To serve, spoon fruit and juices into stemmed goblets.

*Fresh strawberries are available from about March to September.

To do ahead: May be prepared up to 2 hours ahead.

SUMMER MENU

- **Summer Green Salad**

- **Veal with Garden Vegetables**
  Crusty Bread
  Sylvaner Riesling

- **Summer Fruit with Cassis**
  Coffee

For food lovers the glory of summer is the abundance of fresh fruits and vegetables overflowing at the markets and roadside stands. Here's a taste-tempting menu designed to show off the season's bounty.

The salad uses mild butterhead lettuce, radishes, young cucumbers, and fresh dill in the lightest of dressings, a refreshing blend of lemon juice and cream.

All the sparkle of fresh garden vegetables comes through in the delicately seasoned entrée of thin veal cutlets with onions, green pepper, zucchini, yellow summer squash, and tomatoes. A reduction of white wine and vegetable juices moistens and flavors the veal.

The only accompaniments needed with the entrée are bread and wine. A good crusty French or Italian bread or sourdough bread is suitable, as is a California (Sylvaner) Riesling, served chilled. Sylvaner is a wonderful summertime wine, tasty, thirst-quenching, and just right with the veal.

Dessert is a beautiful combination of summer fruits with black currant liqueur, which enhances the fruit flavors superbly. You might want to remember this dessert for the 4th of July for its patriotic colors of red strawberries, white whipped cream (you can also use white Babcock peaches), and blueberries.

SHOPPING LIST FOR SUMMER MENU

Meat, Dairy:

☐ ⅔ lb. veal cutlets, sliced or pounded ¼ inch thick

☐ butter (3 Tbsp. + butter for bread)

☐ whipping cream (⅔ cup)

Produce:

☐ 1 large or 2 small heads butterhead lettuce

☐ 1 small (8-oz.) cucumber (need half)

☐ radishes (⅓ cup sliced)

☐ 1 lemon (need 1½ Tbsp. juice)

☐ dill (2 tsp. chopped), or use dried

☐ parsley (2 tsp. chopped), if using dried dill weed

☐ 1 small (4-oz.) onion

☐ medium-size green pepper (need ½)

☐ 1 small (4-oz.) zucchini

☐ 1 small (4-oz.) yellow summer squash

☐ 1 small (4-oz.) tomato

☐ 2 medium-size peaches (⅔ lb. total)*

☐ strawberries (½ cup sliced)

☐ blueberries (¼ cup)

Grocery:

☐ crusty bread

Liquor:

☐ 1 bottle California (Sylvaner) Riesling (½ cup for cooling)

☐ creme de cassis (2½ Tbsp.)

Check Staples:

☐ salt

☐ white pepper

☐ dried dill weed (½ tsp.), if not using fresh

☐ sugar (2½ Tbsp.)

☐ flour (2 Tbsp.)

☐ coffee

☐ wax paper

☐ plastic wrap

☐ paper towels

*May need to be purchased several days ahead to allow for ripening.

COUNTDOWNS FOR SUMMER MENU

Last-Minute Countdown

Time in   *Activity*
Minutes

60 minutes ahead:
20   Chill wine; Steps 1–2 of salad
15   Steps 1–2 of dessert
25   Steps 1–5 of veal and vegetables
60

Serving:
Serve salad (Step 3).
Reheat veal and vegetables and do Step 6; uncork wine.
Serve veal and vegetables, bread, butter, and wine.
Make coffee.
Serve dessert (Step 3) and coffee.

Plan-Ahead Countdown

Time in   *Activity*
Minutes

One day ahead:
20   Chill wine; Steps 1–2 of salad

40 minutes ahead:
15   Steps 1–2 of dessert
25   Steps 1–5 of veal and vegetables
40

Serving:
Serve salad (Step 3).
Reheat veal and vegetables and do Step 6; uncork wine.
Serve veal and vegetables, bread, butter, and wine.
Make coffee.
Serve dessert (Step 3) and coffee.

SUMMER GREEN SALAD

Working Time: 20 minutes/Chilling Time: 30 minutes/Servings: 2

SALAD INGREDIENTS:

1 large or 2 small heads butterhead lettuce, torn in bite-size pieces

½ small cucumber, peeled, sliced ⅛ inch thick

⅓ cup thinly sliced radishes

2 tsp. chopped fresh dill, or ½ tsp. dried dill weed blended with 2 tsp. finely chopped parsley

LEMON CREAM DRESSING:

¼ tsp. salt

1½ Tbsp. fresh lemon juice

⅓ cup whipping cream

1. Divide lettuce between 2 individual salad bowls. Top with cucumber and radish slices. Sprinkle with dill. Cover with plastic wrap and refrigerate.

2. Place all ingredients for dressing in a ½-pt. jar. Shake to dissolve salt. Refrigerate.

3. To serve, pour dressing over salads.

To do ahead: Do Steps 1–2 up to 1 day ahead.

VEAL WITH GARDEN VEGETABLES

Working and Cooking Time: 30 minutes/Servings: 2

1 small onion, peeled, sliced ⅛ inch thick

½ medium-size green pepper, cut in ¼ inch wide strips

1 small (4-oz.) zucchini, cut in ¼x⅛x3 inch strips

1 small (4-oz.) yellow summer squash, cut in ¼x⅛x3 inch strips

2 Tbsp. flour

¾ tsp. salt, divided

⅛ tsp. ground white pepper

⅔ lb. veal cutlets, sliced or pounded ¼ inch thick, cut in about 8 strips

2 Tbsp. water

½ cup Sylvaner Riesling, or other dry white wine

1 small (4-oz.) tomato, cut in ¼ inch thick wedges

1. Prepare vegetables as indicated. Combine flour, ½ tsp. salt, and the pepper in a bag. Dry veal with paper towels, add to bag, and shake to coat with flour.

2. In a 10-inch skillet with a nonstick surface lightly brown veal in 2 Tbsp. butter over medium-high heat, about 2 minutes on each side.

3. Remove veal to a plate. Add 1 Tbsp. butter to skillet, reduce heat to medium, and add onion and green pepper. Sauté 3 minutes.

4. Mix in squashes and ¼ tsp. salt. Add water, cover, and simmer until vegetables are almost tender, about 5 minutes.

5. Remove vegetables to plate with veal. Add wine to juices in skillet and boil down rapidly to ¼ cup. Return veal and vegetables to skillet.

6. Add tomatoes and mix gently. Cover and heat through, about 3 minutes. Serve on a warm platter.

To do ahead: Do Steps 1–5 up to 30 minutes ahead. Leave at room temperature.

SUMMER FRUIT WITH CASSIS

Working Time: 15 minutes/Chilling Time: 30 minutes/Servings: 2

2 medium-size peaches (⅔ lb. total), peeled
   and cut in bite-size pieces
½ cup thickly sliced strawberries
¼ cup fresh blueberries

2 Tbsp. plus ½ tsp. sugar
2 Tbsp. plus ½ tsp. creme de cassis*
¼ cup whipping cream

1. In a 1½-qt. bowl toss fruit gently with 2 Tbsp. each sugar and cassis. Cover and refrigerate for 30 minutes to 3 hours.

2. In a 3-cup bowl beat cream with a rotary beater until cream is stiff. Beat in ½ teaspoon each sugar and cassis. Cover and refrigerate.

3. To serve, divide fruit and liquid between 2 compotes. Top with whipped cream.

*Creme de cassis is a rich, sweet liqueur made from black currants. Domestic and French versions are available in any liquor store.

To do ahead: Do Steps 1–2 up to 3 hours ahead.

LAMB MENUS

Elegant Menu
East-West Menu
Tunisian Menu
Spring Menu
Armenian Menu

ELEGANT MENU

- Valencia Consommé

- Rack of Lamb with Sherried Mushroom Sauce
- Vegetable Medley with Lemon Crumbs
  Red Rioja

- Raspberry Liqueur Sundaes
  Coffee

Even when you're pressed for time, it's still possible to present a glamorous meal, such as this one that has a sophisticated Spanish flair.

Sweet Valencia oranges flavor the clove- and cinnamon-scented beef broth in Valencia consommé. Garnished with green pepper shreds, this soup is a lovely beginning for an elegant meal.

A roasted rack of lamb, always special, is presented with a delicious, creamy mushroom sauce, accented by a touch of sherry. The roast can be carved in the kitchen and the pink slices arranged on a platter with some of the sauce spooned over them. The vegetable medley can be served on the same platter, becoming a garnish for the meat. The medley consists of cauliflower, green beans, and cherry tomatoes topped with crispy, buttered bread crumbs. Grated lemon peel adds extra zest to the crumbs.

A light, dry red wine, such as Rioja (Viña Lanciano would be perfect) will go well with the lamb.

Dessert is simple, but looks impressive. A sweet raspberry liqueur, such as Chambord of Framboise, is spooned over vanilla ice cream, which is then topped with whipped cream and crushed hazelnuts. It's very attractive served in stemmed crystal compotes.

166

SHOPPING LIST FOR ELEGANT MENU

Meat, Dairy, Eggs:

☐ 1½ lb. rack of lamb

☐ butter (6½ Tbsp.)

☐ half and half (¾ cup), or ¼ cup whipping cream and ½ cup milk

☐ whipping cream (¼ cup)

☐ vanilla ice cream (⅔ pt.)

Produce:

☐ 1 Valencia orange

☐ 1 lemon (need 1 tsp. grated peel)

☐ 1 small green pepper (need ¼, see recipe note)

☐ ⅛ lb. mushrooms

☐ green onions (1)

☐ 1 small head cauliflower (need half)

☐ ⅓ lb. thin green beans

☐ 12 small cherry tomatoes

Grocery:

☐ white bread (1½ slices to make crumbs)

☐ hazelnuts or filberts (1 Tbsp. chopped), or use walnuts

Liquor:

☐ 1 bottle light, dry red wine, such as red Rioja (especially Viña Lanciano)

☐ medium (golden or oloroso) sherry, such as Dry Sack (1 Tbsp.)

☐ raspberry liqueur, such as Chambord or Framboise (2 Tbsp.)

Check Staples:

☐ salt

☐ black pepper

☐ white pepper

☐ whole cloves (2)

☐ stick cinnamon (1 stick)

☐ sugar (½ tsp.)

☐ flour (2 tsp.)

☐ olive oil (1 Tbsp.)

☐ 1 can (14½-oz.) single-strength beef broth

☐ coffee

☐ plastic wrap

COUNTDOWNS FOR ELEGANT MENU

Last-Minute Countdown

Time in   Activity
Minutes

50 minutes ahead:

5   Uncork wine; Step 1 of dessert and chop hazelnuts.

10   Oven to 425°F; Step 1 of soup and prepare garnish.

20   Steps 1–3 of lamb; take soup off heat when done.

15   Steps 1–2 of vegetables; reheat soup.

___

50

Serving :

Serve soup (Step 2).

(When lamb is done, do Step 4.)

Step 3 of vegetables; Step 5 of lamb; Step 4 of vegetables

Serve lamb with sauce, vegetables, and wine.

Make coffee.

Serve dessert (Step 2) and coffee.

Plan-Ahead Countdown

Time in   Activity
Minutes

One day ahead:

10   Step 1 of soup and prepare garnish.

15   Steps 1–2 of vegetables; take soup off heat.

15   Steps 2–3 of lamb (sauce)

___

40

45 minutes ahead:

5   Oven to 425°F; Step 1 of dessert and chop hazelnuts.

35 minutes ahead:

5   Step 1 of lamb

5 minutes ahead:

—   Reheat soup.

Serving:

Serve soup (Step 2).

(When lamb is done, do Step 4.)

Step 3 of vegetables; Step 5 of lamb; Step 4 of vegetables

Serve lamb with sauce, vegetables, and wine.

Make coffee.

Serve dessert (Step 2) and coffee.

VALENCIA CONSOMMÉ

Working Time: 10 minutes/Cooking Time: 15 minutes/Servings: 2

1 can (14½-oz.) single-strength beef broth
1 Tbsp. butter
2 whole cloves
1 inch stick cinnamon

1 Valencia orange (¼ tsp. grated peel; 1
    thin slice, halved; ¼ cup strained juice)
12 green pepper slivers (see Note)

1.   In a 1-qt. saucepan over high heat bring broth to a boil with butter, cloves, cinnamon, and orange peel. Reduce heat to low, cover, and simmer 15 minutes.

2.   To serve, add orange juice to hot broth and pour into 2 soup bowls, discarding cloves and cinnamon. Garnish with orange half-slices and green pepper shreds.

To do ahead: May be done up to 1 day ahead. Remove whole spices, cool, cover, and refrigerate soup; wrap and refrigerate garnishes separately.

Note: Choose a pepper that curves outward so that with a vegetable peeler you can peel off the skin on a portion of the pepper. Then slice the flesh into 1-inch-long slivers.

RACK OF LAMB WITH SHERRIED MUSHROOM SAUCE

Working Time: 25 minutes/Roasting and Resting Time: 40 minutes (425°F)/
Servings: 2

LAMB:
1½ lb. rack of lamb
1 Tbsp. olive oil
½ tsp. salt
¼ tsp. ground black pepper

SHERRIED MUSHROOM SAUCE:
1½ Tbsp. butter
⅛ lb. mushrooms, finely chopped

1 Tbsp. chopped green onion
2 tsp. flour
¼ tsp. salt
Pinch of ground white pepper
¾ cup dairy half and half (or ¼ cup whipping cream and ½ cup milk)
1 Tbsp. medium sherry (golden or oloroso), such as Dry Sack

1.   Preheat oven to 425°F. Trim lamb of all but a thin layer of fat. Rub with oil, salt, and pepper. Roast in lower third of oven until browned, about 35 minutes for medium-rare.

2.   For sauce, heat butter over medium-high heat in an 8-inch skillet. Add mushrooms, onion, ¼ tsp. salt, and a pinch of white pepper. Cook, stirring occasionally, until liquid evaporates and mushrooms are lightly browned.

3.   Stir in flour, cook 1 minute, then whisk in half and half. Boil until thickened, about 2 minutes. Cover and set aside.

4.   When lamb is done, remove from oven, and let rest at least 5 minutes.

5.   Reheat mushroom sauce and add sherry. Carve lamb into chops and arrange down the length of, and on one side of, a serving platter. Spoon a little sauce over lamb and serve the rest in a sauceboat. (Serve vegetables on the other side of platter.)

To do ahead: Do Steps 2–3 up to 2 days ahead. Cool, cover, and refrigerate.

VEGETABLE MEDLEY WITH LEMON CRUMBS

Working and Cooking Time: 20 minutes/Servings: 2

VEGETABLES:
1 qt. water
1¼ tsp. salt, divided
1½ cups cauliflower florets
⅓ lb. thin green beans, cut in 1 inch lengths
2 Tbsp. butter

12 small cherry tomatoes

LEMON CRUMBS:
2 Tbsp. butter
¾ cup fresh bread crumbs, made in blender
1 tsp. grated lemon peel

1.   Bring water to a boil in a 3-qt. saucepan over high heat. Add cauliflower and green beans. Return to a boil and add 1 tsp. salt. Boil, uncovered, until vegetables are tender, about 7 minutes. Drain in a colander.

2.   Meanwhile, in a 5-inch skillet over medium heat brown bread crumbs in 2 Tbsp. butter, stirring occasionally, and watching carefully after they begin to brown. Remove from heat and stir in lemon peel.

3. Melt 2 Tbsp. butter over medium-high heat in saucepan used for vegetables. Add cauliflower and beans and heat through, 3 minutes.

4. Reheat bread crumbs, if necessary. Add tomatoes to cauliflower and beans and heat through, 1 minute. Serve vegetables on same platter as lamb and sprinkle crumbs around and partly over vegetables.

To do ahead: Do Steps 1–2 up to 1 day ahead. Cool vegetables under cold running water, drain well, wrap in plastic wrap, and refrigerate. Cover and refrigerate crumbs separately.

RASPBERRY LIQUEUR SUNDAES

Working Time: 10 minutes/Servings: 2

¼ cup whipping cream
½ tsp. sugar
2 servings vanilla ice cream (about ⅔ pt.)

2 Tbsp. raspberry liqueur*, such as Chambord or Framboise
1 Tbsp. finely chopped hazelnuts** (filberts)

1. In a 3-cup bowl whip cream with a rotary beater until stiff. Blend in sugar. Cover and refrigerate.

2. To serve, place ice cream in individual compotes. Pour 1 Tbsp. raspberry liqueur over each serving, top with whipped cream, and sprinkle with hazelnuts.

*Raspberry liqueurs are available in any liquor store.
**If you have difficulty obtaining hazelnuts, try health food stores. Walnuts may be substituted.

To do ahead: Do Step 1 and chop hazelnuts up to 3 hours ahead.

EAST-WEST MENU

- Romaine, Cucumber, and Carrot Salad
- Lamb Chops, Peppers, and Tomatoes in Spicy Sauce
- Brown Rice
  Oriental Beer
- Pineapple Caramel Sundaes
  Coffee or Tea

East meets West in this delightful dinner that incorporates Eastern flavors in a Western-style menu.

The tossed salad of romaine lettuce, sliced cucumber, and coarsely grated carrot has a light dressing made with Japanese rice vinegar. The dressing's tangy flavor comes from the addition of minced fresh ginger root.

For the main dish, lamb chops are marinated briefly in soy sauce, then pan-broiled and served with stir-fried green peppers, onions, and tomatoes, in a sauce that contains curry powder, tomato catsup, and oyster sauce—an unusual and intriguing combination that turns out to be quite good.

Brown rice is the ideal accompaniment for the lamb, being less bland than white rice. Brown rice takes up to an hour to cook, but if you put it on the stove first, the cooking time presents no problem. Very little attention is required as the rice simmers.

The vibrant, spicy lamb entrée will overwhelm wine, but beer can hold its own. An Oriental beer, such as San Miguel or Kirin, would be the most appropriate.

A touch of the tropics appears in these sundaes of vanilla ice cream atop slices of fresh pineapple, sauced with caramel. The dessert complements nicely the assertive flavors of the main course.

SHOPPING LIST FOR EAST-WEST MENU

Meat, Dairy:

- [ ] 4 loin lamb chops (1¼ lbs. total), 1 inch thick
- [ ] butter (1 Tbsp.)
- [ ] vanilla ice cream (½ pt.)

Produce:

- [ ] 1 medium cucumber (need ½)
- [ ] 1 head romaine lettuce
- [ ] 1 medium-size (4-oz.) carrot
- [ ] fresh ginger (½ tsp. minced)
- [ ] green onions (1)
- [ ] 1 small onion
- [ ] 1 medium-size green pepper (need ½)
- [ ] 1 small (4-oz.) tomato
- [ ] pineapple (2 slices, ¾ inch thick)

Grocery:

- [ ] Japanese rice vinegar (2 Tbsp.)
- [ ] oyster sauce (1 Tbsp.)
- [ ] brown rice (⅔ cup)

Liquor:

- [ ] 2 bottles (or more) Oriental beer, such as San Miguel or Kirin

Check Staples:

- [ ] salt
- [ ] light brown sugar (2 Tbsp.)
- [ ] sugar (2½ Tbsp.)
- [ ] curry powder (1 Tbsp.)
- [ ] soy sauce (2 Tbsp.)
- [ ] salad (not olive) oil (⅓ cup)
- [ ] catsup (¼ cup)
- [ ] 1 can (10¾-oz.) condensed chicken broth
- [ ] plastic wrap
- [ ] coffee or tea

COUNTDOWNS FOR EAST-WEST MENU

Last-Minute Countdown

Time in   Activity
Minutes

60 minutes ahead:

5   Refrigerate beer; Step 1 of rice
20 Steps 1–2 of salad
10 Steps 1–2 of dessert and cut pineapple slices.
25 Oven to 250°F; Steps 1–3 of lamb; put lamb in oven to keep warm; turn off rice and keep warm.
__
60

Serving:
Serve salad (Step 3).
Step 4 of lamb
Serve lamb (Step 5) and rice (Step 2) and beer.
Make coffee or tea.
Serve dessert (Steps 3–4) and coffee or tea.

Plan-Ahead Countdown

Time in   Activity
Minutes

One day ahead:

5   Refrigerate beer; Step 1 of rice
20 Steps 1–2 of salad
5   Steps 1–2 of dessert
__
30 (plus 35 minutes more cooking time for rice)

30 minutes ahead:

5   Cut pineapple slices; oven to 250°F.
25 Steps 1–3 of lamb; put lamb in oven to keep warm; put rice on stove to reheat.
__
30

Serving:
Serve salad (Step 3).
Step 4 of lamb
Serve lamb (Step 5) and rice (Step 2) and beer.
Make coffee or tea.
Serve dessert (Steps 3–4) and coffee or tea.

ROMAINE, CUCUMBER, AND CARROT SALAD

Working Time: 20 minutes/Chilling Time: 30 minutes/Servings: 2

SALAD INGREDIENTS:
½ *medium cucumber, peeled*
3½ *cups bite-size pieces romaine lettuce*
1 *medium-size (4-oz.) carrot, peeled, and*
   coarsely grated

GINGER DRESSING:
¼ *tsp. salt*
1 *Tbsp. light brown sugar*
1 *tsp. minced fresh ginger*
1 *tsp. soy sauce*
2 *Tbsp. Japanese rice vinegar**
1 *Tbsp. chopped green onion*
¼ *cup salad (not olive) oil*

1. Slice cucumber in half lengthwise. If seeds are large, scrape them out with a spoon. Slice cucumber crosswise ⅛ inch thick. Combine with lettuce and grated carrot in a 2-qt. salad bowl. Cover with plastic wrap and refrigerate.

2. Combine all ingredients for dressing, except oil, in a ½-pt. jar. Cover and shake to mix well. Add oil and shake again. Refrigerate.

3. To serve, shake dressing, pour over salad, and toss to blend.

*Japanese rice vinegar is available in Oriental markets and many supermarkets; 1½ tablespoons white vinegar may be substituted for the Japanese vinegar.

To do ahead: May be prepared up to 1 day ahead.

LAMB CHOPS, PEPPERS, AND TOMATOES IN SPICY SAUCE

Working and Cooking Time: 30 minutes/Servings: 2

4 loin lamb chops (1¼ lbs. total), 1 inch thick
½ tsp. salt
1½ Tbsp. soy sauce
1 Tbsp. salad (not olive) oil
1 small onion, peeled, quartered, layers separated
½ medium-size green pepper, cut in 1 inch squares

¼ cup water, divided
1 small (4-oz.) tomato
1 Tbsp. light brown sugar
1 Tbsp. curry powder
¼ cup catsup
1 Tbsp. oyster sauce*

1. Trim lamb chops of excess fat and place on a plate. Season with salt and soy sauce.

2. Heat oil in a 10-inch skillet with a nonstick surface over medium-high heat. Sauté onion and green pepper in oil for 2 minutes. Add 2 Tbsp. water, cover pan, and steam for 2 minutes. Uncover pan and stir until any liquid evaporates. Remove onion and pepper to a bowl.

3. Add lamb chops to pan and reduce heat to medium. Brown chops well, 4 minutes on each side. Meanwhile, cut tomato in 8 wedges and toss in a bowl with the brown sugar; measure out remaining ingredients. Remove lamb chops to serving platter.

4. Over low heat, add curry powder to fat in skillet (add a little more oil if necessary). Add 2 Tbsp. water, the catsup, and oyster sauce. Add onion, pepper, and tomato wedges.

5. Place rice in a ring around lamb. When tomato mixture is heated through, spoon it over and around lamb and serve.

*Oyster sauce is a thick brown sauce made of oyster extractives and other ingredients. It's available in Oriental markets and many supermarkets. It comes in bottles and, tightly covered, keeps indefinitely.

To do ahead: Step 1 can be done up to 30 minutes ahead, and ingredients can be cut up or measured out.

BROWN RICE

Working Time: 5 minutes/Cooking Time: 60 minutes/Servings: 2

⅔ cup brown rice   1 can (10¾-oz.) condensed chicken broth

1.   In a 1-qt. saucepan bring chicken broth to a boil over high heat. Add rice, cover, reduce heat, and simmer until rice is tender and liquid is absorbed, 55 to 60 minutes.

2.   Serve rice on same platter as lamb.

To do ahead: Prepare up to 1 day ahead. Reheat over low heat for 10 minutes, stirring occasionally.

PINEAPPLE CARAMEL SUNDAES

Working and Cooking Time: 10 minutes/Servings: 2

1 Tbsp. butter   2 slices fresh pineapple, ¾ inch thick,
2½ Tbsp. sugar   peeled, cored, halved
¼ cup water   2 scoops vanilla ice cream (about ½ pt.)

1.   Heat butter and sugar in an 8-inch skillet over medium heat until sugar turns a deep tan color. Stir often and watch carefully as soon as sugar begins to caramelize.

2.   When caramel is ready, add water to skillet (stand back) and boil until sugar mass is mostly dissolved, about 3 minutes.

3.   Heat pineapple slices in caramel mixture. Transfer to serving plates and position so as to re-form round slices. Boil down caramel mixture until syrupy and reduced to 3 Tbsp., about 1 minute.

4. To serve, top each pineapple slice with a scoop of ice cream and pour caramel sauce over all.

To do ahead: Do Steps 1–2 up to 1 day ahead. Cover and leave at room temperature.

TUNISIAN MENU

- Chilled Cantaloupe Soup
- Lamb-Chop Couscous
  California Barbera
- Grapes in Honey Cream
  Coffee

This exotic Tunisian Menu offers new taste temptations that will appeal to the nonnative palate. The main course isn't fiercely hot or spicy, just very flavorful.

Summer is a good time to serve this meal when the fresh cantaloupes are at their best and the Perlette grapes and later the Thompson grapes come into the markets. The cantaloupe goes into a lovely chilled soup easily made in the blender with orange juice, lemon juice, and a touch of sugar.

The main dish is couscous, a staple of North African cuisines and a meal in itself. In this version lamb shoulder chops are seasoned with lemon, turmeric, ginger, and red pepper. They are browned, then cooked with onions and garlic until nearly tender. Chick peas, zucchini, and tomatoes are added to finish this stew-like dish. The couscous grain (a semolina of wheat) is prepared separately, like rice, and served with the stew to absorb the flavorful meat juices. ("Couscous" is the name for both the stew and for the grain that is served with the stew.)

A good wine to serve with the couscous is a California Barbera (Sebastiani, Heitz, Martini)—not traditional, but a nice accompaniment for the lamb.

Grapes in honey cream provide a light dessert. The "honey cream" is a blend of sour cream, whipped cream, powdered sugar, orange liqueur, and honey—a very pleasing medium for the slightly tart grapes.

SHOPPING LIST FOR TUNISIAN MENU

Meat, Dairy:

☐ 2 large shoulder lamb chops (1¾ lbs. total)

☐ butter (5½ Tbsp.)

☐ sour cream (¼ cup)

☐ whipping cream (¼ cup)

Produce:

☐ 1 medium-size (2-lb.) cantaloupe*

☐ 2 to 3 oranges (⅔ cup juice)

☐ 1 large lemon (3¼ Tbsp. juice)

☐ ½ lb. seedless green grapes (1 cup)

☐ 1 small onion (½ cup chopped)

☐ garlic (1 tsp. minced)

☐ 1 medium-large (½-lb.) zucchini

☐ 1 medium-size (6-oz.) tomato

☐ fresh mint (1 tsp. chopped), or use dried

Grocery:

☐ ground turmeric (¾ tsp.)

☐ 1 can (8- to 9-oz.) chick peas (garbanzo beans)

☐ couscous (1 cup)

☐ orange blossom honey (1 Tbsp.)

Liquor:

☐ 1 bottle California Barbera (Heitz, Sebastiani, Martini wineries)

☐ orange liqueur, such as Cointreau (1 Tbsp.)

Check Staples:

☐ salt

☐ ground red pepper

☐ ground ginger (¾ tsp.)

☐ dried mint (¼ tsp.), if not using fresh

☐ sugar (2 tsp.)

☐ powdered sugar (¼ cup)

☐ coffee

☐ plastic wrap

*May need to be purchased a few days ahead to allow for ripening.

COUNTDOWNS FOR TUNISIAN MENU

Last-Minute Countdown

Time in   Activity
Minutes

55 minutes ahead:

15 Uncork wine; Steps 1–2 of soup
    (chill in freezer) and squeeze 3½
    tsp. lemon juice for lamb and des-
    sert.
15 Steps 1–3 of lamb
15 Prepare dessert.
10 Baste lamb and do Steps 4–5.
──
55

Serving:
Serve soup (Step 3).
Step 6 of lamb
Serve lamb (Step 7) and wine.
Serve dessert.

Plan-Ahead Countdown

Time in   Activity
Minutes

One day ahead:

15 Steps 1–2 of soup and squeeze ½
    tsp. lemon juice for dessert.
15 Prepare dessert.
──
30

45 minutes ahead:
15 Uncork wine; Steps 1–3 of lamb

10 minutes ahead:
10 Baste lamb; Steps 4–5 of lamb

Serving:
Serve soup (Step 3).
Step 6 of lamb
Serve lamb (Step 7) and wine.
Serve dessert.

CHILLED CANTALOUPE SOUP

Working Time: 15 minutes/Chilling Time: 45 minutes/Servings: 2

1 medium-size (2-lb.) ripe cantaloupe
2 tsp. sugar
⅔ cup fresh orange juice

2 Tbsp. fresh lemon juice
1 tsp. chopped fresh mint, or ¼ tsp. dried

1. Cut cantaloupe in half and scoop out seeds. With melon ball cutter, scoop out 6 large melon balls. Divide melon balls between two wide soup plates.

2. Scoop out remaining cantaloupe and place in blender with sugar and orange and lemon juices. Blend until smooth. Pour into soup plates, cover with plastic wrap, and refrigerate.

3. Sprinkle with mint just before serving.

To do ahead: Prepare through Step 2 up to 1 day ahead. If preparing at the last minute, place soup in freezer for 15 minutes to chill quickly. (Chilling may take up to 30 minutes in freezer if melon and oranges were at room temperature.)

LAMB-CHOP COUSCOUS

Working Time: 30 minutes/Cooking Time: 30 minutes more/Servings: 2

LAMB CHOPS:
2 large shoulder lamb chops (1¾ lbs. total)
1 Tbsp. fresh lemon juice, divided
½ tsp. salt
¾ tsp. ground turmeric*
¾ tsp. ground ginger
⅛ tsp. (or more) ground red pepper
1½ Tbsp. butter

VEGETABLES:
½ cup finely chopped onion
1 tsp. minced garlic

1 can (8- to 9-oz.) chick peas with liquid
1 medium-large (½-lb.) zucchini
1 medium-size (6-oz.) tomato
⅛ tsp. salt

COUSCOUS:
1 cup couscous**
¾ cup boiling water
½ tsp. salt
4 Tbsp. butter

1. Trim lamb of excess fat. Rub lamb with 2 tsp. lemon juice. Mix ½ tsp. salt, turmeric, ginger, red pepper, and 1 tsp. lemon juice in a ½-cup bowl (see Note). Spread mixture on both sides of lamb.

2. In a 10-inch skillet with a nonstick surface brown lamb in 1½ Tbsp. butter over medium heat, about 4 minutes on first side. Turn lamb and add onions and garlic to skillet around lamb. Cook until onion is soft and lamb is browned on second side, 4 minutes.

3. Spoon most of the onion on top of lamb. Add liquid from chick peas to skillet, reduce heat to low, cover, and simmer briskly for 25 minutes. Spoon pan juices over lamb once or twice during cooking.

4. Dissolve salt in boiling water and pour over couscous in a 1½-qt. bowl. Cut zucchini on the diagonal into ⅓-inch-thick slices. Cut tomato into 10 wedges. As soon as couscous has absorbed the water (after about 5 minutes) fluff it with a fork to separate grains.

5. When lamb has cooked 25 minutes, add chick peas and zucchini to skillet, cover, and cook 10 minutes.

6.   Heat 4 Tbsp. butter in a 9-inch skillet over medium heat. Add couscous and heat until warmed through, stirring occasionally, 5 minutes. When zucchini is tender, add tomato and ⅛ tsp. salt to skillet. Cover and heat through, about 2 minutes.

7.   To serve, mound couscous in center of a large platter. Place a lamb chop at each end of platter. With a slotted spoon scoop out vegetables and place around couscous. Pour some of the pan juices over meat and couscous. Serve remaining juices separately in a small pitcher.

*Turmeric is the root of a tropical herb belonging to the ginger family. It's available in Indian grocery stores and many supermarkets.
*Couscous is the name for crushed grain as well as for a finished dish that is a meat or chicken stew served with the grain. One-pound packages of couscous (wheat semolina) are imported from France and can be found in Middle Eastern grocery stores and some supermarkets.

To do ahead: Steps 1 and 4 may be done up to 1 hour ahead. Cover couscous with plastic wrap.

Note: Apply spice paste to lamb with a spoon or butter knife, rather than your hands, as turmeric will (temporarily) stain fingernails on contact.

GRAPES IN HONEY CREAM

Working Time: 15 minutes/Chilling Time: 30 minutes/Servings: 2

1 Tbsp. mild honey, such as orange blossom   ¼ cup sour cream
1 Tbsp. orange liqueur, such as Cointreau   ¼ cup whipping cream
½ tsp. fresh lemon juice   1 cup seedless green grapes
¼ cup powdered sugar

1.   In a 3-cup bowl whisk together honey, orange liqueur, lemon juice, and sugar. Whisk in sour cream just until blended.

2.   In a 2-cup bowl with a rotary beater whip cream until stiff. Gently fold into sour cream mixture. Fold in grapes and spoon into two 6-oz. wine glasses. Cover with plastic wrap and refrigerate.

To do ahead: May be prepared up to 1 day ahead.

SPRING MENU

- Avocado and Bacon Green Salad

- Orange-Glazed Lamb Chops
- Rosemary Rice
- Asparagus Tips
  Médoc (Red Bordeaux)

- Vanilla Mousse with Strawberries
  Coffee

The instinct to celebrate spring seems universal, and the festive foods of spring—fresh asparagus, tender lamb, sweet strawberries—provide a wonderful way to celebrate. Don't worry if you have a touch of spring fever. You can prepare this menu with minimal effort.

The salad of red-leaf lettuce, avocado, and crisp bacon is dressed with a creamy vinaigrette enhanced with Roquefort cheese—an excellent salad-ingredient and dressing combination.

While "spring lamb" is now available all year, it's especially appropriate during its natural season. And what could be easier than these broiled lamb chops topped with orange slices and a piquant mustard, brown sugar, and citrus glaze! Delicious too.

Lamb and rosemary are a classic combination, and here rosemary flavors the rice that accompanies the lamb. It takes just a small amount of rosemary to perfume the rice. Only asparagus, of course, will do for the vegetable—just the tender tips, quickly cooked, and tossed in butter.

For the wine choose one of the less expensive red Bordeaux, such as those labeled simply "Médoc", with no wine district specified.

For dessert, a silken vanilla mousse made with yogurt and whipping cream provides an elegant backdrop to show off the season's fresh strawberries.

SHOPPING LIST FOR SPRING MENU

Meat, Dairy:

☐ 4 loin lamb chops (1⅓ lbs. total), 1 to 1¼ inches thick

☐ bacon (2 slices, 1½ oz. total)

☐ Roquefort cheese (2 Tbsp. crumbled)

☐ whipping cream (⅔ cup)

☐ unflavored yogurt (½ cup)

☐ butter (2 Tbsp.)

Produce:

☐ 1 head red-leaf lettuce

☐ 1 small (⅓-lb.) avocado

☐ 1½ lbs. asparagus

☐ 1 Valencia orange

☐ 1 lemon (need 2 tsp. juice)

☐ fresh rosemary (¼ tsp. chopped), or use dried

☐ 1 pt. strawberries

Liquor:

☐ 1 bottle red Bordeaux, such as Médoc

Check Staples:

☐ salt

☐ black pepper

☐ dried rosemary (a pinch), if not using fresh

☐ vanilla extract (¾ tsp.)

☐ 1 can (10¾-oz.) condensed chicken broth (need 1 cup)

☐ long-grain white rice (½ cup)

☐ sugar (⅓ cup)

☐ light brown sugar (⅓ cup packed)

☐ Dijon mustard (1 Tbsp.)

☐ red wine vinegar (1 Tbsp.)

☐ olive oil (3 Tbsp.)

☐ unflavored gelatin (1 tsp.)

☐ coffee

☐ toothpicks

☐ plastic wrap

COUNTDOWNS FOR SPRING MENU

Last-Minute Countdown

Time in   *Activity*
Minutes

55 minutes ahead:

15 Uncork wine; Steps 1–4 of dessert
20 Steps 1–3 of salad
 5 Steps 1–2 of asparagus
10 Step 1 of lamb
 <u>5</u> Step 1 of rice; Step 4 of salad
55

Serving:
Serve salad.
(6 minutes after serving salad do Step 2 of lamb.)
Transfer dessert to refrigerator; Step 3 of lamb; Step 2 of rice; Step 3 of asparagus; Step 4 of lamb
Serve lamb (Step 5), rice, asparagus, and wine.
Make coffee.
Serve dessert (Step 5) and coffee.

Plan-Ahead Countdown

Time in   *Activity*
Minutes

One day ahead:

 5 Step 1 of rice
15 Steps 2–3 of salad
10 Step 2 of rice; Steps 1, 3, and 4 of dessert (place in refrigerator, not freezer).
<u> </u>
30

30 minutes ahead:

 5 Step 2 of dessert
10 Step 1 of salad; Steps 1–2 of asparagus; uncork wine.
10 Step 1 of lamb; Step 4 of salad
25

Serving:
Serve salad.
(5 minutes after serving salad, put rice on to reheat and do Step 2 of lamb.)
Step 3 of lamb; Step 3 of asparagus; Step 4 of lamb
Serve lamb (Step 5), rice, asparagus, and wine.
Make coffee.
Serve dessert (Step 5) and coffee.

AVOCADO AND BACON GREEN SALAD

Working Time: 20 minutes/Chilling Time: 30 minutes/Servings: 2

SALAD INGREDIENTS:
2 slices (1½ oz. total) bacon, halved
3 cups red-leaf lettuce, torn in bite-size
　　pieces
1 small (⅓-lb.) avocado

ROQUEFORT VINAIGRETTE:
1 Tbsp. red wine vinegar
⅛ tsp. salt
⅛ tsp. ground black pepper
2 Tbsp. whipping cream
3 Tbsp. olive oil
2 Tbsp. crumbled Roquefort cheese

1.　　Cook bacon in an 8-inch skillet over medium heat until crisp. Drain on a paper towel, crumble, and set aside at room temperature.

2.　　Place lettuce in individual salad bowls. Cover with plastic wrap and refrigerate.

3.　　Combine all ingredients for vinaigrette in a ½-pt. jar. Cover and shake well.

4.　　At serving time peel and coarsely chop avocado. Add to salad bowls, pour dressing over, and top with bacon.

To do ahead: Do Steps 2 and 3 up to 1 day ahead. Refrigerate.

ORANGE-GLAZED LAMB CHOPS

Working Time: 15 minutes/Broiling Time: 15 minutes/Servings: 2

ORANGE GLAZE:
1 Tbsp. Dijon mustard
½ tsp. grated orange peel
2 tsp. fresh lemon juice
⅓ cup (packed) light brown sugar

LAMB CHOPS:
4 loin lamb chops (1⅓ lbs. total), 1 to 1¼
　　inches thick
½ tsp. salt
⅛ tsp. ground black pepper
2 Valencia* orange slices, ⅛ inch thick, cut
　　in half

1.   Combine all ingredients for glaze in a 1-cup bowl. Trim lamb chops of excess fat. Place on rack in small broiler pan.

2.   Sprinkle chops with salt and pepper. Spread ½ Tbsp. glaze on top of each chop. Broil 3 inches from heat for 5 minutes.

3.   Turn chops and spread each with ½ Tbsp. glaze. Broil 5 minutes more (for medium).

4.   Place an orange half-slice on each chop and spread with remaining glaze. Broil until bubbly and brown, about 3 minutes.

5.   To serve, place lamb on one end of a large platter. Spoon pan juices over lamb to glaze. Put rice in center of platter and asparagus opposite lamb.

*Valencia oranges remain sweet when cooked, whereas navel oranges may become slightly bitter.

To do ahead: Do Step 1 up to 1 hour ahead.

ROSEMARY RICE

Working Time: 5 minutes/Cooking Time: 15 minutes/Servings: 2

1 cup canned, condensed chicken broth
½ cup long-grain white rice

¼ tsp. chopped fresh rosemary or a pinch of
   dried
1 Tbsp. butter

1.   In a 1-qt. saucepan over high heat bring broth to a boil. Add rice, reduce heat to low, cover, and simmer until rice is tender and liquid absorbed, 15 minutes.

2.   Stir rosemary and butter into rice. Serve on a platter, flanked by lamb and asparagus.

To do ahead: Prepare up to 1 day ahead. Cool, cover, and refrigerate.

ASPARAGUS TIPS

Working Time: 5 minutes/Cooking Time: 6 minutes/Servings: 2

1 qt. water
1½ lbs. asparagus

1¼ tsp. salt, divided
1 Tbsp. butter

1. Bring water to a rapid boil in a wide 2-qt. saucepan over high heat. Cut stalks off asparagus leaving 5-inch-long tips.

2. Add tips to boiling water. Add 1 tsp. salt. Cook until asparagus is tender when tested with a toothpick, about 6 minutes. Drain in a colander.

3. Melt butter over medium heat in same saucepan. Add asparagus and ¼ tsp. salt. Shake pan to coat asparagus with butter. Cover and heat a few minutes.

To do ahead: Prepare through Step 2 up to 2 hours ahead.

Note: Tender parts of cut-off asparagus stalks may be saved for another use, such as in a Chinese stir-fry dish.

VANILLA MOUSSE WITH STRAWBERRIES

Working time: 15 minutes/Chilling Time: 1 hour/Servings: 2

1 tsp. (part of a packet) unflavored gelatin
¼ cup cold water
¼ cup plus 1 Tbsp. sugar
1 pt. strawberries

½ cup whipping cream
½ cup unflavored yogurt
¾ tsp. vanilla extract

1. Sprinkle gelatin over water in a 1-cup metal measuring cup. Let stand 2 minutes. Place over medium-low heat, stirring frequently, until gelatin dissolves. (It will still look a little foamy.) Add ¼ cup sugar and heat until dissolved.

2. Meanwhile, wash and slice enough strawberries to make 1 cup. In a 3-cup bowl mix strawberries with 1 Tbsp. sugar. Cover and refrigerate 30 minutes or up to 2 hours.

3. Put cream in a 1-qt. bowl. Pour gelatin mixture into cream, stirring with a whisk. Stir in yogurt and vanilla until mixture is smooth.

4. Pour into individual compotes and place in freezer for about 50 minutes, or just until top of mixture begins to freeze slightly. Transfer to refrigerator.

5. To serve, spoon strawberries with liquid over chilled mousse.

To do ahead: Do Steps 1, 3, and 4 up to 3 days ahead. Cover and refrigerate (skip freezer chilling). Do Step 2 up to 2 hours ahead.

ARMENIAN MENU

- **Bulgur Yogurt Soup**
- **Lamp-Chop Oven Dinner**
  Crusty Bread
  Côtes du Rhône
- **Honey Almond Turnovers**
  Coffee

The influence of Armenian cuisine has been lasting and significant throughout the world in spite of the small number of Armenians and their history of upheavals and hardships. Armenian food has a simple, tasty Middle Eastern style, as illustrated by the menu suggested here.

A nourishing soup, made with beef or chicken broth, cracked wheat (bulgur), yogurt, and mint, introduces the meal. It's delicious and easy to make.

The lamb-chop oven dinner is a quick version of an Armenian stew. Browned lamb shoulder chops are placed in individual gratin dishes, topped with vegetables, and seasoned with lemon, oregano, and thyme. The dishes are covered with foil and baked at high heat. The resultant "stew" is infused with the flavors of onions, garlic, mushrooms, green peppers, and tomatoes. Zucchini and yellow squash add their colorful accents, and the fragrant juices call for crusty bread to absorb them.

The traditional beverage is *tan*, a lightly salted mixture of yogurt and water. If you prefer to serve wine, a good selection would be a Côtes du Rhône (at least five years old), a big, sturdy, substantial red wine.

Flaky turnovers filled with homemade almond paste and drizzled with honey provide the satisfying finale to this dinner. They are perfect to serve with rich, strong coffee.

SHOPPING LIST FOR ARMENIAN MENU

Meat, Dairy, Eggs:

☐ 2 shoulder lamb chops, (1½ lbs. total), about 1 inch thick

☐ unflavored yogurt (⅓ cup)

☐ butter (3½ Tbsp. + butter for bread)

☐ eggs (2)

Produce:

☐ 1 medium-size (6-oz.) tomato

☐ 1 small (⅓-lb.) yellow summer squash

☐ 1 small (¼-lb.) zucchini

☐ 1 small (¼-lb.) green pepper

☐ 8 medium-size mushrooms (¼ lb.)

☐ 1 lemon (need 1 Tbsp. juice)

☐ 1 medium-size (⅓-lb.) onion

☐ garlic (1 tsp. minced)

☐ mint (2 tsp. chopped), or use dried mint and parsley

☐ parsley (2 tsp. chopped), if using dried mint

Grocery:

☐ Ala cracked wheat (2 Tbsp.)

☐ crusty bread

☐ slivered almonds (⅓ cup)

☐ mild honey, such as orange blossom (2 Tbsp.)

☐ frozen Pepperidge Farm patty shells (2 each)

Liquor:

☐ 1 bottle robust red wine, such as Côtes du Rhône

Check Staples:

☐ salt

☐ black pepper

☐ white pepper

☐ dried oregano (¼ tsp.)

☐ dried thyme (¼ tsp.)

☐ dried mint (½ tsp.), if not using fresh

☐ almond extract (¼ tsp.)

☐ sugar (1 Tbsp.)

☐ flour (¼ cup)

☐ olive oil (1 Tbsp.)

☐ 1 can (14½-oz.) single-strength beef or chicken broth

☐ coffee

☐ paper towels

☐ aluminum foil

COUNTDOWNS FOR ARMENIAN MENU

Last-Minute Countdown

Time in 　　　 *Activity*
Minutes

70 minutes ahead:
30　Patty shells (for dessert) out of freezer; uncork wine; Steps 1–5 of lamb-chop dinner (400°F oven)

30 minutes ahead:
15　Steps 1–3 of soup and chop mint.
15　Steps 1–4 of dessert
——
30

Serving:
Serve soup (Step 4).
(Dessert out of oven; bread in oven to warm)
Serve lamb-chop dinner, bread, butter, and wine.
Make coffee.
Serve dessert (Step 5) and coffee.

Plan-Ahead Countdown

Time in 　　　 *Activity*
Minutes

One day ahead:
30　Patty shells (for dessert) out of freezer; Steps 1–5 of lamb-chop dinner
10　Steps 1–2 of soup
15　Steps 1–4 of dessert
——
55　(plus 45 minutes more cooking and cooling time for lamb-chop dinner)

30 minutes ahead:
5　Oven to 350°F; uncork wine; Step 3 of soup and chop mint.

15 minutes ahead:
—　Lamb-chop dinner in oven to reheat

10 minutes ahead:
—　Soup on stove to reheat

Serving:
Serve soup (Step 4).
(Bread in oven to warm)
Serve lamb-chop dinner, bread, butter, and wine.
Reheat dessert in 300°F oven; make coffee.
Serve dessert (Step 5) and coffee.

BULGUR YOGURT SOUP

Working Time: 15 minutes/Cooking Time: 15 minutes/Servings: 2

2 Tbsp. butter
2 Tbsp. flour
1 can (14½-oz.) single-strength beef or
  chicken broth
Pinch of salt
Pinch of ground white pepper

2 Tbsp. cracked wheat*
⅓ cup unflavored yogurt
1 egg yolk
2 tsp. chopped fresh mint, or ½ tsp. dried
  mint mixed with 2 tsp. chopped parsley

1. Melt butter in a 1½-quart saucepan over medium heat. Stir in flour and cook 1 minute. Turn heat to medium-high and gradually whisk in beef or chicken broth.

2. Add salt and pepper and bring mixture to a boil, whisking frequently. Add cracked wheat, reduce heat, and simmer, uncovered, until wheat is tender but still firm to the bite, 15 minutes. Stir occasionally.

3. In a 3-cup bowl whisk together yogurt and egg yolk.

4. When soup is done, remove from heat and whisk in yogurt mixture. Pour into soup bowls, sprinkle with mint, and serve.

*Cracked wheat, also called bulgur, is a Middle Eastern staple commonly sold in this country under the brand name "Ala." Look for it in the rice section of supermarkets or ethnic grocery stores.

To do ahead: Do Steps 1–2 up to 1 day ahead. To serve, reheat, then proceed with Steps 3–4. If soup is too thick, add a few tablespoons of water.

LAMB-CHOP OVEN DINNER

Working Time: 30 minutes/Baking Time: 50 minutes (400°F)/Servings: 2

2 shoulder lamb chops (1½ lbs. total), about
   1 inch thick
1¼ tsp. salt, divided
⅛ tsp. ground black pepper
1 Tbsp. butter
1 Tbsp. olive oil
1 medium-size (⅓-lb.) onion, peeled, sliced
   ⅛ inch thick
1 tsp. minced garlic
8 medium-size mushrooms (¼ lb.)
1 small (¼-lb.) green pepper, cut in eighths
1 small (⅓-lb.) yellow summer squash, cut
   in 1 inch cubes
1 small (¼-lb.) zucchini, sliced 1 inch thick
1 medium-size (6-oz.) tomato, cut in 6
   wedges
¼ tsp. dried oregano
¼ tsp. dried thyme
1 Tbsp. fresh lemon juice
Crusty bread

1.   Dry lamb with paper towels and trim off excess fat. Season with ½ tsp. salt and the pepper. In a 10-inch skillet over medium-high heat brown lamb in butter and oil, about 5 minutes on each side.

2.   Turn oven to 400°F. When lamb is browned, remove each chop to a separate gratin dish (10 inches long). Add onion and garlic to skillet and sauté over medium heat until lightly browned, about 5 minutes.

3.   Remove skillet from heat. Add remaining vegetables to skillet, along with ¾ tsp. salt, the oregano, and thyme. Mix well.

4.   Pour lemon juice over lamb. Spoon vegetables over and around meat. Cover dishes tightly with aluminum foil.

5.   Bake in center of oven for 50 minutes.

6.   Remove foil from gratin dishes (be careful of steam) and let food cool a few minutes. Serve directly from dishes with crusty bread to soak up the juices.

To do ahead: Prepare up to 1 day ahead, cool, recover with foil, and refrigerate. To serve, reheat in a 350°F oven for 25 minutes.

HONEY ALMOND TURNOVERS

Thawing Time: 30 minutes/Working Time: 15 minutes/Baking Time: 15 minutes (400°F)/Cooling Time: 10 minutes/Servings: 2

ALMOND FILLING:
⅓ cup slivered almonds
½ Tbsp. butter, melted
1 Tbsp. sugar
¼ tsp. almond extract
1 Tbsp. mild honey, such as orange blossom
1 egg yolk

PASTRY:
2 frozen patty shells* (⅓ of a 10-oz. pkg.), thawed
2 Tbsp. (about) flour for rolling out pastry
1 Tbsp. egg white
2 tsp. mild honey, such as orange blossom

1. Turn oven to 400°F. For filling, grind almonds in blender and empty into a 1-cup bowl. Add remaining filling ingredients, stirring to combine well.

2. On a lightly floured surface roll out each patty shell (with side marked "TOP" up) to 7 inches in diameter. Turn pastry over and make 3 radial slits ½ inch long on one half of each patty shell. Spread other half with the almond filling to within 1 inch of edge.

3. Brush edges of pastry with egg white. Fold pastry in half and seal edges well by pressing together with the tines of a fork. Brush pastry with egg white.

4. Carefully transfer to a small baking sheet. Bake at once in upper third of oven until puffed and brown, 12 to 15 minutes. Cool 10 minutes before serving.

5. To serve, place turnovers on dessert plates and drizzle each with 1 tsp. honey.

*Patty shells are made by Pepperidge Farm and can be found in the frozen dessert section of most grocery stores.

To do ahead: Do Steps 1–4 up to 1 day ahead. Cool completely, cover with foil, and leave at room temperature. To reheat, uncover and place directly on oven rack in a 300°F oven until warmed through, 3 to 5 minutes.

PORK MENUS

Texas Menu
Chinese Menu
Autumn Menu
New England Menu
Mexican Menu

TEXAS MENU

- **Tex-Mex Salad**
- **Spiced Pork with Peaches**
- **Herbed Lima Beans**
  Iced Tea
- **Coconut Pecan "Pie"**

This is a lovely summer menu from Texas with a good bit of influence from Mexico, as seen in the salad and in the spicing of the pork.

The salad is a mixture of shredded vegetables—romaine lettuce, tomato, green pepper, and green onion—tossed in a vinaigrette dressing flavored with oregano and chili powder. The salad can be made shortly before dinner if you place it in the freezer for a few minutes just before serving to give it a frosty crispness.

For the entrée, sirloin pork chops are dusted with cinnamon, cloves, salt, and flour, then sautéed in butter with onions. A little sugar, lemon juice, and water are added, and the chops are simmered until tender. Just before serving the pork is topped with fresh peach slices, heated in butter, and a dollop of sour cream—delicious!

An excellent vegetable selection for the pork dish is lima beans seasoned with summer savory and parsley. For the beverage iced tea is suitable for the menu as well as the season.

Dessert is a coconut and pecan delight that's not really a pie, since it doesn't have a pastry crust, but it's baked in a pie plate, looks like a pie, and is served as a pie. It can be prepared in only ten minutes.

SHOPPING LIST FOR TEXAS MENU

Meat, Dairy, Eggs:

☐ 2 large sirloin pork chops (about 1 lb. total)

☐ butter (5½ Tbsp.)

☐ sour cream (about ¼ cup)

☐ milk (⅔ cup)

☐ eggs (2)

Produce:

☐ 1 small head romaine lettuce

☐ 1 medium-size (6-oz.) tomato (need ½)

☐ 1 medium-size (4-oz.) green pepper (need ¼)

☐ parsley (1 Tbsp. chopped)

☐ green onions (1 small)

☐ 1 small onion (⅓ cup chopped)

☐ garlic (¼ tsp. minced)

☐ ½ lb. peaches (1 large or 2 small)*, or use frozen

☐ 1 or 2 lemons (need 5 tsp. juice plus any needed for iced tea)

Grocery:

☐ 10-oz. pkg. frozen lima or baby lima beans (need ½)

☐ frozen, unsweetened peaches (8 slices), if not using fresh

☐ chopped pecans (¼ cup)

☐ packaged, sweetened, flaked coconut (½ cup)

Check Staples:

☐ salt

☐ black pepper

☐ chili powder (½ tsp.)

☐ ground cinnamon (½ tsp.)

☐ ground cloves (½ tsp.)

☐ dried summer savory (¼ tsp.)

☐ dried oregano (¼ tsp.)

☐ baking powder (½ tsp.)

☐ vanilla extract (½ tsp.)

☐ red wine vinegar (1½ Tbsp.)

☐ salad oil (¼ cup)

☐ flour (⅓ cup)

☐ sugar (about ⅔ cup)

☐ tea (for iced tea)

☐ wax paper

☐ plastic wrap

*May need to be purchased several days ahead to allow for ripening.

COUNTDOWNS FOR TEXAS MENU

Last-Minute Countdown

Time in   Activity
Minutes

60 minutes ahead:

 5 Oven to 350°F; make iced tea.
10 Prepare dessert.
20 Steps 1–4 of pork (squeeze 2 tsp. lemon juice for beans)
20 Steps 1–2 of salad; pie out of oven when ready
20 Steps 1–2 of salad
 5 Baste pork; Step 1 of beans and chop parsley; salad in freezer to crisp
___
60

Serving:

Serve salad (Step 3).
Step 5 of pork; Step 2 of beans
Serve pork, beans, and iced tea.
Serve pie (and more iced tea if desired).

Plan-Ahead Countdown

Time in   Activity
Minutes

One day ahead:

 5 Oven to 350°F; make iced tea.
10 Prepare dessert.
20 Steps 1–2 of salad
___
35 (plus 35 minutes for pie to finish cooking and cool before being refrigerated)

45 minutes ahead:

20 Steps 1–4 of pork (squeeze 2 tsp. lemon juice for beans)

5 minutes ahead:

 5 Baste pork; Step 1 of beans and chop parsley.

Serving:

Serve salad (Step 3).
Oven to 350°F (to warm pie); Step 5 of pork; Step 2 of beans
Serve pork, beans, and iced tea.
(When oven is hot, put pie in.)
Serve pie (and more iced tea if desired).

TEX-MEX SALAD

Working Time: 20 minutes/Servings: 2

SALAD INGREDIENTS:
2 cups shredded romaine lettuce (¼-inch-
   wide shreds)
½ medium-size tomato (cut in half through
   stem)
¼ medium-size (4-oz.) green pepper
1 small green onion

CHILI VINAIGRETTE:
¼ tsp salt
¼ tsp. dried oregano
½ tsp. chili powder
¼ tsp. minced garlic
1½ Tbsp. red wine vinegar
¼ cup salad oil

1.   Divide lettuce between two salad bowls. Cut pepper into thin julienne strips and green onion into very fine strips. Scatter tomato, pepper, and onion strips over lettuce. Cover with plastic wrap and refrigerate.

2.   Combine all dressing ingredients, except oil, in a 1-cup jar. Cover and shake until salt dissolves. Add oil and shake again. Refrigerate.

3.   To serve, shake dressing and spoon over salads.

To do ahead: Do Steps 1-2 up to 1 day ahead. If preparing salad at the last minute, place in freezer about 5 minutes to chill and crisp.

SPICED PORK WITH PEACHES

Working Time: 20 minutes/Cooking Time: 40 minutes/Servings: 2

PORK:
2 large sirloin pork chops (about 1 lb. total)
½ tsp. salt
½ tsp. ground cinnamon
½ tsp. ground cloves
1 Tbsp. butter
⅓ cup finely chopped onion
2 tsp. sugar

1 Tbsp. fresh lemon juice
¼ cup water

PEACHES:
1 large or 2 small peaches* (½ lb. total)
1 Tbsp. butter
¼ cup (about) sour cream

1. Trim pork of any excess fat. Combine salt, cinnamon, cloves, and flour on a piece of wax paper. Press chops into mixture, coating them on both sides.

2. In a 10-inch skillet with a nonstick surface brown chops in 1½ Tbsp. butter over medium heat, about 2 minutes on first side. Turn chops and add onion to skillet around pork. Cook 2 minutes.

3. Sprinkle pork with sugar, then lemon juice. Spoon most of the onion over the pork. Turn heat to low, add water around chops, cover, and simmer 40 minutes. Spoon pan juices over pork halfway through cooking.

4. Peel peach(es) and slice thickly. Melt butter in a 7-inch skillet and coat slices with butter to prevent darkening.

5. When pork is done, heat peach slices about 3 minutes, just until hot. Place pork on a small platter and spoon pan juices on top. Arrange peach slices in a row over chops and top with a dollop of sour cream.

*Peaches are most readily available from June to September. Frozen unsweetened peach slices are available through a longer season and are a good substitute in this recipe. (Use about 10 peach slices.)

To do ahead: Prepare through Step 5 up to 30 minutes ahead. Cover and leave at room temperature. Reheat pork and complete Step 5.

Note: When this dish is cooking it may smell overspiced at first, but don't worry—the resulting flavor is subtle and pleasing.

HERBED LIMA BEANS

Working Time: 10 minutes/Cooking Time: 15 minutes/Servings: 2

½ cup water
½ of a 10-oz. pkg. frozen lima or baby lima
  beans
½ tsp. (scant) salt
1 Tbsp. butter

Pinch of ground black pepper
¼ tsp. dried summer savory
1 Tbsp. chopped parsley
2 tsp. fresh lemon juice

1. In a 1-qt. saucepan bring water to a boil over high heat. Add lima beans and salt. Bring to a boil again, reduce heat to low, cover, and cook until beans are tender, 12 to 15 minutes.

2. Drain beans in a colander. Melt butter in saucepan. Add beans, pepper, savory, and parsley. Remove from heat and add lemon juice.

To do ahead: Step 1 may be done up to several hours ahead.

COCONUT PECAN "PIE"

Working Time: 10 minutes/Baking Time: 30 minutes (350°F)/Cooling Time: 15 minutes/Servings: 3

2 Tbsp. butter	¼ cup flour
¼ cup chopped pecans	½ tsp. baking powder
2 eggs	⅛ tsp. salt
⅔ cup milk	½ tsp. vanilla extract
½ cup sugar	½ cup packaged flaked coconut (sweetened)

1. Turn oven to 350°F. Place butter and pecans in a 6-inch glass pie plate and put on low rack in oven. After butter melts, stir to coat pecans (leave in oven).

2. Place remaining ingredients in blender and blend for 30 seconds. When pecans are lightly toasted and butter is beginning to brown, remove pie plate from oven and cool a minute or two.

3. Pour coconut mixture over pecans (they will float to top) and return to oven. Bake until top of pie is golden and evenly puffed, 30 minutes. Cool at least 15 minutes before serving (pie will settle).

To do ahead: May be prepared up to 2 days ahead. To serve, rewarm in a 350°F oven about 15 minutes.

Note: Six-inch glass pie plates (actually about 5 inches across the bottom and 7 inches across the top) are obtainable, but if you have difficulty finding one, some 2-qt. glass casserole dishes have a pie-plate-shaped top that makes a good substitute.

CHINESE MENU

- Spinach and Mushroom Egg Drop Soup
- Stir-Fried Pork, Snow Peas, Lychees, and Tomatoes
- Boiled Rice
  Oolong Tea

- Kumquat Walnut Sundaes

This meal is organized in the same way as most Chinese restaurant meals (in the United States), with the soup served as a first course and tea accompanying the meal. As an extra treat, a dessert with Chinese overtones is also included. You can try a more authentic arrangement, if you like, by serving the soup as the beverage with the meal and offering tea only at the end of the meal.

The soup can easily stand alone, with its attractive garnish of spinach shreds, mushroom slices, and egg yolk flowers. The soup base is chicken broth seasoned with garlic, soy sauce, pepper, and sesame oil. Unlike many Chinese dishes, this soup can be prepared ahead of time and will still be good when reheated.

For an unusual stir-fry dish, pork is flavored with hoisin sauce (a slightly sweet Chinese barbecue sauce), which is played against the perfumed sweetness of lychees, the crisp texture of fresh snow peas, and the bright color and slight acidity of tomatoes. The components are contrasting, yet harmonious and pleasing. Plain boiled rice is the appropriate accompaniment.

For dessert, candied walnuts and julienne strips of preserved kumquats are heated in syrup and spooned over vanilla ice cream. Easy, delicious, and refreshing.

SHOPPING LIST FOR CHINESE MENU

Meat, Dairy, Eggs:

☐ 1 lb. pork chops or ½ lb. boneless pork chops

☐ vanilla ice cream (⅔ pt.)

☐ butter (1 tsp.)

☐ eggs (1 yolk)

Produce:

☐ 16 small (⅛ lb.) snow peas

☐ 1 small (¼-lb.) tomato

☐ 1 medium-size onion (need half)

☐ 2 medium-size mushrooms

☐ spinach (¼ cup shredded)

☐ garlic (¼ tsp. minced)

Grocery:

☐ Oriental sesame oil (½ tsp.)

☐ 1 can (11-oz.) lychees (need half)

☐ hoisin sauce (2 tsp.)

☐ walnuts (2 Tbsp. chopped)

☐ preserved kumquats (3 + 3 Tbsp. syrup)

Check Staples:

☐ salt

☐ white pepper

☐ soy sauce (4 tsp.)

☐ cornstarch (4 tsp.)

☐ sugar (5 tsp.)

☐ salad (not olive) oil (2 Tbsp.)

☐ 1 can (14½-oz.) single-strength chicken broth

☐ long-grain white rice (¾ cup)

☐ oolong tea

COUNTDOWNS FOR CHINESE MENU

Last-Minute Countdown

Time in   *Activity*
Minutes

50 minutes ahead:
10	Steps 1–3 of dessert
20	Steps 1–3 of pork dish
15	Steps 1–3 of soup
5	Steps 1–2 of rice
50	

Serving:
Serve soup (Step 4).
Step 3 of rice; heat water for tea; Steps 4–5 of pork dish; make tea; Step 6 of pork dish
Serve pork dish, rice, and tea.
Serve dessert (Step 4) and more tea, if desired.

Plan-Ahead Countdown

Time in   *Activity*
Minutes

One day ahead:
10	Steps 1–3 of dessert
15	Steps 1–3 of soup
25	

25 minutes ahead:
20	Steps 1–3 of pork dish
5	Reheat soup; Steps 1–2 of rice
25	

Serving:
Serve soup (Step 4).
Step 3 of rice; heat water for tea; Steps 4–5 of pork dish; make tea; Step 6 of pork dish
Serve pork dish, rice, and tea.
Serve dessert (Step 4) and more tea, if desired.

SPINACH AND MUSHROOM EGG DROP SOUP

Working and Cooking Time: 15 minutes/Servings: 2

1 can (14½-oz.) single-strength chicken
   broth
¼ tsp. minced garlic
1 tsp. soy sauce
Dash of ground white pepper
2 tsp. cornstarch
1 Tbsp. plus ½ tsp. cold water

2 medium-size mushrooms, thinly sliced
   (about ½ cup)
¼ cup (packed) finely shredded spinach
   leaves
1 egg yolk
½ tsp. Oriental sesame oil*

1. In a 1-qt. saucepan over medium-high heat bring chicken broth to a boil with garlic, soy sauce, and pepper.

2. In a ½-cup bowl mix cornstarch with 1 Tbsp. cold water. Whisk mixture into boiling broth and boil a minute until mixture is clear.

3. Add mushrooms and spinach and boil 2 minutes. Reduce heat to medium-low. In a ½-cup bowl mix egg yolk with ½ tsp. water. Drizzle mixture into soup, wait 30 seconds, then stir.

4. Serve soup in individual soup bowls and sprinkle sesame oil over each serving.

*Oriental sesame oil is a brown oil extracted from toasted sesame seeds and used as a seasoning in Oriental dishes. It's available in bottles in Oriental markets. Omit if unavailable.

To do ahead: Prepare through Step 3 up to 1 day ahead. Cool, cover, and refrigerate. To serve, reheat over low heat about 10 minutes, then proceed with Step 4.

STIR-FRIED PORK, SNOW PEAS, LYCHEES, AND TOMATOES

Working and Cooking Time: 30 minutes/Servings: 2

PORK AND VEGETABLES:

1 lb. pork chops or ½ lb. boneless pork
   chops
½ medium-size onion, peeled
16 small (⅛ lb.) snow peas
6 to 8 lychees* (half of an 11-oz. can)
1 small (¼-lb.) tomato
2 Tbsp. salad (not olive) oil, divided
2 Tbsp. water

SEASONING MIXTURE:

2 tsp. cornstarch
½ tsp. salt
¼ tsp. sugar
2 tsp. hoisin sauce**
1 Tbsp. soy sauce
¼ cup water

1. Bone pork chops, if necessary, and trim off fat. Cut meat into 1½ x ½ x ⅛-inch slices.

2. Quarter onion half and separate layers. Remove tips and any strings from snow peas. Halve lychees and cut tomato into ⅓-inch-thick wedges.

3. Place separate mounds of pork and vegetables on a plate. Measure out oil and water. Combine all ingredients for seasoning mixture in a ½-cup bowl, stirring to blend well.

4. Heat a wok (or 10-inch skillet) over high heat. Add 1 Tbsp. oil and immediately add pork. Stir-fry about 3 minutes or until pork is opaque. Remove to a small bowl.

5. Add onion to wok and 1 Tbsp. oil. Stir-fry 1 minute. Reduce heat to medium high. Add snow peas and stir-fry 1 minute. Add 2 Tbsp. water, cover, and steam 2 minutes.

6. Stir seasoning mixture to recombine and pour it over the cooked pork. Add pork mixture to wok and cook until liquid thickens, about 1 minute. Add lychees and tomatoes and heat through, 2 minutes.

7. Serve on a small platter with boiled rice alongside.

*Lychees (also spelled litchis) are the fruit of a large tropical tree native to southeastern Asia. Canned lychees are available in Oriental markets and some supermarkets.
**Hoisin sauce is a thick, reddish brown, barbecue-flavored sauce, used in small quantities in Chinese cooking. It is available in cans or jars in Oriental markets. It will keep indefinitely in a jar in the refrigerator.

To do ahead: Do Steps 1–3 up to 1 hour ahead. Cover ingredients and leave at room temperature.

BOILED RICE

Working Time: 5 minutes/Cooking Time: 20 minutes/Servings: 2

¾ cup long-grain white rice   1¼ cups water

1.   Place rice in a 1-qt. saucepan. Wash rice in several changes of water, rubbing the grains between your fingers to remove excess starch. Pour off rinse water.

2.   Add 1¼ cups water to rice and bring to a boil over high heat. Reduce heat to medium and boil, uncovered, until no bubbles appear on surface of rice, about 10 minutes.

3.   Turn heat to very low, cover pan, and let steam 10 minutes more. Serve.

To do ahead: Step 1 can be done up to 1 hour ahead.

KUMQUAT WALNUT SUNDAES

Working Time: 10 minutes/Servings: 2

1 tsp. butter   3 preserved kumquats*
1½ Tbsp. sugar   3 Tbsp. syrup from preserved kumquats
2 Tbsp. finely chopped walnuts   2 servings (⅔ pt.) vanilla ice cream

1.   Melt butter in a ¾-qt. saucepan over medium heat. Add sugar and walnuts. When sugar begins to melt, stir frequently until walnuts begin sticking together.

2. Meanwhile, slit kumquats lengthwise, pull out and discard pulp and seeds. Cut kumquat rind lengthwise into slivers.

3. Add kumquat syrup to melted sugar and walnut mixture (stand back). Boil until walnuts separate again and mixture is syrupy. Add kumquat slivers.

4. To serve, place ice cream in individual compotes and spoon warm kumquat walnut sauce over ice cream.

*Kumquats are orange-colored, oval citrus fruits about 2 inches long and 1 inch in diameter. Kumquats preserved in sugar syrup are available in jars in gourmet shops and some supermarkets. Preserved kumquats keep indefinitely in the refrigerator.

To do ahead: Prepare through Step 3 up to 1 day ahead. Cool, cover, and refrigerate. Reheat before serving.

AUTUMN MENU

- **Romaine, Chick Pea, and Tomato Salad**
- **Sicilian Pork and Peppers**
- **Parmesan Corncakes**
  Chianti Classico
- **Pears in Red Wine with Whipped Cream**
  Coffee

Autumn is the time of year when appetites and energy increase, and the colorful offerings of the produce markets are an exciting invitation to great meals. This menu, which has a Sicilian accent, takes advantage of the season's abundant bright-red peppers (in the meat dish) and Bartlett pears (in the dessert).

The salad contains chick peas that are marinated in Italian salad dressing, then, just before serving, are tossed with romaine lettuce, tomato wedges, salami strips, and chopped green onions.

Sicilian pork and peppers is a succulent dish of pork chops, onions, garlic, red and green peppers, and black olives, in a rich sauce. It goes together quickly and is excellent served alongside oven-baked Parmesan flavored corncakes. The cakes take the place of polenta and are faster to make.

The popular Italian Chianti goes well with the pork and peppers and also complements the cheesy corncakes. One that's labeled "Riserva" is almost sure to be good Chianti.

The Chianti is excellent too, for poaching the pears for dessert. The wine takes on a different character when it's boiled down, spiced with ginger, and sweetened. It's mellow, yet zesty—a great companion for pears and whipped cream.

213

SHOPPING LIST FOR AUTUMN MENU

Meat, Dairy, Eggs:

☐ 2 rib pork chops (1 lb. total), 1 inch thick

☐ salami (8 thin slices, 1 oz.)

☐ Parmesan cheese (¼ cup grated)

☐ butter (1 Tbsp.)

☐ whipping cream (⅓ cup)

Produce:

☐ 1 small head romaine lettuce

☐ 1 medium-size (6-oz.) tomato

☐ green onions (2 Tbsp. chopped)

☐ 1 small onion

☐ green pepper (½ medium-size)

☐ red pepper (½ medium-size)

☐ garlic (1 tsp. minced)

☐ 1 lemon (1 strip peel + 1 Tbsp. juice)

☐ 2 medium-size pears (¾ lb. total)*

Grocery:

☐ canned chick peas (⅓ cup)

☐ bottled Italian salad dressing, such as Wish-Bone (¼ cup)

☐ canned tomato paste (1 Tbsp.)

☐ bottled gravy browner, such as Wilson's B-V Beefer-Upper or Kitchen Bouquet (¼ tsp.)

☐ canned black olives (8)

☐ yellow cornmeal (½ cup)

Liquor:

☐ 1 bottle Chianti Classico (need 1 cup for cooking)

Check Staples:

☐ salt

☐ ground red pepper

☐ ground ginger (⅛ tsp.)

☐ dried thyme (¼ tsp.)

☐ flour (2 tsp.)

☐ olive oil (1½ Tbsp.)

☐ shortening (1 Tbsp.)

☐ sugar (½ cup)

☐ 1 can (14½-oz.) single-strength chicken broth

☐ coffee

☐ toothpicks

☐ plastic wrap

☐ wax paper

*May need to be purchased several days ahead to allow for ripening.

COUNTDOWNS FOR AUTUMN MENU

Last-Minute Countdown

Time in   Activity
Minutes

60 minutes ahead:
15 Uncork wine; Step 1 of salad
10 Steps 1–2 of dessert
15 Steps 1–4 of pork and peppers
 5 Oven to 450°F; Step 4 of dessert;
     Steps 5–6 of pork and peppers
 5 Steps 5 and 3 of dessert
10 Steps 1–3 of corncakes
——
60

Serving:
Serve salad (Step 2).
Serve pork and peppers, corncakes, and
  wine.
Make coffee.
Serve dessert (Step 6) and coffee.

Plan-Ahead Countdown

Time in   Activity
Minutes

One day ahead:
10 Steps 1–2 of dessert
15 Step 1 of salad
15 Step 4 of dessert; Step 1 of corn-
     cakes; Step 5 of dessert; Step 2 of
     corncakes
——
40

35 minutes ahead:
20 Oven to 450°F; uncork wine; Steps
     1–6 of pork and peppers
 5 Step 3 of corncakes; Step 3 of des-
     sert
——
25

Serving:
Serve salad (Step 2).
Serve pork and peppers, corncakes, and
  wine.
Make coffee.
Serve dessert (Step 6) and coffee.

ROMAINE, CHICK PEA, AND TOMATO SALAD

Working Time: 15 minutes/Chilling Time: 30 minutes/Servings: 2

⅓ cup canned chick peas, drained
¼ cup (about) bottled Italian salad dressing, such as Wish-Bone Italian
8 thin slices salami (1 oz.), cut in ¼ inch wide strips

2 Tbsp. chopped green onions
1 medium-size tomato (6-oz.), cut in 10 wedges
1 small head romaine lettuce, torn in bite-size pieces (3 cups)

1. In a 2-qt. salad bowl toss chick peas with dressing until well coated. Sprinkle salami and green onions over chick peas (do not toss). Add tomato wedges and place lettuce on top. Cover with plastic wrap and refrigerate at least 30 minutes.

2. Just before serving, toss ingredients to coat with dressing. Add a little more dressing if needed.

To do ahead: Do Step 1 up to 2 days ahead.

SICILIAN PORK AND PEPPERS

Working Time: 20 minutes/Cooking Time: 25 minutes more/Servings: 2

2 rib pork chops (1 lb. total), 1 inch thick
½ tsp. plus ⅛ tsp. salt
⅛ tsp. ground red pepper
¼ tsp. dried thyme
2 tsp. flour
1½ Tbsp. olive oil
1 small onion
½ medium-size green pepper

½ medium-size red pepper*
1 tsp. minced garlic
½ cup single-strength chicken broth
1 Tbsp. fresh lemon juice
1 Tbsp. tomato paste
¼ tsp. gravy browner**
6 to 8 black olives, halved

1. Dry pork chops on paper towels and trim off excess fat. On a piece of wax paper combine ½ tsp. salt, ground red pepper, thyme, and flour. Coat chops with the mixture.

2. In a 10-inch skillet with a nonstick surface brown chops on one side in oil over medium-high heat, about 4 minutes.

3. Meanwhile, peel, halve, and thinly slice the onion. Cut peppers into ¼-inch-wide strips and mince the garlic.

4. Turn chops over, push to side of pan, and add onion, garlic, peppers, and ⅛ tsp. salt. Sauté over medium heat until vegetables are wilted, about 5 minutes.

5. For sauce, blend chicken broth, lemon juice, tomato paste, and gravy browner in measuring cup.

6. Pour sauce mixture over chops, and cover chops with some of the onions and peppers. Scatter olive halves on top. Simmer, covered, over low heat until cooked through, 25 minutes. Serve on a small platter with corncakes alongside.

*Sweet (that is, not hot) red bell peppers are most readily available during late summer and fall.
**Gravy browner is sold under such trade names as Wilson's B-V Beefer-Upper or Kitchen Bouquet. It can be found near the steak sauces in most grocery stores.

To do ahead: May be prepared through Step 6 up to 30 minutes ahead. Remove from heat and leave covered.

Note: A 14½-oz. can of single-strength chicken broth is enough for this recipe and the corncakes.

PARMESAN CORNCAKES

Working Time: 10 minutes/Baking Time: 15 minutes (450°F)/Servings: 2

1¼ cups single-strength chicken broth
¼ tsp. salt
⅛ tsp. sugar
1 Tbsp. butter

½ cup yellow cornmeal
1 Tbsp. shortening, for greasing baking pan
2 Tbsp. freshly grated Parmesan cheese

1. Turn oven to 450°F. In a 1-qt. saucepan bring broth, salt, sugar, and butter to a boil over high heat. Quickly whisk in cornmeal and remove from stove. Mixture should be thickened, but not solid.

2.   Grease a large baking sheet. Drop heaping tablespoons of cornmeal mixture close together on baking sheet. Flatten slightly. (Makes 12 to 15.) Top each cake with a pinch of grated cheese.

3.   Bake in upper third of oven until cakes brown slightly around the edges, 15 minutes. Serve on same platter as pork.

To do ahead: Prepare through Step 2 up to 2 days ahead. Cover with plastic wrap and refrigerate.

Note: A 14½-oz. can of single-strength chicken broth is enough for this recipe and the pork and peppers.

PEARS IN RED WINE WITH WHIPPED CREAM

Working Time: 15 minutes/Cooking Time: 20 minutes/Servings: 2

1 cup Chianti Classico, or other dry red
  wine
1 strip lemon peel, ½ inch x 1 inch
⅓ cup plus ½ tsp. sugar

⅛ tsp. ground ginger
2 medium-size ripe pears (¾ lb. total)
⅓ cup whipping cream

1.   Put wine, lemon peel, and ⅓ cup sugar mixed with ginger in a 1½-qt. saucepan. Bring to a boil over high heat, stirring occasionally to dissolve sugar.

2.   Peel pears with vegetable peeler, cut into thick lengthwise slices, and core. Add to wine mixture, lower heat, and simmer, uncovered, until tender when tested with a toothpick, 10 to 15 minutes.

3.   In a 3-cup bowl with a rotary beater whip cream until stiff. Beat in ½ tsp. sugar. Cover and refrigerate.

4.   With a slotted spoon remove cooked pears to two compotes. Rapidly boil down wine to ⅓ cup, about 5 minutes.

5.   Remove lemon peel. Cool wine slightly and pour over pears.

6.   Serve warm, cool, or chilled, topped with whipped cream.

To do ahead: Steps 1, 2, 4, and 5 may be done up to 2 hours ahead and left at room temperature or up to 1 day ahead and refrigerated, covered. (The pears are prettiest if made ahead, because they will absorb the red color of the wine on standing.) Step 3 may be done up to 3 hours ahead.

NEW ENGLAND MENU

- Cream of Clam Soup

- Stuffed Pork Chops
- Sweet Potatoes with Apples
- Buttered Green Cabbage
  Hard Cider or Sparkling Cider

- Deep-Dish Blueberry Pies
  Coffee

Traditional New England recipes represent old-fashioned country cooking at its best. The down-to-earth goodness of this menu is especially appealing on a cold night. You might begin the meal in front of a cozy fire, serving the clam soup from mugs. The soup isn't a filling chowder, but rather a puréed clam broth to be sipped as a first course.

You could move to the dining room for the main course of stuffed pork chops, sweet potatoes with apples, and cabbage. The stuffed chops are easier to fix than most, since the bread crumb, celery, and sage stuffing is mounded on top of the chops instead of being pushed into pockets and skewered closed.

The few simple ingredients of the sweet potato and apple casserole combine to produce a dish of extraordinary natural flavor that needs no spicing. The alternating slices of sweet potato and apple are quite attractive too. For the green vegetable sliced cabbage is boiled briefly, then tossed with butter and parsley.

Cider is a nice beverage for this menu because it blends well with all the main course dishes. Most dinner wines would taste excessively dry against the sweetness of the sweet potatoes and apples.

The deep-dish blueberry pies are made in custard cups and take only fifteen minutes to assemble. The crust can be shaped in your hands—no rolling required. The pies are served warm, topped with vanilla ice cream.

SHOPPING LIST FOR NEW ENGLAND MENU

Meat, Dairy, Eggs:

☐ 2 rib or loin pork chops (about 1 lb. total), 1 inch thick

☐ butter (1 stick + ½ Tbsp.)

☐ whipping cream (⅓ cup)

☐ vanilla ice cream (2 scoops)

☐ eggs (1 yolk)

Produce:

☐ 1 lemon (need 2 Tbsp. juice)

☐ 1 small onion (need ¼ cup chopped)

☐ celery (⅓ cup chopped)

☐ 1 medium-size (⅔-lb.) slender sweet potato

☐ 1 medium-size (⅓-lb.) green apple

☐ green cabbage (need ½ lb.)

☐ parsley (2 Tbsp. chopped)

Grocery:

☐ 1 can (6½-oz.) clams, such as Gorton's brand

☐ white bread (2 slices)

☐ minute tapioca (1 tsp.)

☐ frozen (unsweetened) blueberries (1 cup)

☐ 1 bottle sparkling cider, if not using hard cider

Liquor:

☐ 1 bottle hard cider, if not using sparkling cider

Check Staples:

☐ salt

☐ black pepper

☐ white pepper

☐ paprika (2 dashes)

☐ ground sage (¼ tsp.)

☐ ground nutmeg (⅛ tsp.)

☐ sugar (¼ cup)

☐ light brown sugar (2 Tbsp.)

☐ flour (⅓ cup)

☐ cornstarch (1½ tsp.)

☐ 1 can (10¾-oz.) condensed chicken broth

☐ coffee

COUNTDOWNS FOR NEW ENGLAND MENU

Last-Minute Countdown

Time in   *Activity*
Minutes

65 minutes ahead:

5   Chill cider; Steps 1–2 of potato dish
5   Step 1 of cabbage
10 Oven to 350°F; Steps 1–2 of soup
     (squeeze 2 tsp. lemon juice for des-
     sert)
10 Steps 3–5 of potato dish
20 Steps 1–5 of pork chops
15 Steps 1–3 of dessert; Step 3 of soup
65

Serving:
Serve soup.
Step 2 of cabbage; pork chops and po-
     tato dish out of oven; oven to
     425°F; Step 4 of dessert
Serve pork chops, potato dish, cabbage,
     and cider.
Dessert out of oven; make coffee.
Serve dessert (Step 5) and coffee.

Plan-Ahead Countdown

Time in   *Activity*
Minutes

One day ahead:

15 Chill cider; Steps 1–5 of potato dish
     (oven to 350°F)
15 (plus 1 hour cooking time)

50 minutes ahead:

10 Steps 1–2 of soup
5   Step 1 of cabbage
20 Steps 1–5 of pork chops (oven to
     350°F)
15 Steps 1–3 of dessert; potato dish in
     oven to reheat; Step 3 of soup
50

Serving:
Serve soup.
Step 2 of cabbage; pork chops and po-
     tato dish out of oven; oven to
     425°F; Step 4 of dessert
Serve pork chops, potato dish, cabbage,
     and cider.
Dessert out of oven; make coffee.
Serve dessert (Step 5) and coffee.

CREAM OF CLAM SOUP

Working and Cooking Time: 10 minutes/Servings: 2

1 can (6½-oz.) clams*
1 cup canned condensed chicken broth, divided
⅛ tsp. ground white pepper

1 egg yolk
1 Tbsp. fresh lemon juice
⅓ cup whipping cream
2 dashes paprika

1.   Purée clams (with their liquid) in blender with ½ cup chicken broth and pepper. Pour into a 1-qt. saucepan. Rinse blender with remaining ½ cup chicken broth and add to pan.

2.   In a 3-cup bowl, whisk together egg yolk, lemon juice, and cream.

3.   Bring clam mixture to a boil and remove from heat. Whisk in cream mixture. Pour into 2 mugs (or soup bowls), garnish with a dash of paprika, and serve.

*Use a reliable brand of canned clams, such as Gorton's, for this soup. Strong, off-flavored clams will spoil it.

To do ahead: Prepare through Step 2 up to 1 hour ahead.

Notes:
1. A 10¾-oz. can of condensed chicken broth is enough for this recipe and the pork chops.
2. If soup is too salty for your taste, add about ¼ cup water to broth and heat slightly (do not boil) before serving.

STUFFED PORK CHOPS

Working Time: 20 minutes/Baking Time: 25 minutes (350°F)/Servings: 2

2 rib or loin pork chops (about 1 lb. total), 1
  inch thick
½ tsp. salt
⅛ tsp. ground black pepper
2½ Tbsp. butter, divided
¼ cup finely chopped onion

⅓ cup finely chopped celery
1 cup fresh white bread crumbs, made in
  blender
¼ tsp. ground sage
¼ cup canned condensed chicken broth

1.   Season chops with salt and pepper and brown in ½ Tbsp. butter in 10-inch skillet over medium-high heat, about 4 minutes on each side. Remove chops to a gratin dish (about 9 inches long).

2.   Turn oven to 350°F.

3.   Reduce heat under skillet to medium, add 2 Tbsp. butter, chopped onion, and celery. Cook until softened, about 3 minutes. Add bread crumbs and cook until toasted, about 3 minutes, stirring frequently.

4.   Stir in sage and chicken broth and remove from heat. With a spoon shape stuffing mixture against side of skillet into 2 portions. Transfer stuffing to top of chops, mounding it smoothly over them.

5.   Bake, uncovered, in center of oven until chops are cooked through, 25 minutes.

To do ahead: Do Steps 1, 3, and 4 up to 30 minutes ahead. Cover and leave at room temperature.

Note: A 10¾-oz. can of condensed chicken broth is enough for this recipe and the clam soup.

SWEET POTATOES WITH APPLES

Working Time: 15 minutes/Cooking Time: 15 minutes more/Baking Time: 45 minutes (350°F)/Servings: 2

1 medium-size (⅔-lb.) slender sweet potato
⅓ cup plus 1 Tbsp. water
2 Tbsp. butter
⅛ tsp. salt

3 Tbsp. sugar
1½ tsp. cornstarch
1 medium-size (⅓-lb.) green apple

1. Peel sweet potato and halve crosswise. Cover with water in a 2-qt. saucepan. Bring to a boil over high heat. Reduce heat to low, cover, and simmer 20 minutes.

2. Bring ⅓ cup water to a boil in a ¾-qt. saucepan, adding butter, salt, and sugar. Mix cornstarch with 1 Tbsp. water in a ½-cup bowl. Add to boiling mixture and stir until thickened, 2 minutes. Set aside.

3. Turn oven to 350°F. Peel apple and cut in half through stem. Core and slice crosswise ¼ inch thick. When potato is done, drain, and slice crosswise ¼ inch thick.

4. Alternate apple and potato slices, overlapping them, in a 7-inch quiche dish. Pour sugar mixture over, making sure apples are coated.

5. Bake, uncovered, in middle of oven for 45 minutes. Cool a few minutes before serving.

To do ahead: Prepare through Step 5, cool, cover, and refrigerate. To serve, reheat, uncovered, in 350°F oven for 10 minutes.

BUTTERED GREEN CABBAGE

Working Time: 5 minutes/Cooking Time: 5 minutes/Servings: 2

1 qt. water
3 cups sliced (¼-inch-wide strips) green cabbage

1 tsp. salt
2 Tbsp. butter
2 Tbsp. chopped parsley

1. Bring water to a boil in a 2-qt. saucepan over high heat. Add cabbage, bring to a boil again, and add salt. Cook, uncovered, 5 minutes. Drain cabbage in a colander.

2. Melt butter in same saucepan over low heat. Add cabbage and parsley, mixing well. Heat through and serve.

To do ahead: Do Step 1 up to 1 hour ahead. Leave at room temperature.

DEEP-DISH BLUEBERRY PIES

Working Time: 15 minutes/Baking Time: 25 minutes (425°F)/Cooling Time: 15 minutes/Servings: 2

1 cup frozen (unsweetened) blueberries
4 tsp. sugar
1 tsp. minute tapioca
2 tsp. fresh lemon juice
⅓ cup all-purpose white flour (do not sift)
Pinch of salt

⅛ tsp. ground nutmeg
2 Tbsp. (packed) light brown sugar
2 Tbsp. butter, slightly softened
2 tsp. (about) cold water
2 scoops vanilla ice cream

1. Turn oven to 425°F. Divide blueberries between 2 buttered 10-oz. custard cups. Sprinkle with sugar, tapioca, and lemon juice.

2. In a 1-qt. bowl mix flour, salt, nutmeg, and brown sugar. Cut in butter with a pastry blender until evenly distributed.

3. With a fork stir in just enough water to enable you to press the mixture together. Shape into 2 equal balls. Flatten each ball with your fingers into a disc just large enough to cover blueberries. Place discs over blueberries.

4. Bake in center of oven until top is browned, about 25 minutes.

5. Cool 15 minutes. Serve warm, topped with ice cream.

To do ahead: Do Steps 1–3 up to 30 minutes ahead.

Note: The blueberries will cook down, leaving plenty of space for big scoops of ice cream.

MEXICAN MENU

- Apple Green Salad

- Pork Chops in Olive Sauce
- Corn, Zucchini, and Tomatoes
  Tortillas
  Beaujolais

- Kahlua Parfaits
  Coffee

Mexican food isn't all enchiladas, tacos, burritos, and tamales—the Mexican repertoire includes more than 2,000 dishes! There must be something for a fresh, fast, flavorful meal. Indeed, the menu selected here meets these criteria splendidly.

For an excellent salad, a crisp chopped apple and a trio of greens—romaine, red-leaf lettuce, and parsley sprigs—are dressed with an unusual chamomile dressing. The chamomile flavor, which is mild and apple-like, is obtained by steeping chamomile tea in cider vinegar and using the flavored vinegar to make the salad dressing.

Pork is a favorite meat in Mexico, and here it's prepared with a Spanish accent in a sauce containing sliced, pimiento-stuffed green olives. The rich sauce glazes the meat attractively and is surprisingly easy to produce. Balancing the pork is a colorful, cumin-flavored sauté of New World vegetables—corn, zucchini, and tomatoes.

A chilled, fruity, young Beaujolais is just right with the pork, as long as you don't increase the hot red pepper in the recipe by too much.

Kahlua parfaits are assemblies of chocolate cookie crumbs, vanilla ice cream, and Kahlua liqueur. Though easy, the combined effect is elegant and delicious.

SHOPPING LIST FOR MEXICAN MENU

Meat, Dairy:

☐ 4 pork chops (1⅓ lbs. total), cut ½ to ¾ inch thick

☐ butter (3 Tbsp. + butter for tortillas)

☐ vanilla ice cream (⅔ pt.)

Produce:

☐ 1 small head Romaine lettuce

☐ 1 small head red-leaf lettuce

☐ parsley (½ cup sprigs)

☐ 1 medium-size (⅓-lb.) apple

☐ 2 small (½ lb. total) onions

☐ 1 medium (6-oz.) tomato

☐ 1 medium (8-oz.) zucchini

☐ 1 lemon (need 1 Tbsp. juice)

Grocery:

☐ chamomile tea (1 tea bag), such as Lipton Quietly Chamomile

☐ pimiento-stuffed green olives (2 Tbsp. sliced)

☐ flour tortillas (4 to 6)

☐ chocolate cookies, such as Pepperidge Farm Chocolate Nut (4 cookies) or Nabisco Chocolate Wafers (6 wafers)

☐ frozen corn (⅓ of a 10-oz. package)

Liquor:

☐ 1 bottle light red wine, such as Beaujolais

☐ Kahlua (2 Tbsp.)

Check Staples:

☐ salt.

☐ black pepper

☐ ground red pepper

☐ ground cumin (¼ tsp.)

☐ paprika (¼ tsp.)

☐ Dijon mustard (½ tsp.)

☐ cider vinegar (¼ cup)

☐ salad oil (⅓ cup)

☐ flour (3 Tbsp.)

☐ coffee

☐ aluminum foil

☐ plastic wrap

☐ paper towels

COUNTDOWNS FOR MEXICAN MENU

Last-Minute Countdown

Time in   *Activity*
Minutes

60 minutes ahead:
15 Chill wine; Steps 1–3 of salad
20 Steps 1–4 of pork
10 Prepare parfaits.
10 Oven to 350° F (for tortillas); Steps
    1–2 of vegetables; take pork off
    heat.
 5 Step 4 of salad; tortillas (wrapped in
    foil) in oven
___
60

Serving:
Serve salad.
Reheat pork; Step 3 of vegetables; un-
    cork wine; Step 5 of pork
Serve pork, vegetables, tortillas, butter,
    and wine.
Make coffee.
Serve parfaits and coffee.

Plan-Ahead Countdown

Time in   *Activity*
Minutes

One day ahead:
15 Chill wine; Steps 1–3 of salad
10 Prepare parfaits.
___
25

35 minutes ahead:
20 Steps 1–4 of pork
10 Oven to 350°F (for tortillas); Steps
    1–2 of vegetables
 5 Step 4 of salad; tortillas (wrapped in
    foil) in oven
___
35

Serving:
Serve salad.
Step 3 of vegetables; uncork wine; Step
    5 of pork
Serve pork, vegetables, tortillas, butter,
    and wine.
Make coffee.
Serve parfaits and coffee.

APPLE GREEN SALAD

Working Time: 20 minutes/Chilling Time: 30 minutes/Servings: 2

CHAMOMILE DRESSING:
¼ cup cider vinegar
1 chamomile tea bag*
¼ tsp. salt
½ tsp. Dijon mustard
¼ cup salad oil

SALAD INGREDIENTS:
1½ cups bite-size pieces red-leaf lettuce
1½ cups bite-size pieces romaine lettuce
½ cup (lightly packed) parsley sprigs, large stems removed
1 medium-size (⅓-lb.) red apple

1. Heat vinegar in a 1-cup metal measuring cup until it bubbles. Add tea bag, remove from heat, and steep 5 minutes.

2. Combine mustard, salt, and 4 tsp. only of the spiced vinegar in a ½-pt. jar. Cover and shake to dissolve salt. Add oil and shake again. Refrigerate.

3. Place salad greens in individual salad bowls. Cover with plastic wrap and refrigerate.

4. At serving time peel, core, and chop apple. Add to salads. Shake dressing and pour over salads.

*Chamomile is a plant of the aster family that is used in herbal teas as a relaxant. It has a mild, apple-like flavor. Chamomile blends are available in supermarkets and health food stores. Lipton makes a blend of chamomile, rosehips, orange peel, hibiscus flowers, and allspice, called "Quietly Chamomile," which is fine for this recipe.

To do ahead: Prepare through Step 3 up to 1 day ahead.

Note: Leftover, spiced vinegar may be saved for another time.

PORK CHOPS IN OLIVE SAUCE

Working Time: 20 minutes/Cooking Time: 20 minutes/Servings: 2

PORK CHOPS:

4 pork chops (1⅓ lbs. total), cut ½ to ¾
  inch thick
½ tsp. salt
⅛ tsp. ground black pepper
⅛ tsp. (or more) ground red pepper
2 Tbsp. flour
1 Tbsp. salad oil
1 Tbsp. butter

OLIVE SAUCE:

¼ cup finely chopped onion
1 Tbsp. flour
¼ tsp. paprika
½ cup water
1 Tbsp. fresh lemon juice
2 Tbsp. sliced pimiento-stuffed green olives

1. Slash fat around chops at 1 inch intervals to prevent curling (trim away excess fat). Dry chops with paper towels. Mix salt, black and red pepper, and 2 Tbsp. flour in a bag. Add chops, two at a time, and shake bag.

2. In a 12-inch skillet or electric frying pan brown chops in oil and butter over medium-high to high heat, about 5 minutes on each side. Remove to a plate.

3. Sauté onion in fat in skillet over low heat for 3 minutes. Stir in 1 Tbsp. flour and the paprika. Cook 1 minute. Add water and lemon juice, stirring until thickened.

4. Return chops to pan, coat with a little sauce, cover, and simmer over low heat for 20 minutes.

5. Place chops on a small platter. Add sliced olives to sauce, spoon over chops, and serve.

To do ahead: Prepare through Step 4 up to 1 hour ahead. Cover and leave at room temperature. Reheat over low heat before continuing with Step 5.

CORN, ZUCCHINI, AND TOMATOES

Working Time: 10 minutes/Cooking Time: 6 minutes more/Servings: 2

2 Tbsp. butter
1 small onion, peeled, quartered, layers separated
⅔ cup frozen corn
¼ tsp. ground cumin

1 medium-large (8-oz.) zucchini
1 Tbsp. water
¼ tsp. salt, divided
1 medium-size (6-oz.) tomato

1. In a 9-inch skillet over medium heat sauté onion, corn, and cumin in but-ter until onion softens slightly, 5 minutes.

2. Cut zucchini in half lengthwise, then on the diagonal to make ½-inch-wide slices. Cut tomato in 8 wedges.

3. Add zucchini, water, and ⅛ tsp. salt to skillet. Cover and steam 5 minutes. Sprinkle tomato with ⅛ teaspoon salt. Add to skillet, cover, and heat 1 minute. Transfer to a small serving dish.

To do ahead: Prepare through Step 2 up to 1 hour ahead. Cover and leave at room temperature.

KAHLUA PARFAITS

Working Time: 10 minutes/Servings: 2

4 to 6 chocolate cookies*, crushed in
  blender
2 Tbsp. Kahlua**

4 large scoops vanilla ice cream (about ⅔
  pt.)

1. Layer ingredients into 8-oz. wine or parfait glasses as follows (for each glass):

> 1 Tbsp. cookie crumbs
> ½ tsp. Kahlua
> 1 scoop ice cream (pack down)
> 2 Tbsp. cookie crumbs
> 1 tsp. Kahlua
> 1 scoop ice cream (pack down)
> 1½ tsp. Kahlua
> ¼ tsp. cookie crumbs

2. Serve at once or cover with plastic wrap and store in freezer.

*Use 4 Pepperidge Farm Chocolate Nut Cookies (preferably) or 6 Nabisco Chocolate Wafers.
**Kahlua is a sweet coffee liqueur produced in Mexico and available in any liquor store.

To do ahead: May be prepared several days ahead.

SAUSAGE AND CURED-MEAT MENUS

Swiss Menu
German Menu
Southern Italian Menu
Polish Menu
Southern Menu
Irish Menu

SWISS MENU

- Lemon Barley Soup

- Swiss Bratwurst with Winter Vegetables
  California Gewürztraminer

- Sugar-Topped Baked Apples with Cream
  Coffee

For proof that sausage can make a handsome meal, try this Swiss menu that features delicate veal sausages.

The dinner begins with a lemon barley soup that's enriched with cream and an egg yolk, but that's not too filling for a first course. Chopped tomato, added at the last minute, provides color and flavor.

Sausages are a great favorite in Switzerland, including the flavorful Swiss-style bratwurst. It's a cooked, lightly spiced, almost white, unsmoked sausage made of lean veal and pork. It's similar to German bockwurst, except that the German sausage has onion and parsley added. The vegetables called for are brussels sprouts, red-skinned potatoes, carrots, and parsnips. They are quite attractive piled on a platter with the bratwurst, drizzled with butter, and topped with chopped parsley.

Too elegant for beer, this meal deserves a pleasantly spicy wine. A California Gewürztraminer on the dry side, such as that made by Simi or Louis Martini wineries, would be perfect.

Baked apples are a comforting, nostalgic dessert enjoyed by almost everyone. In this version the apples are peeled completely, then topped with a sugar mixture that forms a light crust and also creates a sauce. For total indulgence, serve the apples with heavy cream to be poured over them.

SHOPPING LIST FOR SWISS MENU

Meat, Dairy, Eggs:

☐ ⅔ lb. Swiss-style bratwurst or German bockwurst

☐ butter (6 Tbsp.)

☐ whipping cream (¾ cup)

☐ eggs (1 yolk)

Produce:

☐ 1 small (4-oz.) tomato

☐ 1 lemon (need 5 tsp. juice)

☐ parsley (4 tsp. chopped)

☐ 8 medium-size (⅓ lb.) brussels sprouts, or use frozen

☐ 1 large (⅓-lb.) carrot

☐ 2 small parsnips (½ lb. total)

☐ 2 small red-skinned potatoes (½ lb. total)

☐ 2 medium-size green apples (⅔ lb. total)

Grocery:

☐ pearl barley (¼ cup)

☐ 1 pkg. (10-oz.) frozen brussels sprouts (need ½), if not using fresh

Liquor:

☐ 1 bottle spicy white wine, such as California Gewürtztraminer (especially Simi or Martini)

Check Staples:

☐ salt

☐ black pepper

☐ ground cinnamon (¼ tsp.)

☐ 1 can (10¾-oz.) condensed chicken broth

☐ sugar (⅓ cup)

☐ mustard, such as Dijon or Düsseldorf (as condiment)

☐ horseradish (as condiment)

☐ coffee

☐ toothpicks

COUNTDOWNS FOR SWISS MENU

Last-Minute Countdown

Time in   Activity
Minutes

55 minutes ahead:

15   Steps 1–3 of soup (squeeze 2 Tbsp.
     lemon juice for dessert, chop 1
     Tbsp. parsley for vegetables)
20   Steps 1–4 of dessert (oven to 375°F)
<u>20</u>   Steps 1–4 of sausage and vegetables
55

Serving:

Serve soup (Step 4).

Step 5 of sausage and vegetables (remove dessert from oven when done).

Serve sausage and vegetables, mustard,
horseradish, and wine.

Make coffee.

Serve dessert (Step 5) and coffee.

Plan-Ahead Countdown

Time in   Activity
Minutes

One day ahead:

20   Steps 1–4 of dessert (oven to 375°F)
15   Steps 1–3 of soup
<u>35</u>   plus 30 minutes more cooking time
     for dessert

20 minutes ahead:

20   Steps 1–4 of sausage and vegetables;
     reheat soup.

Serving:

Serve soup (Step 4).

Oven to 350°F (for dessert); Step 5 of
sausage and vegetables

Serve sausage and vegetables, horseradish, and wine.

(15 minutes before serving dessert put in
oven to reheat.)

Make coffee.

Serve dessert (Step 5) and coffee.

LEMON BARLEY SOUP

Working Time: 15 minutes/Cooking Time: 40 minutes/Servings: 2

1 can (10¾-oz.) condensed chicken broth	1 egg yolk
⅔ cup water	1 Tbsp. fresh lemon juice
1 small (4-oz.) tomato	¼ cup whipping cream
¼ cup pearl barley*	1 tsp. finely chopped parsley

1. In a heavy 1½-qt. saucepan bring chicken broth and water to a boil over high heat. Put tomato in broth and roll around for 30 seconds. Remove tomato. Add barley, cover, reduce heat, and simmer until barley is chewy-tender, about 35 minutes.

2. Slip skin off tomato. Seed and chop tomato and set aside.

3. In a 1-cup bowl whisk together egg yolk, lemon juice, and cream.

4. When barley is done, whisk in egg mixture. Do not allow to boil. Add chopped tomato and heat through, 1 minute. Pour into soup bowls and garnish with parsley.

*Pearl barley is the barley grain after the outer and inner husks have been removed and the grain polished. It's available in the rice section of grocery stores.

To do ahead: Do Steps 1–3 up to 1 day ahead. Cover and refrigerate (separately).

SWISS BRATWURST WITH WINTER VEGETABLES

Working Time: 20 minutes/Cooking Time: 10 minutes more/Servings: 2

1 qt. water	8 medium-size (⅓ lb.) brussels sprouts,
2 tsp. salt	fresh or frozen
1 large (⅓-lb.) carrot	4 Tbsp. butter, divided
2 small parsnips (½ lb. total)	1 Tbsp. finely chopped parsley
2 small red-skinned potatoes (½ lb. total), quartered	Mustard, such as Dijon or Düsseldorf Horseradish
⅔ lb. Swiss-style bratwurst or German bockwurst*	

1.   Bring water to a rapid boil in a 3-qt. saucepan, adding salt. Peel carrot and parsnips. Slice on the diagonal ½ inch thick. Add carrot, parsnips, and potatoes to boiling water. Cover, reduce heat, and simmer 7 minutes.

2.   Bring ½ cup water to a boil in an 8-inch skillet. Prick sausages with a fork in several places. Add to skillet, cover, and simmer 3 minutes.

3.   If using fresh brussels sprouts, trim them and cut a ¼-inch-deep "X" in stem end. Melt 3½ Tbsp. butter in a ½-cup metal measuring cup over low heat.

4.   Drain sausages and add ½ Tbsp. butter to skillet. Brown sausages over medium-high heat, about 10 minutes total time. Cover and keep warm over low heat.

5.   Meanwhile, when root vegetables have boiled 7 minutes, uncover, raise heat to high, and add brussels sprouts. Boil until all vegetables are tender when tested with a toothpick, 8 minutes.

6.   Pour contents of saucepan into a colander. Place sausages on a platter and surround with vegetables. Pour melted butter over vegetables and sprinkle with parsley. Serve with mustard and horseradish.

*Swiss-style bratwurst is a cooked, lightly spiced, unsmoked, fine-textured, almost white sausage made of lean veal and pork, milk, and eggs. German bockwurst is similar, but has chopped green onions and parsley added. These sausages are available in some delicatessens and supermarkets. Regular bratwurst, which is German in origin, is a different sausage that is darker in color and comes in fresh (uncooked) or smoked versions.

To do ahead: Prepare vegetables for cooking and chop parsley up to 1 hour ahead. Cover and leave at room temperature.

SUGAR-TOPPED BAKED APPLES WITH CREAM

Working Time: 15 minutes/Baking Time: 45 minutes (375°F)/Cooling Time: 15 minutes/Servings: 2

2 Tbsp. butter, slightly softened
¼ cup sugar
¼ tsp. ground cinnamon
2 Tbsp. flour
1 tsp. water

2 medium-size green apples (⅔ lb. total)
2 tsp. fresh lemon juice
2 Tbsp. water
½ cup (about) whipping cream

1. Turn oven to 375°F. In a 3-cup bowl cream together butter, sugar, cinnamon, and flour until smooth. Mix in water.

2. Peel apples and core them with a melon-ball cutter without cutting through at the blossom end. Divide lemon juice and water between two 10-oz. custard cups. Roll apples around in liquid to coat.

3. Place 1 Tbsp. sugar mixture in each apple cavity. Shape remaining mixture into 2 balls, flatten, and press over tops of apples.

4. Bake in center of oven until apples are tender when pierced with a toothpick, 35 to 45 minutes.

5. Serve warm, passing a small pitcher of cream to pour over apples.

To do ahead: Prepare through Step 4 up to 1 day ahead. Cool, cover, and refrigerate. To serve, warm in a 350°F oven for 15 minutes.

Note: During baking, part of the sugar mixture will melt from the apples to form a sauce.

GERMAN MENU

- Caraway Mushroom Bouillon
- Knockwurst with Red Cabbage
- Herbed New Potatoes and Peas
  German Beer

- Gingerbread Oven Pancakes with Banana Sauce
  Coffee

Hearty German fare is a good choice when the weather is cool and a substantial meal seems in order.

Begin with a warming soup, quickly made—beef broth flavored with caraway, marjoram, chives, and grated mushrooms. The raw mushrooms give the soup a unique, earthy flavor.

Follow with a main dish of baked sausages on a bed of sweet and sour red cabbage. Knockwurst or garlic sausages can be used and are a great favorite in Germany. The red cabbage (finely sliced) is first sautéed in butter with a little onion, then cooked briefly with a chopped tart apple, red wine vinegar, sugar, and cloves, before going into the oven.

Serve boiled potatoes and peas on the side with plenty of butter and sautéed green onions, some parsley and thyme. A bay leaf added to the water in which the potatoes cook gives them a nice fresh flavor.

Drink a good German beer (such as Lowenbrau, Heineken, or Beck's), the natural accompaniment for this meal.

Finish with a German oven pancake, in this case individual gingerbread pancakes made in 4-inch pie pans. The pancakes puff up around the edges as they bake. When removed to serving plates, they can be filled with a hot topping—ideally, sliced bananas in a butterscotch syrup.

SHOPPING LIST FOR GERMAN MENU

Meat, Dairy, Eggs:

- [ ] 2 knockwurst or garlic sausages (⅔ lb. total)
- [ ] butter (7 Tbsp.)
- [ ] whipping cream (¼ cup)
- [ ] eggs (1)

Produce:

- [ ] 2 medium-large mushrooms (⅛ lb. total)
- [ ] 1 lemon (need 2 tsp. juice)
- [ ] chives (2 tsp. chopped), or use frozen
- [ ] 1 small onion (need 2 Tbsp. chopped)
- [ ] green onions (2 Tbsp. chopped)
- [ ] 1 small red cabbage (need 2 cups finely sliced)
- [ ] 1 small (4-oz.) green apple
- [ ] 2 medium-size new potatoes (⅔ lb. total)
- [ ] parsley (2 Tbsp. chopped)
- [ ] 1 medium-size banana*

Grocery:

- [ ] frozen chives (2 tsp.), if not using fresh

- [ ] 1 pkg. (10-oz.) frozen green peas (need ½ cup)
- [ ] light molasses (¼ cup)

Liquor:

- [ ] 2 bottles (or more) German beer, such as Lowenbrau, Heineken, or Beck's

Check Staples:

- [ ] salt
- [ ] white pepper
- [ ] caraway seeds (½ tsp.)
- [ ] dried marjoram (⅛ tsp.)
- [ ] dried thyme (⅛ tsp.)
- [ ] bay leaves (1)
- [ ] ground cloves (⅛ tsp.)
- [ ] ground ginger (½ tsp.)
- [ ] ground cinnamon (¼ tsp.)
- [ ] sugar (2 Tbsp.)
- [ ] light brown sugar (¼ cup)
- [ ] flour (¼ cup)
- [ ] red wine vinegar (1½ Tbsp.)
- [ ] 1 can (14½-oz.) single-strength beef broth
- [ ] coffee

*May need to be purchased several days ahead to allow for ripening.

COUNTDOWNS FOR GERMAN MENU

Last-Minute Countdown

Time in   Activity
Minutes

50 minutes ahead:

15 Chill beer; Steps 1–2 of sausage
    dish
10 Turn oven to 400°F; Steps 1–2 of
    soup
 5 Step 3 of sausage dish
10 Steps 2 and 4 of dessert
10 Step 1 of potatoes and peas (chop
__ onions and parsley)
50

Serving:

Serve soup (Step 3).
Steps 2–3 of potatoes and peas
Serve sausage dish (leave oven on for
    dessert), potatoes and peas, and beer.
(20 minutes before serving dessert do
    Steps 1 and 3.)
Make coffee.
Serve dessert (Step 5) and coffee.

Plan-Ahead Countdown

Time in   Activity
Minutes

One day ahead:

15 Chill beer, Steps 1–2 of sausage
    dish
10 Steps 1–2 of soup
25

35 minutes ahead:

10 Turn oven to 400°F; Steps 2 and 4
    of dessert
 5 Step 3 of sausage dish
15

10 minutes ahead:

10 Step 1 of potatoes and peas (chop
    onions and parsley)

Serving:

Serve soup (Step 3).
Steps 2–3 of potatoes and peas
Serve sausage dish (leave oven on for
    dessert), potatoes and peas, and beer.
(20 minutes before serving dessert do
    Steps 1 and 3.)
Make coffee.
Serve dessert (Step 5) and coffee.

CARAWAY MUSHROOM BOUILLON

Working and Cooking Time: 10 minutes/Servings: 2

1 can (14½-oz.) single-strength beef broth
½ tsp. caraway seeds
⅛ tsp. dried marjoram
Pinch of ground white pepper

2 medium-large mushrooms (⅛ lb. total)
1 tsp. fresh lemon juice
2 tsp. fresh or frozen chopped chives

1. In a 1-qt. saucepan bring broth to a boil over high heat while adding caraway, marjoram, and pepper. Reduce heat, cover, and simmer 5 minutes.

2. Finely grate mushrooms and divide between two soup bowls. Add ½ tsp. lemon juice to each bowl and mix. Sprinkle each with 1 tsp. chives.

3. To serve, pour hot broth into soup bowls, leaving caraway seeds in saucepan.

To do ahead: Do Steps 1–2 up to 1 day ahead. Cover and refrigerate separately.

KNOCKWURST WITH RED CABBAGE

Working Time: 20 minutes/Cooking Time: 10 minutes/Baking Time: 30 minutes (400°F)/Servings: 2

1 Tbsp. butter
2 Tbsp. finely chopped onion
2 cups finely sliced red cabbage (⅓ lb.)
1 small (4-oz.) green apple, peeled, cored, and finely chopped
½ tsp. salt

2 Tbsp. sugar
⅛ tsp. ground cloves
1½ Tbsp. red wine vinegar
2 knockwurst* or garlic sausages (⅔ lb. total)

1. Sauté onion in butter in a 2-qt. saucepan over medium heat for 3 minutes. Add cabbage and sauté 3 minutes.

2. Turn oven to 400°F. Add remaining ingredients to cabbage, except sausage. Cover and cook for 10 minutes.

3. Make 3 diagonal gashes about ¼ inch deep along one side of sausage. Transfer cabbage mixture to a gratin dish (about 10 inches long). Place sausage over cabbage, slit side up. Bake in upper third of oven until sausage browns, about 30 minutes. Serve from gratin dish.

*Knockwurst (sometimes spelled knackwurst) is a meaty German sausage available in most delicatessens and supermarkets.

To do ahead: Do Steps 1–2 up to 2 days ahead. Cover and refrigerate.

Note: The cooked red cabbage mixture freezes well, so if you wish to use up a whole small red cabbage, you can triple or quadruple the recipe and freeze the extra amount. Cook the mixture another 20 minutes if you wish to have it completely cooked before freezing. (In this recipe the cooking is finished in the oven.)

HERBED NEW POTATOES AND PEAS

Working Time: 15 minutes/Cooking Time: 20 minutes/Servings: 2

2 cups water
1½ tsp. salt
1 bay leaf
2 medium-size new potatoes (⅔ lb. total),
    peeled and quartered

½ cup frozen green peas
3 Tbsp. butter
2 Tbsp. chopped green onions
2 Tbsp. finely chopped parsley
⅛ tsp. dried thyme

1. In a 1½-qt. saucepan bring water to a boil over high heat, adding salt, bay leaf, and potatoes. Reduce heat to low, cover, and simmer until potatoes are just tender, 12 to 15 minutes.

2. Add peas to saucepan with potatoes. Cook until peas are hot and potatoes tender, about 3 minutes. Drain in a colander.

3. Melt butter in same saucepan over medium heat. Add green onions, parsley, and thyme. Cook until onion is soft, 2 minutes. Add potatoes and peas and toss to coat with butter. Serve in a small vegetable dish.

To do ahead: Best if made just before serving.

GINGERBREAD OVEN PANCAKES WITH BANANA SAUCE

Working Time: 15 minutes/Baking Time: 20 minutes (400°F)/Servings: 2

GINGERBREAD PANCAKES:
1 Tbsp. butter
¼ cup water
¼ cup light molasses
1 egg
¼ cup flour
1 Tbsp. sugar
½ tsp. ground ginger
¼ tsp. ground cinnamon

BANANA SAUCE:
2 Tbsp. butter
¼ cup (packed) light brown sugar
¼ cup whipping cream
1 tsp. fresh lemon juice
1 medium-size ripe banana, peeled, sliced ¼
  inch thick

1. Turn oven to 400°F. Put ½ Tbsp. butter in each of two 4-inch pie pans. Set on a baking sheet and put in center of oven.

2. Place ingredients for pancakes (except butter) in blender and blend, scraping down sides of blender as necessary.

3. When butter has melted, reblend batter a few seconds, if necessary, and pour into pans. Bake until brown and puffed around the edges, about 20 minutes.

4. Meanwhile, put 2 Tbsp. butter, brown sugar, and cream in a ¾-qt. saucepan and boil 2 minutes. Remove from heat and add sliced banana and lemon juice.

5. When pancakes are almost ready, reheat banana sauce. When pancakes are done, slide from pans and place on serving plates. Fill with hot banana sauce and serve.

To do ahead: Do Steps 2 and 4 up to 1 hour ahead. Cover and leave at room temperature.

SOUTHERN ITALIAN MENU

- Cucumber, Tomato, Watercress, and Anchovy Salad
- Roasted Italian Sausages, Potatoes, and Peppers
  Italian Bread
  Lambrusco
- Lemon Gelato
  Lemon Nut Cookies
  Coffee

Southern Italian cooking tends to be simpler and more robust than Northern Italian cooking; it depends on olive oil more than butter, tomatoes more than cream. The menu selected here is one of the easiest in this book to execute, yet it's attractive, delicious, and satisfying.

The first course is a cucumber and tomato salad, mixed with sprigs of watercress and anchovy fillets. An herbed Italian dressing enhances and blends the flavors of the salad.

The sausage and vegetable entrée takes only fifteen minutes to have oven-ready. "Italian sausage" refers to the wonderful, fresh, fennel-flavored sausage available in this country. Roasting the sausages allows them to yield their excess fat while browning. The vegetables—potatoes, sweet red and green peppers, and onions—are cut up and tossed in olive oil and chopped rosemary and roasted alongside the sausages. In half an hour the sausages are ready to be served, surrounded by the colorful vegetables.

Crusty Italian (or French) bread is a good accompaniment for this meal, as is Lambrusco (borrowed from Northern Italy), a light, zingy, slightly sparkling red wine, best served chilled.

Gelato is the Italian word for ice cream, and this lemon version is light and refreshing and bursting with flavor. You can purchase the crisp lemon nut cookies, which are nice to serve with the gelato.

SHOPPING LIST FOR SOUTHERN ITALIAN MENU

Meat, Dairy, Eggs:

☐ 4 mild Italian sausages (⅔ lb. total)

☐ whipping cream (⅓ cup)

☐ butter (for bread)

☐ eggs (1)

Produce:

☐ 1 small (8-oz.) cucumber

☐ 1 medium-size (6-oz.) tomato

☐ 1 bunch watercress (1 cup)

☐ 1 medium-large (8-oz.) baking potato

☐ 1 small green pepper

☐ 1 small red pepper (not hot)

☐ 1 small onion

☐ garlic (1 tsp. minced)

☐ fresh rosemary (1 tsp.), or use dried

☐ 1 large or 2 medium-size lemons (need ½ tsp. grated peel + ¼ cup juice)

Grocery:

☐ anchovy fillets (4)

☐ Italian salad dressing, such as Wish-Bone (¼ cup)

☐ crusty Italian (or French) bread

☐ Lemon Nut Crunch cookies (Pepperidge Farm)

Liquor:

☐ 1 bottle Lambrusco wine

Check Staples:

☐ salt

☐ black pepper

☐ dried rosemary (¼ tsp.)

☐ sugar (½ cup)

☐ olive oil (1 Tbsp.)

☐ coffee

☐ plastic wrap

COUNTDOWNS FOR SOUTHERN ITALIAN MENU

Last-Minute Countdown
Time in   Activity
Minutes

90 minutes ahead:
10   Steps 1–2 of dessert

45 minutes ahead:
15   Chill wine; Steps 1–2 of salad
15   Steps 1–2 of sausages and vege-
___   tables (oven to 425°F)
30

Serving:
Serve salad (Step 3).
(Turn sausages.)
Uncork wine.
Serve sausages and vegetables (Step 3),
   bread, butter, and wine.
Make coffee.
Serve dessert (Step 3) and serve coffee
   with or after dessert.

Plan-Ahead Countdown
Time in   Activity
Minutes

One day ahead:
15   Steps 1–2 of salad
10   Steps 1–2 of dessert
25

30 minutes ahead:
15   Chill wine; Steps 1–2 of sausages
      and vegetables (oven to 425°F)

Serving:
Serve salad (Step 3).
(Turn sausages.)
Uncork wine.
Serve sausages and vegetables (Step 3),
   bread, butter, and wine.
Make coffee.
Serve dessert (Step 3) and serve coffee
   with or after dessert.

CUCUMBER, TOMATO, WATERCRESS, AND ANCHOVY SALAD

Working Time: 15 minutes/Chilling Time: 30 minutes/Servings: 2

1 small (8-oz.) cucumber
1 medium-size (6-oz.) tomato, cut in thin
   wedges
1 cup (lightly packed) watercress, large
   stems removed

4 anchovies, drained on a paper towel, each
   cut in 4 pieces
¼ cup (about) Italian salad dressing, such as
   Wish-bone
Freshly ground black pepper

1. Peel cucumber and score lengthwise with a fork. Slice in half lengthwise and scoop out seeds. Slice crosswise ¼ inch thick.

2. Divide cucumber, tomato, watercress, and anchovies between 2 salad bowls. Cover with plastic wrap and refrigerate.

3. To serve, pour dressing over salads. Pass peppermill at the table.

To do ahead: Prepare up to 1 day ahead.

ROASTED ITALIAN SAUSAGES, POTATOES, AND PEPPERS

Working Time: 15 minutes/Roasting Time: 30 minutes (425°F)/Servings: 2

1 medium-large (8-oz.) baking potato,
   peeled, cut in ¾ inch dice
1 Tbsp. olive oil
1 small onion, peeled, quartered, layers separated
1 small green pepper, cut in 1 inch squares
1 small red pepper (not hot), cut in 1 inch
   squares

1 tsp. chopped fresh rosemary, or ¼ tsp.
   dried
¼ tsp. salt
⅛ tsp. ground black pepper
4 mild Italian sausages (⅔ lb. total)

1. Turn oven to 425°F. In a shallow 2-qt. baking dish toss potato cubes with olive oil. Add remaining ingredients, except sausages, and mix well.

2.   With a fork prick sausages in a few places. Lay on a rack in a small broiling pan. Roast sausages and vegetables, uncovered, turning sausages over after 20 minutes. Roast until sausages are lightly browned and edges of some of the vegetables start to char, about 30 minutes total.

3.   Serve sausages on a small platter surrounded by the roasted vegetables.

To do ahead: Do Step 1 up to 1 hour ahead. Leave at room temperature.

LEMON GELATO

Working Time: 10 minutes/Freezing Time: 2½ hours/Servings: 2

1 egg
½ cup sugar
¼ cup cold water
½ tsp. grated lemon peel

¼ cup strained fresh lemon juice
⅓ cup whipping cream
Lemon Nut Crunch cookies (Pepperidge Farm)

1.   Combine egg, sugar, water, and lemon peel and juice in blender, whirling at high speed for 1 minute. Add cream and blend a few seconds.

2.   Pour into freezer tray and freeze at least 2½ hours. Pack into a freezer container for storage.

3.   Serve gelato in small compotes, accompanied by the cookies.

To do ahead: May be prepared up to 1 week ahead.

POLISH MENU

- Red Beet Soup
- Kielbasa, Cabbage, Mushroom, and Tomato Sauté
- Poppy Seed Biscuits
  California Gewürtztraminer

- Buttered Rum Fruit Compotes
  Coffee

Polish cooking is hearty and hospitable, the kind of food you can feel at home with. Try this country-style menu for an informal, happy occasion.

The soup is made quickly in the blender from canned beets and tomato juice. Green onion, lemon juice, sour cream, pepper, and dill perk up the flavor. For such an easy soup, it's remarkably good.

Kielbasa is a smoked, garlic-flavored Polish sausage made from ground pork and beef. It becomes a complete meal when sliced and sautéed with mushrooms, onions, cabbage, and chopped tomato. The acidity of the tomato balances the richness of the sausage and is colorful too.

Bread fresh from the oven is a welcome accompaniment to any meal, and these homemade biscuits sprinkled with poppy seeds are especially appropriate for this one.

A nice choice for the wine is a Gewürtztraminer with a touch of sweetness, such as those made by Almaden and Buena Vista wineries in California.

A dried fruit compote in hot buttered rum sauce makes a delightful dessert. The fruit might be a combination of dried pears, peaches, apricots, and prunes. The dessert is topped with plain whipped cream to mellow the intensity of the fruit flavors.

SHOPPING LIST FOR POLISH MENU

Meat, Dairy:

- ☐ ⅔ lb. kielbasa (Polish sausage)
- ☐ butter (2½ Tbsp. + butter for biscuits)
- ☐ sour cream (⅔ cup)
- ☐ whipping cream (⅓ cup)
- ☐ milk (⅓ cup)

Produce:

- ☐ ¼ lb. mushrooms
- ☐ 1 medium-size (6-oz.) tomato
- ☐ green cabbage (½ lb., 3 cups sliced)
- ☐ 1 lemon (need 1 tsp. juice)
- ☐ 1 orange (need 1 slice)
- ☐ 1 medium-size onion
- ☐ green onions (1 Tbsp. chopped)
- ☐ parsley (2 Tbsp. chopped)
- ☐ dill (1 tsp. chopped), or use dried

Grocery:

- ☐ 1 can (8-oz.) sliced beets
- ☐ 1 can (6-oz.) tomato juice
- ☐ ¼ lb. mixed, dried fruit (4 prunes and 2 each pear, peach, and apricot halves)

Liquor:

- ☐ 1 bottle Gewürztztraminer, such as that from Almaden or Buena Vista wineries
- ☐ light rum (2 Tbsp.)

Check Staples:

- ☐ salt
- ☐ white pepper
- ☐ whole cinnamon (1 stick)
- ☐ dried dill weed (¼ tsp.), if not using fresh
- ☐ poppy seeds (2 tsp.)
- ☐ sugar (¼ cup)
- ☐ all-purpose white flour (1¼ cups)
- ☐ baking powder (1½ tsp.)
- ☐ lard or shortening (3 Tbsp.)
- ☐ coffee

COUNTDOWNS FOR POLISH MENU

Last-Minute Countdown

Time in Minutes	Activity

60 minutes ahead:

15 Chill wine; Steps 1–2 of dessert
10 Step 1 of soup; Step 2 of biscuits
10 Step 3 of dessert; Steps 1–2 of kielbasa and slice onion.
10 Step 1 of biscuits (oven to 450°F); Steps 3–4 of kielbasa
10 Step 3 of biscuits; remove cabbage from heat; Step 4 of biscuits
5 Step 2 of soup; uncork wine.
60

Serving:
Serve soup.
Biscuits out of oven; Step 5 of kielbasa
Serve kielbasa, biscuits, and wine.
Make coffee.
Serve dessert (Step 4) and coffee.

Plan-Ahead Countdown

Time in Minutes	Activity

One day ahead:

20 Chill wine; Step 1 of dessert
10 Step 1 of soup; Step 2 of biscuits; Step 3 of dessert
20 (plus 10 minutes more cooking time for dessert)

40 minutes ahead:

5 Step 2 of dessert
10 Steps 1–2 of kielbasa and slice onion.
10 Step 1 of biscuits (oven to 450°F); Steps 3–4 of kielbasa
10 Step 3 of biscuits; remove cabbage from heat; Step 4 of biscuits
5 Step 2 of soup; uncork wine.
40

Serving:
Serve soup.
Biscuits out of oven; Step 5 of kielbasa
Serve kielbasa, biscuits, and wine.
Make coffee and warm fruit for dessert.
Serve dessert (Step 4) and coffee.

RED BEET SOUP

Working and Cooking Time: 10 minutes/Servings: 2

1 can (8-oz.) sliced beets
1 Tbsp. chopped green onion
1 can (6-oz.) tomato juice
⅛ tsp. salt
Dash of ground white pepper

1 tsp. fresh lemon juice
3 Tbsp. (about) sour cream
1 tsp. chopped fresh or frozen dill weed, or
    ¼ tsp. dried

1.   Purée beets (with liquid from can) and green onion in blender. Pour into a 1-qt. saucepan and add tomato juice, salt, white pepper, and lemon juice.

2.   Heat beet mixture to boiling. Pour into 2 soup bowls. Top each serving with a large dollop of sour cream and sprinkle with dill weed.

To do ahead: Do Step 1 up to 1 day ahead. Cover and refrigerate.

Note: This soup is also good served chilled.

KIELBASA, CABBAGE, MUSHROOM, AND TOMATO SAUTÉ

Working Time: 20 minutes/Cooking Time: 10 minutes more/Servings: 2

¼ lb. mushrooms, sliced ⅛ inch thick
1½ Tbsp. butter
⅔ lb. kielbasa*, sliced ⅓ inch thick
1 medium-size onion, peeled, halved, and
    sliced ⅛ inch thick
3 cups finely sliced green cabbage

⅛ tsp. salt
1 medium-size (6-oz.) tomato, cut in ½ inch
    dice
2 Tbsp. finely chopped parsley
⅓ cup (about) dairy sour cream

1.   In a 10-inch skillet with a nonstick surface sauté mushrooms in butter over medium-high heat until lightly browned, about 4 minutes. Remove to a plate.

2.   Brown sausage slices on both sides in same skillet over medium heat, about 6 minutes. Remove to plate with mushrooms.

3.   Discard all but 1½ Tbsp. sausage fat. Sauté onion in fat until soft, 5 minutes.

4.   Add cabbage and salt to skillet and sauté 5 minutes more.

5.   Return mushrooms and sausage to skillet, and add tomato and parsley. Toss and heat through. Serve in wide soup plates, with sour cream on the side.

*Kielbasa is a smoked, garlic-flavored Polish sausage made from ground pork and beef. It's available in delicatessens and supermarkets.

To do ahead: May be prepared through Step 4 up to 30 minutes ahead. Leave at room temperature.

POPPY SEED BISCUITS

Working Time: 15 minutes/Baking Time: 12 minutes (450°F)/Yield: 8 to 9 biscuits/Servings: 2 to 3

1 cup all-purpose white flour (do not sift)	*⅓ cup milk*
1½ tsp. baking powder	*Flour for rolling out biscuits*
½ tsp. salt	*1 Tbsp. (about) sour cream*
3 Tbsp. lard or shortening	*2 tsp. (about) poppy seeds*

1.   Turn oven to 450°F.

2.   In a 1-qt. bowl stir together flour, baking powder, and salt. With a pastry blender cut in lard or shortening until evenly distributed.

3.   With a fork stir milk into dry mixture and form into a ball. On a floured surface knead mixture a few strokes, then roll out to ½-inch thickness. Cut out 4 to 5 two-inch biscuits. Reroll and cut out remaining biscuits.

4.   Spread top of each biscuit with about ⅓ tsp. sour cream and sprinkle with ¼ tsp. poppy seeds. Place on a small baking sheet and bake in upper third of oven until lightly browned, 10 to 12 minutes.

To do ahead: Do Step 2 up to 1 day ahead. Cover and leave at room temperature.

BUTTERED RUM FRUIT COMPOTES

Working Time: 15 minutes/Cooking Time: 20 minutes/Servings: 2

1 cup water
¼ cup sugar
¼ lb. mixed dried fruit*
1 cinnamon stick

1 orange slice
⅓ cup whipping cream
1 Tbsp. butter
2 Tbsp. light rum

1.   In a ¾-qt. saucepan combine water, sugar, dried fruit, cinnamon stick, and orange slice. Bring to a boil, lower heat, cover, and simmer 10 minutes.

2.   In a 3-cup bowl with a rotary beater whip cream until stiff. Cover and refrigerate.

3.   Uncover saucepan, remove cinnamon stick and orange slice. Boil down liquid over medium-high heat until reduced to ¼ cup, 8 to 10 minutes.

4.   Remove from heat and stir in butter and rum. Divide fruit and juices between two compotes and serve warm, topped with whipped cream.

*From a package of mixed, dried fruit select 4 prunes and 2 each pear, peach, and apricot halves (or make your own choice). Quarter the pear and peach halves and cut apricot halves in half.

To do ahead: Do Steps 1 and 3 up to 2 days ahead. Cool, cover, and refrigerate. Do Step 2 up to 3 hours ahead. Reheat fruit before serving.

SOUTHERN MENU

- Celery Leaf and Carrot Salad
- Ham with Apricots and Bananas
- Green Beans with Pecans
  Dinner Rolls
  Mateus

- Cointreau Custards
  Coffee

Southerners seem to have a knack for taking ordinary foods and creating extraordinary meals. Here's an example of such a meal. Good things happen to plain old celery, ham, green beans, and custard with a little Creole mustard, chutney, pecans, and Cointreau.

Celery is not often thought of as a salad green, but the bright green, leafy tops (along with part of the stalks) can be used that way and make a wonderfully refreshing, crunchy salad. The celery is marinated with grated carrot in a Creole vinaigrette dressing—and it stays crisp!

Southern menus often feature baked ham, and a leftover slice of ham (or a purchased slice) can make a quick main dish for two. One easy and different idea is to top the ham with apricot halves and sliced bananas, coat with a chutney sauce, and glaze under the broiler. The fruit cuts the saltiness of the ham and is visually pleasing and tasty too.

Green beans make a fine accompaniment for the ham and are marvelous with a topping of butter-browned pecans.

For the beverage a chilled rosé wine on the sweet side would be appropriate, especially a Mateus from Portugal. It's easy to find and easy to drink.

Dessert is a delicate custard that's lifted out of the ordinary by the addition of Cointreau. Serve it with good, strong coffee.

SHOPPING LIST FOR SOUTHERN MENU

Meat, Dairy, Eggs:

☐ 1 fully cooked ham slice (¾ lb.), ¼ inch thick

☐ dairy half and half (1 cup), or ⅔ cup milk + ⅓ cup whipping cream

☐ butter (4 Tbsp. + butter for rolls)

☐ eggs (1 + 1 yolk)

Produce:

☐ 1 bunch celery with fresh leafy tops

☐ 1 small (3-oz.) carrot

☐ 1 small banana*

☐ ½ lb. thin green beans

☐ 1 lemon (need 3 Tbsp. juice)

Grocery:

☐ dinner rolls

☐ Creole mustard, or any coarse-grained mustard (1 tsp.)

☐ mango chutney (2 Tbsp.)

☐ 1 can (8-oz.) apricot halves

☐ pecans (2 Tbsp. chopped)

Liquor:

☐ 1 bottle rosé wine, such as Mateus

☐ Cointreau (1½ Tbsp.)

Check Staples:

☐ salt

☐ black pepper

☐ ground nutmeg (2 dashes)

☐ ground cinnamon (¼ tsp.)

☐ curry powder (½ tsp.)

☐ sugar (⅓ cup)

☐ light brown sugar (1 Tbsp.)

☐ red wine vinegar (½ Tbsp.)

☐ salad oil (3 Tbsp.)

☐ coffee

*May need to be purchased several days ahead to allow for ripening.

COUNTDOWNS FOR SOUTHERN MENU

Last-Minute Countdown

Time in   Activity
Minutes

60 minutes ahead:

10 Chill wine; Steps 1–2 of dessert
     (oven to 325°F)
20 Prepare salad (squeeze 5 tsp. lemon
     juice for ham and green beans).
15 Steps 1–3 of ham
15 Step 3 of dessert; turn oven to broil;
     Steps 1–2 of green beans; uncork
     wine; Step 4 of ham
___
60

Serving:

Serve salad.
Reheat green beans; take ham from
     broiler, turn oven to 325°F, and heat
     rolls.
Serve ham, green beans (Step 3), rolls,
     butter, and wine.
Make coffee.
Serve dessert and coffee.

Plan-Ahead Countdown

Time in   Activity
Minutes

One day ahead:

10 Chill wine; Steps 1–2 of dessert
     (oven to 325°F)
20 Steps 1–2 of salad
___
30 (plus 15 minutes more cooking
     time, then do Step 3 of dessert.)

60 minutes ahead:

— Step 3 of salad

30 minutes ahead:

15 Steps 1–3 of ham
15 Turn oven to broil; Steps 1–2 of
     green beans; uncork wine; Step 4 of
     ham
___
30

Serving:

Serve salad.
Reheat green beans; take ham from
     broiler, turn oven to 325°F, and heat
     rolls.
Serve ham, green beans (Step 3), rolls,
     butter, and wine.
Make coffee.
Serve dessert and coffee.

CELERY LEAF AND CARROT SALAD

Working Time: 20 minutes/Standing Time: 30 minutes/Servings: 2

CREOLE DRESSING:
½ Tbsp. red wine vinegar
1 Tbsp. fresh lemon juice
½ tsp. salt
⅛ tsp. ground black pepper
1 tsp. Creole mustard*
3 Tbsp. salad oil

SALAD INGREDIENTS:
1 bunch celery with fresh leafy tops
1 small (3-oz.) carrot, peeled and coarsely
   grated

1.   In a 1-qt. bowl whisk together vinegar, lemon juice, salt, pepper, and mustard until salt dissolves. Whisk in oil.

2.   Trim off dried ends of celery (do not separate stalks). Wash only if dirty and dry thoroughly. Cut across celery stalks from the leaf end in ¼ inch thick slices to make 1½ cups celery with leaves.

3.   Add celery and grated carrot to dressing, mixing well. Transfer to individual salad bowls. Let stand at room temperature 30 minutes to 1½ hours before serving.

*Creole mustard is a coarse, brownish mustard made from crushed or ground mustard seeds, vinegar, and salt. It's available in gourmet shops and some supermarkets. Other grainy mustards may be substituted.

To do ahead: Do Steps 1–2 up to 1 day ahead. Cover and refrigerate dressing and vegetables separately.

HAM WITH APRICOTS AND BANANAS

Working Time: 15 minutes/Broiling Time: 10 minutes/Servings: 2

2 Tbsp. butter
¼ tsp. ground cinnamon
½ tsp. curry powder
1 Tbsp. (packed) light brown sugar
1 Tbsp. fresh lemon juice
2 Tbsp. mango chutney*, solid pieces finely
  chopped

1 fully cooked ham slice (¾ lb.), ¼ inch
  thick
1 can (8-oz.) apricot halves, drained
1 small, ripe banana

1. Melt butter in a 1-cup metal measuring cup. Remove from heat and add chutney, curry powder, brown sugar, and lemon juice.

2. Cut ham slice in half, trim off any fat, and place in a gratin dish (12 inches long). Peel banana and slice diagonally ⅓ inch thick.

3. Arrange alternating rows of apricot halves (cut side down) and banana slices on top of ham. Pour chutney mixture over all, making sure banana slices are well coated.

4. Preheat broiler at highest setting. Broil 6 inches from heat until lightly browned, 8 to 10 minutes. Serve from gratin dish.

*Chutney is a sort of relish, usually made with fruit, spices, and an acid such as vinegar or lemon juice. Mango chutney is available commercially, the most popular type being Major Grey's. It can be found in grocery and gourmet stores.

To do ahead: Do Steps 1–3 up to 30 minutes ahead.

GREEN BEANS WITH PECANS

Working Time: 10 minutes/Cooking Time: 6 minutes/Servings: 2

6 cups water
½ lb. green beans*
2⅛ tsp. salt, divided

2 Tbsp. butter
2 Tbsp. finely chopped pecans
2 tsp. fresh lemon juice

1. Bring water to a rapid boil in a wide 2-qt. saucepan. Break off stem ends of green beans and add to boiling water. Add 2 tsp. salt. Boil, uncovered, until beans are tender when pierced with a toothpick, about 6 minutes. Drain.

2. In a 5-inch skillet over medium heat cook pecans in butter until butter is browned and pecans are well toasted, about 5 minutes. Be careful not to burn them. Remove from heat and add lemon juice and ⅛ tsp. salt.

3. Place hot beans in a small warm vegetable dish and pour pecan butter over them.

*Select small green beans that feel tender and crisp, rather than fibrous.

To do a head: Do Steps 1–2 up to 2 hours ahead. Leave at room temperature. To serve, reheat beans in 1 tsp. butter in same saucepan. Reheat pecan butter and proceed with Step 3.

COINTREAU CUSTARDS

Working Time: 10 minutes/Baking Time: 35 minutes (325°F)/Cooling Time: 15 minutes/Servings: 2

1 cup dairy half and half, or ⅔ cup milk plus
   ⅓ cup whipping cream
⅓ cup sugar

1 egg plus 1 egg yolk
1½ Tbsp. Cointreau*
2 dashes ground nutmeg

1. Turn oven to 325°F. Warm half and half in a 1½-qt. saucepan until it feels hot to the touch. Remove from heat, add sugar, and whisk to dissolve. Whisk in egg and extra yolk. Add Cointreau.

2. Pour into two 6-oz. soufflé dishes or custard cups (unbuttered). Dust with nutmeg. Half fill an 8- or 9-inch cake pan with hottest tap water and place in center of oven. Set custards in water and bake until top feels like soft gelatin when you touch it, about 35 minutes.

3. Carefully remove custards from oven. Tip pan to drain off some of the water and remove custards. Serve warm or chilled.

*Cointreau is a clear, orange-flavored liqueur of excellent quality, produced in France and available in any liquor store.

To do ahead: Prepare up to 1 day ahead. Cool, cover, and refrigerate.

IRISH MENU

- **Kipper Paté**
- **Corned Beef and Cabbage Soup**
- **Irish Soda Bread**
  Beaujolais

- **Lemon Puddings**
- **Irish Coffee**

The best dishes of Ireland are the simple, traditional ones that are tried and true, handed down from one generation to the next. Here's a menu in the best Irish tradition, tailored for the twosome. Try it for St. Patrick's Day or any cold day when you'd like a hearty, warming meal.

The kipper paté is made in minutes by mashing kippers (smoked herrings), softened butter, lemon juice, and mace to a smooth paste. Spread on crackers, it makes an excellent appetizer.

Corned beef and cabbage, a typical Irish dish, becomes a quick soup for two in this menu. You make it with cooked corned beef (from the delicatessen), green cabbage, chicken broth, and root vegetables like potatoes, carrots, and rutabagas. The soup is paired with the wonderful Irish soda bread—surely one of the world's easiest-to-make breads. This version contains golden raisins for a distinctive touch of sweetness.

If you feel the need for a beverage accompaniment to the meal, a fresh and fruity young red wine, such as a Beaujolais, served lightly chilled, would be very good.

Lemon pudding is a delicious dessert, moist and spongelike with a velvet lemon custard at the bottom. Serve it with Irish coffee (coffee with sugar, whiskey, and whipped cream), a modern-day tradition all over Ireland.

SHOPPING LIST FOR IRISH MENU

Meat, Dairy, Eggs:

☐ 2 small slices corned beef (⅓ lb.)
    from delicatessen

☐ butter (8 Tbsp. + butter for bread)

☐ buttermilk (5 oz.)

☐ whipping cream (½ cup)

☐ eggs (1)

Produce:

☐ 1 small (¼-lb.) onion

☐ 1 medium-size (⅓-lb.) potato

☐ 1 small (⅓-lb.) rutabaga

☐ 1 large (⅓-lb.) carrot

☐ green cabbage (need ⅓ lb.)

☐ 1 lemon (need ½ tsp. grated peel +
    2 Tbsp. juice)

☐ parsley (½ tsp. chopped)

Grocery:

☐ 1 can (3- to 4-oz.) kipper fillets or
    "kipper snacks"

☐ plain crackers (about 16), such as
    saltines or Waverly Wafers

☐ golden raisins (¼ cup)

Liquor:

☐ 1 bottle Beaujolais

☐ Irish whiskey (¼ cup)

Check Staples:

☐ salt

☐ black pepper

☐ white pepper

☐ ground mace (¼ tsp.)

☐ dried thyme (¼ tsp.)

☐ baking powder (1 tsp.)

☐ baking soda (¼ tsp.)

☐ sugar (½ cup)

☐ all-purpose white flour (1¼ cups)

☐ 2 cans (10¾-oz. each) condensed
    chicken broth

☐ coffee

COUNTDOWNS FOR IRISH MENU

Last-Minute Countdown

Time in   *Activity*
Minutes

55 minutes ahead:

20   Butter out of refrigerator (for paté); Steps 1–4 of soup

10   Chill wine; oven to 375°F; make bread.

10   Step 5 of soup; Step 1 of paté; take soup off heat; Step 2 of paté (grate ½ tsp. lemon peel and squeeze 1 Tbsp. juice for dessert)

15   Steps 1–3 of dessert; reduce oven to 350°F, take bread from oven, and wrap in a cloth napkin.

___

55

Serving:

Serve paté and crackers.

Reheat soup and do Step 6.

Serve soup, bread, butter, and wine.

(Take dessert from oven and keep warm in waterbath.)

Make Irish coffee.

Serve dessert and Irish coffee.

Plan-Ahead Countdown

Time in   *Activity*
Minutes

One day ahead:

20   Butter out of refrigerator (for paté); Steps 1–4 of soup

10   Make paté.

5   Steps 5–6 of soup

___

35

35 minutes ahead:

10   Chill wine; paté out of refrigerator; oven to 375°F; make bread.

15 minutes ahead:

15   Steps 1–3 of dessert; reduce oven to 350°F, take bread from oven, and wrap in a cloth napkin; put soup on to reheat.

Serving:

Serve paté and crackers.

Serve soup, bread, butter, and wine.

(Take dessert from oven and keep warm in waterbath.)

Make Irish coffee.

Serve dessert and Irish coffee.

KIPPER PATÉ

Working Time: 10 minutes/Servings: 2 to 3

6 Tbsp. butter, softened
1 can (3- to 4-oz.) kipper fillets* or "kipper
  snacks," drained
Pinch of ground black pepper
⅛ tsp. plus a pinch of ground mace

1 Tbsp. fresh lemon juice
½ tsp. finely chopped parsley
Plain crackers (about 16), such as saltines
  or Waverly Wafers

1. On a dinner plate mash together with a fork the butter, kippers, pepper, and ⅛ tsp. mace until well blended.

2. Stir lemon juice into mixture. Pack into an 8-oz. crock or soufflé dish. Dust with mace and sprinkle with chopped parsley. Provide individual butter knives for spreading paté onto crackers.

*Kippers are herring that have been split, salted, and smoked. They are available canned in most supermarkets. (Look for them near the sardines and smoked oysters.)

To do ahead: Prepare up to 1 hour ahead and leave at room temperature, or prepare up to 2 days ahead, cover, and refrigerate. Let soften at room temperature at least 30 minutes before serving.

CORNED BEEF AND CABBAGE SOUP

Working Time: 20 minutes/Cooking Time: 20 minutes/Servings: 2 to 3

1 cup finely chopped onion
1 Tbsp. butter
2 cans (10¾-oz. each) condensed chicken
  broth
1 medium-size (⅓-lb.) potato
1 small (⅓-lb.) rutabaga

1 large (⅓-lb.) carrot
¼ tsp. ground white pepper
¼ tsp. dried thyme
⅓ lb. wedge green cabbage
2 small slices corned beef, ¼ inch thick
  (about ⅓ lb.), from delicatessen

1. In a 2-qt. saucepan over medium heat sauté onion in butter until soft, 5 minutes. Add chicken broth and bring to a boil over high heat.

2. Meanwhile, peel potato and rutabaga and cut into ½-inch dice. Peel carrot and slice ¼ inch thick.

3. Add potato, rutabaga, carrot, pepper, and thyme to saucepan. Bring to a boil, turn heat to low, cover, and simmer until potatoes are nearly tender, 12 minutes.

4. Slice cabbage into ¼-inch-wide shreds to make about 2 cups packed. Cut corned beef into 1-inch squares.

5. When vegetables are nearly done, add cabbage, raise heat, and simmer, uncovered, until all vegetables are tender, 5 minutes.

6. Add corned beef to soup and heat through, 1 minute. Serve in large soup plates.

To do ahead: Prepare up to 2 days ahead. Cool, cover, and refrigerate. To serve, reheat over medium heat just until hot. (If soup is too salty, add a little water.)

IRISH SODA BREAD

Working Time: 10 minutes/Baking Time: 25 minutes (375°F)/Servings: 2 to 3

1 cup all-purpose white flour (do not sift)
1 tsp. baking powder
¼ tsp. baking soda
½ tsp. salt

1 Tbsp. sugar
¼ cup golden raisins
½ cup plus 1 Tbsp. buttermilk
Flour for kneading (about 2 Tbsp.)

1. Turn oven to 375°F. In a 1½-qt. bowl stir together flour, baking powder, soda, salt, and sugar. Stir in raisins and ½ cup buttermilk.

2. Dust mixture with flour and form into a ball. Knead about 10 strokes, just until smooth. Shape into a ball and flatten into a 4½-inch disc.

3. Brush top with 1 Tbsp. buttermilk. With a sharp knife slash a large "X" about ¼ inch deep across the disc. Transfer to a small greased baking sheet. Bake in center of oven until browned, about 25 minutes. Serve with lots of butter.

To do ahead: This is best prepared fresh. However, leftover bread is good split, buttered, and toasted under the broiler.

LEMON PUDDINGS

Working Time: 15 minutes/Baking Time: 30 minutes (350°F)/Cooling Time: 5 minutes/Servings: 2

1 Tbsp. butter
1 egg, separated
⅓ cup sugar
1 Tbsp. flour

¼ cup whipping cream
½ tsp. grated lemon peel
1 Tbsp. fresh lemon juice

1. Turn oven to 350°F. Melt butter in a metal measuring cup. Separate egg, putting white in a 1-cup bowl and yolk in a 1-qt. bowl. To yolk add sugar, flour, cream, lemon peel, and juice. Whisk smooth. Stir in melted butter.

2. With a rotary beater beat egg white until stiff. With a rubber spatula thoroughly fold egg white into yolk mixture. Pour into two 6-oz. soufflé dishes or custard cups.

3. Half fill an 8- or 9-inch cake pan with hottest tap water and place in center of oven. Set puddings in water. Bake until puffed and brown on top, about 30 minutes.

4. Carefully remove puddings from oven. Tip pan to drain off some of the water. Remove puddings from pan and cool 5 minutes before serving.

To do ahead: May be prepared up to 30 minutes ahead and kept warm in the waterbath.

IRISH COFFEE

Working Time: 10 minutes/Servings: 2

2 cups strong, black coffee
¼ cup whipping cream

1 Tbsp. sugar
2 jiggers (¼ cup) Irish whiskey

1. Make the coffee. With a rotary beater whip cream in a 3-cup bowl until stiff.

2. Put ½ Tbsp. sugar in each of two 10-oz. stemmed glasses or clear glass mugs. Pour in enough coffee to dissolve sugar. Add whiskey and enough coffee to come within one inch of top of glasses. Top with whipped cream and serve at once.

To do ahead: Cream may be whipped up to 3 hours ahead. Cover and refrigerate.

INDEX